T0030148

Baring Witness

Figure 1. Daniel and Stephanie Lauritzen, March 2007, Salt Lake City, Utah

Stephanie writes: "When we were first married and both active members, I took comfort in this image. We were small parts of a big eternal plan, and that plan, like the temple, was far more striking and impressive than the two tiny humans before it. Later, I saw that huge temple as oppressive. Daniel and I are so small compared to our surroundings that we become almost featureless. We could be any Mormon couple, molded into idealized carbon copies with identical gender roles and spiritual paths.

Now I'm at peace with it all. Mormonism is who I was. I'm happy for the version of my past self who was thrilled to be married in the temple, but even happier with the current self who was brave enough to walk away."

Baring Witness

*36 Mormon Women Talk Candidly
about Love, Sex, and Marriage*

Edited by Holly Welker

University of Illinois Press
URBANA, CHICAGO, AND SPRINGFIELD

Portions of "I Do . . . to You and You and You"
by Nancy Ellsworth was previously published under a
different title and in a different form by Doves & Serpents
at http://www.dovesandserpents.org/wp/2012/
gp-the=everlasting-covenant/. Reprinted with permission.

Library of Congress Cataloging-in-Publication Data
Names: Welker, Holly, editor.
Title: Baring witness: 36 Mormon women talk candidly about love,
    sex, and marriage / edited by Holly Welker.
Other titles: Baring witness: thirty-six Mormon women talk
    candidly about love, sex, and marriage
Description: Urbana; Chicago; Springfield: University of Illinois
    Press, [2016] | Includes bibliographical references and index.
Identifiers: LCCN 2015047428 (print) | LCCN 2015049981 (ebook) |
    ISBN 9780252040344 (cloth : alk. paper) | ISBN 9780252081781
    (pbk. : alk. paper) | ISBN 9780252098598 (ebook)
Subjects: LCSH: Women in the Mormon Church. | Mormon
    women. | Marriage. | Marriage—Religious aspects—Mormon
    Church.
Classification: LCC BX8643.W66 B37 2016 (print) | LCC BX8643.W66
    (ebook) | DDC 289.3082—dc23
LC record available at http://lccn.loc.gov/2015047428

For Marilyn, my mother

Contents

Acknowledgments

I must first thank all the women who discussed their marriages with me and wrote essays for this volume, even those whose work, for one reason or another, is not included here. It was a privilege to learn about their experiences, one that enriched me and taught me more than I can say.

Thanks to the women who generously allowed their photographs to be included in the book.

Thanks to Lynn Matthews Anderson, Carol Hamer, Mary Ellen Robertson, and Alison Udall for help evaluating the manuscript and preparing it for submission.

Thanks to friends and family who provided support and encouragement as I worked on this project, especially Matt Dann, Kathryn Hess, LoraLee Jesperson, Joan Marcus, Robert Raleigh, and Sheryl Schindler.

Thanks to Amanda Wicks, editorial assistant at University of Illinois Press, for help shepherding the book through the editorial and production process. Thanks as well to the other staff at the press who helped me prepare the book for publication.

Thanks to my agent, Linda Roghaar, who has offered so much encouragement, advice, and help and been a staunch advocate of my work.

Thanks to my mother, Marilyn, for being such a remarkable woman, and to my father, Dudley, for material and emotional support in this effort to honor Mom.

And thanks to Dawn Durante, my editor, for her enthusiastic support, encouragement, guidance, and feedback. From the moment she took on this project, I knew it was in the right hands. It has been a pleasure to work with her.

Baring Witness

Introduction

Attempting Mormon Marriage

HOLLY WELKER

I was born and raised in southern Arizona in a town so Mormon we held our high school proms in the cultural hall of our LDS meetinghouse instead of the school gym. Girls I'd gone to church with began marrying before they were out of their teens. I remember listening in confused silence to a college roommate (like most of my roommates, she was both Mormon and a relative) weep over the fact that she was almost twenty-two, weeks from graduation, and without any prospects for marriage. It had never occurred to her, she told me through her tears, that she would be single when she graduated from college—in 1983, a time when there was no great stigma to getting a college diploma before you got an engagement ring. In contrast, it had never occurred to me that I might marry before graduating—or why I would even want to. Somehow, with one exception I'll discuss below, I never wanted to be married simply to be married. Instead, I have wanted several times to marry a specific person I was in love with, and when things didn't work out, well, it was the relationship I mourned, rather than my marital status itself. I don't know whether this was due to something in my own nature or, say, the fact that in my youth I'd read enough romance novels, from Jane Austen to cheap potboiler paperbacks, to figure out that while Charlotte Lucas from *Pride and Prejudice* might not be right in her cynical insistence that "happiness in marriage is entirely a matter of chance" (16), there were certainly no guarantees of marital bliss. In any event, like Jane Austen (whose birthday I share), I ended up a spinster who thinks and writes a great deal about marriage.

It's hard to be Mormon and not think a lot about marriage. In general, people marry because they think it will make them happy, and because, as Andrew J. Cherlin notes in his study of contemporary American practices and attitudes regarding marriage, "Marriage, although optional, remains the most highly valued form of family life in American culture, the most prestigious way to live your

Figure 2. Marilyn and Dudley Welker, September 1960, Tucson, Arizona

life" (9). But for members of The Church of Jesus Christ of Latter-day Saints, marriage is much more than an institution, a relationship, and a good idea. All the ways it can bring people happiness—such as through companionship or by providing a stable environment for raising well-adjusted children—are subsumed by the fact that it's a commandment, an absolutely necessary prerequisite for salvation and exaltation. Marrying "for time and all eternity"—which happens when a couple is "sealed" in an LDS temple in a special ordinance that yokes people together in a covenanted relationship intended to survive death—is both the reward for living a righteous life and a primary method by which righteousness is demonstrated.

This is something I have understood implicitly for as long as I can remember, even if I couldn't articulate it that directly. But in 2010, I became hungry for stories about how Mormon women see their marriages. One reason for that was the fact that I had moved to Utah in 2008, just in time to watch up close the church's participation in the successful campaign to pass California's Proposition 8 amending that state's constitution to ban gay marriage; I thought more carefully than I had before about why the church felt so threatened by gay marriage.[1] I also began to suspect that Mormons in Utah didn't see marriage quite the same way as Mormons elsewhere: attitudes about marriage, relationships, and family seemed amplified, or perhaps slightly skewed.

One Sunday afternoon in August 2009, I called my mother. She didn't feel well, but that wasn't remarkable: she'd long suffered from Crohn's disease; plus the removal of her gall bladder over twenty years earlier had for some reason caused scarring in her liver, and it just kept spreading. Every so often, a stent had to be inserted in her bile duct to keep it open enough to drain. We all knew she would someday die of cirrhosis or a related illness, despite never having consumed a drink in her life. But we also knew what a fighter Mom was—born with an extra vertebra, she literally had a lot of backbone—and we'd also seen how well her resourceful, dedicated doctors could patch her up each time she had a bad spell. Somehow, though, something signaled to me during that conversation that she had less than a year to live—even though her prognosis suggested she should have longer than that. In particular, we hoped she would make it to September 2010, so she and my father could celebrate their fiftieth wedding anniversary. But that day I knew, I absolutely *knew*, that we had to begin preparing for the end. After we said goodbye but before I had even hung up the phone, I burst into tears. "I have got to find a husband. I have got to find a husband. I cannot watch my mother die alone," I repeated through my sobs. That reaction shocked me almost as much as the knowledge that my mother would be gone in mere months. As it turned out, I neither found a husband nor even looked for one—but I did file the experience away as one more reason people marry: it can make mortality easier to bear.

And then there was the Saturday in March 2010, when I gave a tour of Salt Lake City to a Canadian friend who'd grown up in the Reorganized Church of Jesus Christ of Latter Day Saints (now the Community of Christ), where beliefs about marriage are quite different.[2] As we strolled through Salt Lake's beautiful cemetery, a place I loved visiting for its views of the city, its landscaping, its peacefulness, and its history, she asked me about the fact that so many Mormons have an image of a temple engraved on their tombstones. I was certainly aware of this myself, but I had never stopped to analyze it; I told her that the engravings were not any sort of universal symbol of the church as much as an explicit depiction of the temple a couple was married in and thus an announcement of what their marriage led them to expect about the hereafter. It was perhaps an odd conversation to have just then: less than twenty-four hours earlier, my mother had finally died. Her fierce heart beat steadily as her other organs shut down; it didn't stop until there was nothing else left to support. Too grieved by all that to want to be alone, I was also too dutiful a tour guide to omit so important a location when my friend said she would enjoy spending a beautiful spring day visiting some of the city's significant sites. In any event, I was grateful for a sensitive, thoughtful companion who helped me begin to comprehend that enormous loss and listened as I voiced questions about my mother's life that she would have been reluctant to discuss when she was still alive.[3]

I had read a handful of memoirs on the topic of Mormon marriage; following my mother's death, I began reading books and articles about marriage in general. I also asked snoopy questions of friends and acquaintances. Still my curiosity was not sated. I soon realized that what I really wanted was the variety and breadth of an essay anthology—say, a Mormon version of Cathi Hanauer's collection *The Bitch in the House*. I knew of several anthologies of works by Mormon women on motherhood, and I could have read any number of Mormon mommy blogs. But none of those provided the perspective I sought. I saw that I would have to take Toni Morrison's oft-quoted advice: "If there is a book you really want to read but it hasn't been written yet, then you must write it"—or, in this case, solicit, edit, and compile the essays it comprises. Although I hadn't yet articulated it when I first sent out a call for submissions, the question I was pursuing was this: given that a particular emphasis on marriage is one of the things distinguishing The Church of Jesus Christ of Latter-day Saints, what distinguishes LDS marriages for the women in them?

What follows in this introduction is an overview of Mormon doctrine about marriage and a bit of background to help readers make sense of the topics and perspectives explored in this collection. The essays themselves are where readers will find subjective answers to the question underlying this volume.

Section 132 of the Doctrine and Covenants,[4] recorded July 12, 1843, is purportedly Christ's response when LDS church founder Joseph Smith inquired how such prophets as Abraham, Isaac, Jacob, Moses, David, and Solomon could be "justified" in "having many wives and concubines." It announces a form of marriage that is "a new and everlasting covenant." Because it allows spouses to be married not merely until "death do us part" but forever, provided the marriage is "sealed unto them by the Holy Spirit of promise, by him who is anointed," it is often called eternal marriage. It is sometimes called celestial marriage, because it enables spouses to "inherit thrones, kingdoms, principalities, and powers, dominions, all heights and depths" (D&C 132:19) in what Latter-day Saints call the celestial kingdom. And because such a marriage must be performed in an

LDS temple, it is often called temple marriage. Eternal or celestial or temple marriage underlies the Mormon belief that intimate relationships will continue beyond the grave, which is seen by many as a major appeal of Mormonism.

This idea of marriage didn't spring merely from Joseph Smith's curiosity about Old Testament polygamy. It's also one strain in the evolution of marriage within Christianity and American society. Detailing that evolution is beyond the scope of this introduction, but a bare bones outline is certainly in order.

In 1 Corinthians 7, Saint Paul famously declared that celibacy is superior to marriage, but that "it is better to marry than to burn." That was the conventional wisdom regarding marriage throughout Christendom—until Martin Luther came along and started the Protestant Reformation in the sixteenth century. Luther believed that far from being "merely the second-best choice for those who lacked the self-discipline to remain celibate, [marriage] was rather the highest form of personal life." But it was still "part of what Luther called the 'earthly kingdom' rather than the 'heavenly kingdom': it was, in his words, 'a secular and outward thing'" (Cherlin 42).

Luther's ideas about marriage influenced the English Puritans who colonized New England, where "the marriage-based family of husband, wife, and children was not just the backbone of New England colonial society, in large part, it *was* society" (Cherlin 40). So in many ways it's not surprising that in the religion started in 1830 by Joseph Smith, a descendent of those Puritan colonists, the marriage-based family of husband, wife, and children is not just the backbone of the church, but, in large part, the church itself, the moral and spiritual ideal not just on earth but in heaven.

Furthermore, LDS ideas about marriage have continued to evolve throughout the existence of the church. Although the first work of scripture produced by Joseph Smith, the Book of Mormon, expressly forbids polygamy (see Jacob 2:27), the justification of polygamy, or "plural marriage," as it is often called, is presented in subsequent scripture in very legalistic and proprietary terms:

> if any man espouse a virgin, and desire to espouse another, and the first give her consent, and if he espouse the second, and they are virgins, and have vowed to no other man, then is he justified; he cannot commit adultery for they are given unto him; for he cannot commit adultery with that that belongeth unto him and to no one else. (D&C 132:61)

The punishment threatened a mere three verses later for any wife who rejects the "law" of polygamy seriously undercuts the notion of consent:

> if any man have a wife, who holds the keys of this power, and he teaches unto her the law of my priesthood, as pertaining to these things, then shall she believe and administer unto him, or she shall be destroyed, saith the Lord your God; for I will destroy her. (D&C 132:64)

The mainstream Utah church formally abandoned the practice of polygamy, once in 1890 and again in 1904 after it became clear that the first renunciation wasn't quite sincere, in order to avoid reprisals from the federal government.[5] Nonetheless, polygamy remains an undeniable—and complicated—aspect of Mormon eschatology. Even today, a man who divorces or becomes a widower can be sealed to each and every one of his successive wives, with the possibility if not the expectation that he will be married to all of them at once in the next life.[6] However, in order for a woman to be sealed to a second husband, as after a civil divorce, she must first obtain a sealing cancellation, also known as a temple divorce, which renders her sealing null and void. Sealing cancellations, although not rare, are also not routine. And if a woman is widowed, even very shortly after her wedding, after which she marries a man with whom she has children and grandchildren, she remains sealed to her dead husband, and what's more, her children are sealed as well to their mother's dead husband as his spiritual offspring. Only after she is dead may she and her children be sealed by proxy to the man she actually had a family with.[7]

The church's current stance on marriage is put forth in a 1995 document titled "The Family: A Proclamation to the World." Published as the LDS church battled efforts in Hawaii to obtain legal recognition for same-sex unions, the Proclamation on the Family, as it is popularly known, is both religious counsel and a political statement. Its title may announce that it is directed to the world, but its primary audience has been Latter-day Saints, who are expected to show agreement with it by shaping their lives according to it and by displaying a copy prominently in their homes.[8] It states that

> marriage between a man and a woman is ordained of God and that the family is central to the Creator's plan for the eternal destiny of His children. . . . The divine plan of happiness enables family relationships to be perpetuated beyond the grave. Sacred ordinances and covenants available in holy temples make it possible for individuals to return to the presence of God and for families to be united eternally.

Furthermore, "All human beings—male and female—are created in the image of God. Each is a beloved spirit son or daughter of heavenly parents"—heavenly parents who have divine physical bodies that are quite literally the images in which human beings were created. This means that God the Father/Father in Heaven is partnered with/married to God the Mother/Mother in Heaven, a shadowy and insubstantial figure about whom little is known or said.[9] The best known expression of this doctrine is from a hymn titled "Oh My Father" by Eliza R. Snow (reputedly a plural wife of both Joseph Smith and Brigham Young):

> In the heavens are parents single?
> No, the thought makes reason stare!

Truth is reason; truth eternal
tells me I've a mother there. (lines 21–24)

The LDS church has been called a "gospel of emulation" (Callister), and the beings Latter-day Saints are to emulate are their heavenly parents—even though next to nothing is known about Heavenly Mother, and knowledge of Heavenly Father is also very limited. The most salient point, however, is that Mormons believe that by marrying and having children, they *are* emulating their perfect heavenly parents. "The commandment to multiply and replenish the earth," Boyd K. Packer, president of the Quorum of the Twelve Apostles, reminded the Saints in 2015, "is essential to the plan of redemption and is the source of human happiness. Through the righteous exercise of this power, we may come close to our Father in Heaven and experience a fulness of joy, even godhood. The power of procreation is not an incidental part of the plan; it is the plan of happiness; it is the key to happiness." Furthermore, Mormons believe that their unions, like that of their heavenly parents, can be eternal.

Faced with a decision designed to endure for eternity, many people would proceed slowly, deliberate carefully, and weigh as many options as possible before making a final choice. But that's not how Mormons are told to approach selecting a mate. A few major criteria must be met: any appropriate spouse should be a devout Latter-day Saint who displays his or her devotion through righteous living and obedience to church leaders and who is therefore worthy to go to the temple. Beyond that, other considerations are almost beside the point. One president of the church told students at Brigham Young University that "while every young man and young woman will seek with all diligence and prayerfulness to find a mate with whom life can be most compatible and beautiful, yet it is certain that almost any good man and any good woman can have happiness and a successful marriage if both are willing to pay the price," which is to "love the Lord more than their own lives and then love each other more than their own lives, working together in total harmony with the gospel program as their basic structure," as if those were easy things to do (Kimball). Another president of the church stated, "Being happily and successfully married is generally not so much a matter of marrying the right person as it is *being the right person*" (Hunter 130, emphasis in original).

Provided a potential spouse is LDS, more important than the specific individual one marries are the place (the temple) and time of marriage: Latter-day Saints are encouraged to marry young and warned that "postponing marriage until money is sufficient to sustain a stylish living is not wise. So much of life together—struggling, adjusting, and learning to cope with life's challenges—is lost when that happens" (Tingey). As a result, and because sex outside marriage is strictly forbidden, Mormons tend to marry a couple of years before their peers in the rest of the United States ("College Students"). And, while such commands are less frequent than they were a generation ago, LDS couples are still sometimes instructed not to "postpone having your children" or to "curtail the number of your children for personal or selfish reasons" such as a lack of money or the emotional resources necessary to support a large family (Benson).[10]

Although marriage is important for both men and women, LDS women are instructed from infancy in ways that men are not that marriage and parenthood are their primary callings and must be their ultimate goals, even as they pursue additional goals encouraged by the church, such as education. In a 2007 speech, Julie B. Beck, general president of the Relief Society (the women's organization of the LDS church), reminds women that "all the education women attain will avail them nothing if they do not have the skill to make a home." In a 2013 survey of Mormon women about the lessons they received in the Young Women's program, the church's curriculum for girls ages twelve to eighteen, 75.2 percent answered that they were "taught in YW that [their] main objective in life is to marry in the temple"—higher than the 60.1 percent who answered that they were "taught in YW that [their] main objective in life is to live the gospel" or the 50.7 percent taught that their "main objective in life is to have a testimony of [the] Saviour and a relationship with [our] Heavenly Father" ("Survey Results"). The temple is accessible only to Latter-day Saints who meet specific criteria, including being a member of record for at least a year; paying a tithe of 10 percent of their income; abstaining from tobacco, alcohol, illicit drugs, and extramarital sex; and passing a worthiness interview delving into orthodoxy and sexual behavior. Thus, believing that your main objective in life is to marry there entails a very great deal—including, ideally, a belief that traditional gender roles are divinely decreed, as stated in the Proclamation on the Family:

> By divine design, fathers are to preside over their families in love and righteousness and are responsible to provide the necessities of life and protection for their families. Mothers are primarily responsible for the nurture of their children. In these sacred responsibilities, fathers and mothers are obligated to help one another as equal partners.

That passage is crucial, for it articulates a contradiction the church refuses to acknowledge: fathers and mothers are to be "equal partners" over which men preside, a situation that makes an equal partnership impossible. Not only is this contradiction somehow immune to recognition or acknowledgment by the church hierarchy, it is also immune to change or adjustment, since it exists "by divine design."

Counterintuitive as it might seem, these expectations and contradictions help explain the existence of Mormon feminism. Given that young Mormon women are encouraged to get educations, get married, and start families, it's no surprise that many intelligent, ambitious Mormon women end up as wives and mothers sooner than their secular counterparts. They find themselves with questions about the great calling of homemaking, especially when it fails to meet their expectations, while being equipped with analytical skills, a vocabulary, and texts to critique the institutions and attitudes that shaped their choices. It's also one reason I knew that I could gather essays of the type I wanted to read: while not every woman who has contributed to this volume identifies as a Mormon feminist (though many do), they are part of a community where analyzing the details of one's marriage from a variety of perspectives is, if not quite commonplace, at least not strange.

In other words, it's not only the LDS church but the world at large that shapes Mormon women's ideas and expectations about marriage. A discussion of general attitudes about marriage is beyond the scope of this introduction; many readers will already be familiar with the topic, and those who want to know more can find a few titles listed in the Bibliography section. I'll limit myself to quoting Stephanie Coontz's insightful conclusion in *Marriage, A History*:

> The historical transformation in marriage over the ages has created a similar paradox for society as a whole. Marriage has become more joyful, more loving, and more satisfying for many couples than ever before in history. At the same time it has become optional and more brittle. These two strands of change cannot be disentangled. (306)

The catch for Latter-day Saints is that while marriage has grown more brittle, so much in the church is aimed at cementing it—not just until death parts a couple, but for all eternity. Certainly Mormons blessed with loving, successful marriages often feel enriched and inspired by the promise that their marriage may last forever. But things can be very different for couples in unhappy or difficult marriages. In the words of one church president, "Without proper and successful marriage, one will never be exalted" (Kimball). Informing couples that marriage will provide them not only earthly joy but also eternal salvation and exaltation *if they do it right* but will consign them to eternal inferiority *if they do it wrong* may or may not make marriage more brittle—but it certainly increases the pressure on troubled marriages and the people in them.

This is especially true when a marriage begun as an eternal or celestial marriage between two devout Mormons turns into a marriage between one devout Mormon and a spouse who has lost faith. In such a case, the spouse who has lost faith often ceases to be a top priority for the other—instead, the devout spouse's highest obligations and deepest loyalties are often to the church.[11] And marriages between a committed Mormon and someone of another religion have been shown to have among the highest divorce rates in the country.[12]

Although I have no statistical data to support any claim on the topic, extensive anecdotal evidence (including several essays in this volume) suggests the fragility of marriages in which one spouse "apostasizes" or "loses their testimony" or "goes inactive," to use common LDS ways of describing the situation. It also suggests that the experience can be extremely traumatic for both spouses—which is one reason so many essays collected here discuss it.

From the beginning, I knew I wanted this collection to address topics especially fraught within Mormonism, including polygamy, race, sexual orientation, and marrying outside the temple. In fact, I wanted at least two essays on major topics so that readers would have a variety of perspectives. But it hasn't worked out that way: I had considerable trouble finding writers willing to tackle certain subjects. This is particularly true on the topic of race. The primary demographic represented here—Western, white, middle class, educated, straight—is the demographic Mormon marriage was created to fit, but that hasn't stopped the church from expecting the entire planet to adapt to the model. In fact, aggressive missionary efforts around the world ensure that the issue of race in the LDS church remains complicated, as teachings created by and for white English speakers are translated into a vast array of languages and taught to people of color. Still, only one essay, "Across Racial and Cultural Divides" by Jamie Davis, discusses race in any detail, and it's from the perspective of a white American woman married to a Brazilian man of color. While Gina Colvin is Maori and a scholar of race and religion, her essay doesn't address the question of race in Mormon marriages because critical race questions were, in her words, "superfluous to her response to the subject at hand."[13] I solicited essays from women of color; among other things, I contacted bloggers who write about race and Mormonism, but I got no reply. Having served a mission in Taiwan with Chinese women who now write in English, I hoped to find someone who would write about the intersection of race, culture, and faith involved in a Chinese Mormon marriage, but I failed in that as well. I hope and expect that future volumes of this nature can correct these omissions.

I also wanted LDS perspectives on situations by no means unique to Mormons, including divorce, widowhood, staying single, and the ways marriage can limit other options and possibilities. I was grateful for any writer willing to talk about sex, though I certainly respected a writer's desire to keep some things secret. A few essays don't foreground Mormon attitudes—for example, Amy Sorensen's essay about a rocky but committed marriage, or Rebekah Orton's essay about how being married to a husband with a very different body type affects her sense of self—but Mormon expectations still underlie issues complicating the writers' lives, including marrying young, starting a family soon after marriage, and having large families.

One of the readers who evaluated an early version of this collection noted that several essays focus "on issues that will seem dated to many readers." This is undeniably true and is important to understanding Mormon belief, Mormon culture, and Mormons themselves: as a whole, they are extremely conservative. Not only did the church's leaders embrace the male-breadwinner, father-knows-best, love-based marriage of the 1950s, today, church leaders and discourse claim that that model is enshrined by divine decree as the eternal ideal we must all strive to attain. It's not shocking that an ambitious young woman in graduate school would be warned in 1961 that if she wants a happy marriage she should purposely acquire less education and plan to earn less money than her intended husband; it is shocking that it happened in 2001, as Alisa Curtis Bolander describes in her essay. Mormon women in the twenty-first century struggle to reconcile the demands and expectations of contemporary reality with ideals firmly rooted in the past.

Given that literature typically relies on conflict for narrative tension, it's no surprise that most of the essays are about problems in a marriage. But I wanted if at all possible to include a portrait of a consistently happy marriage. As I sought essays from people who felt their marriage fit that description, I got two main responses: "The fact that my marriage is happy means it's not interesting enough to write about," and "I wouldn't know what to say. I certainly couldn't give advice. I just got lucky." But the idea that luck plays any part in marital happiness is frankly radical in an LDS context: happy marriages are supposedly the result of righteousness and hard work, which means, conveniently for those dispensing advice, that bad marriages happen only to the unrighteous and the lazy. So I am grateful to Rachel Whipple for articulating and exploring this unorthodox idea in her essay.

I was happy to collaborate with writers who had an interesting story but not a lot of writing experience; we just kept working on drafts until we were both satisfied with the essay, or until someone decided it was time to give up. I cared very much about the quality of the prose—I started my writing life as a poet—and I wanted the collection to succeed on aesthetic terms. It's therefore not surprising that women who studied English in college are overrepresented in this collection. But I am happy to showcase some very fine writing here and a variety of stylistic approaches to the personal essay.

In arranging the collection, I wanted to group essays that shared major thematic elements while trying to build dramatic and narrative tension into the structure of the anthology. "Complicated Paths to the Temple (Or Not Getting There at All)," the second section, might therefore have been a logical place to open the collection, but I wanted to give readers some idea of common LDS expectations about marriages before presenting essays that focus on courtship or the decisions and challenges involved in getting to the temple, because those expectations most definitely influence courtship. I therefore begin with a section called "For Better or for Worse." This phrase, derived from the marriage ceremony in the English

Book of Common Prayer, is not used in LDS ceremonies, but it seems an apt description of a fundamental commitment one makes in marriage, which is not to leave as soon as things get difficult. Several of these essays explore an issue not at all limited to marriage but also common in friendships, families, and even professional settings: what do you do when someone you have a relationship with evolves into a different person, one you don't like nearly as much as the person you knew before? People in such situations often feel a great sense of betrayal and confront the question of whose betrayal is greater: the one who changed in the first place, or the partner who resists change when presented with a new normal.

Divorce has never been forbidden in Mormonism; Brigham Young, for instance, married six women who were divorced from other men, and ten of his wives divorced him (Johnson 62). But absence of a prohibition does not always translate into approval. President David O. McKay's 1969 address "Structure of the Home Threatened by Irresponsibility and Divorce" includes a still oft-quoted passage stating, "To look upon marriage as a mere contract that may be entered into at pleasure in response to a romantic whim, or for selfish purposes, and severed at the first difficulty or misunderstanding that may arise, is an evil meriting severe condemnation, especially in cases wherein children are made to suffer because of such separation." What's important in the address is not to understand divorce—after all, it's frankly foolish to imagine that people who take the trouble to marry really end their marriages "at the first difficulty or misunderstanding," especially since, as common wisdom has long pointed out, "breaking up is hard to do" even when couples are not married. Instead, the purpose is to condemn divorce: "conditions that cause divorce are violations of [Christ's] divine teachings. Except in cases of infidelity or other extreme conditions, the Church frowns upon divorce, and authorities look with apprehension upon the increasing number of divorces among members of the Church." It is therefore extremely important to look at why LDS women do divorce and just how bad things have to be before they will end a marriage they expected to endure for all eternity. That is the primary ending explored in the third section, "Divorce and Other Endings," the longest section in the book. Another ending is widowhood, portrayed in Anita Tanner's lovely lyric essay "Sole." I had hoped to have other essays on this topic, but no one chose to write about it, though Bernadette Echols does compare the two situations in "Departures." This comparison underscores an ending implicit in some Mormon divorces: the end of belief that the eternal ideal is possible.

From there we move to "Second Chances," or stories of successful second marriages. These essays explore both the useful and destructive lessons women learn from failed marriages. They consider negative lessons women must unlearn and where and how those lessons were taught. They also portray the faith and hope that enable women to remarry with the belief that the second marriage will be more successful than the first.

The final section, "Expectations: Met, Unmet, or Exceeded," is as close as the volume comes to "happily ever after." Several essays here deal with successful marriages that Mormon culture predicts will be difficult: marriages to non-Mormons or to someone of another race or in which traditional gender roles are inverted in some way. The entire collection is about leaps of faith—it seems to me that falling in love and marriage are almost always leaps of faith—but the essays in this section are by women who, if they didn't quite manage to stick the landing after such a leap, still somehow mustered the gracefulness or good luck to avoid serious injury when they hit the ground.

I'll conclude with a few words about truthfulness, truth-telling, and form. Literary nonfiction and its various subcategories are not merely genres; invoking nonfiction involves invoking a set of propositions about aesthetics and the "truth." Every so often I encounter the claim that "fiction contains deeper truths than nonfiction," a modern restatement of Aristotle's claim that "poetry is a more philosophical and a higher thing than history: for poetry tends to express the universal, history the particular" (636). For Aristotle, poetry's important feature is not that it's in verse (he acknowledges that "the poet and the historian differ not by writing in verse or in prose. The work of Herodotus might be put into verse, and it would still be a species of history, with meter no less than without it" [635]) but that it's *imaginative*, not something that really did happen but what *could* happen. That, he claims, makes it universal—and superior.

I find the question of which genre is inherently superior as tedious and beside the point as the question of how many angels can dance on the head of a pin, or, more to the point for this collection, the question of exactly what our relationships will be like in the afterworld if indeed there is a life beyond this one: while it would certainly be nice to have an answer from on high sufficiently definitive and clear that all humanity would have no choice but to recognize and accept it, we must make do instead with conjecture, speculation, and opinion, which often have very little effect on the ideas or preferences of others. Rather than assert the superiority of nonfiction, I will simply say that I am a fan of narrative, and I am interested in stories that purport to be true as well as in the demands of trying to tell the truth and claiming that you are doing so, which is something literary essays frequently do.

Essay, which is French for *attempt*, exists as the name of a literary form because in the sixteenth century Michel de Montaigne called his writings *essais*, attempts at understanding, explorations, not resolutions. That is how these texts should be read: after all, marital status and one's feeling about one's spouse can be subject to change, as Mary Ellen Robertson's essay underscores. Still, the writers in this collection worked very hard with me to ask difficult questions about certain aspects of their lives and answer those questions as honestly as possible, striving to arrive at worthy insights as the essays evolved through multiple revisions. We faced the fact that we could not ask readers to respect decisions that even the woman who made them had come to see as foolish and destructive, but we wanted to command respect for mature attempts to learn from decisions and to deal responsibly with their consequences—even as future decisions could reshape the way a woman saw and understood her past.

Wallace Stegner, a non-Mormon who wrote fiction and history about Mormons, once declared, "It is almost impossible to write fiction about the Mormons, for the reason that Mormon institutions and Mormon society are so peculiar that they call for constant explanation" (347). I both suspect and hope that he is wrong, but I do grant that in a volume like this one, where the goal is not merely telling a story but explaining the forces that shape it, some attention to the peculiarity of Mormonism is in order. I have worked to make the collection accessible and intelligible to a non-Mormon audience by providing this introduction and a glossary and by providing explanations as necessary in the essays themselves. I hope the volume is valuable and interesting to non-Mormon readers—for the insights it offers into Mormonism, for considerations of what marriage means in our society today. At the same time, I acknowledge that this volume is not just by and about Mormons; it is directed to them in many ways and is shaped by Mormon rhetoric.

Along with prayer, bearing testimony is one of the most common rhetorical practices in Mormonism, with a slew of conventions and assumptions informing how, when, and where it's done, and how it should be received.[14] The verb in the phrase, *to bear*, means "to transmit at large; relate," though I've always thought "to bare" is more emotionally accurate in a Mormon context, given that sharing one's testimony often involves baring one's soul. Certainly that is the pun the title plays on.

For my purposes, the most salient points regarding testimony are this: a testimony is not merely something you bear or bare or share, either orally or in writing; it is also a specific discrete entity you "have," and you can "have" a testimony of many things: the Book of Mormon, Joseph Smith, temple marriage, etc. To have a testimony is to experience some sort of visceral conviction of the truthfulness or significance of something. In Mormon rhetoric, one can "lose" a testimony as well—but there are those who say that anyone who could lose a testimony must not have really had one in the first place. In any event, it's a way of thinking about one's values and beliefs not as mere attributes of one's character, but as a distinct, unique, precise possession one must cultivate and guard.

I discouraged conventional testimony-bearing in these essays. Both despite and because of Mormons' aggressive proselytizing program, I did not want this volume to seem like some sort of Mormon missionary effort. Religious orthodoxy was not a concern as I gathered these essays; instead, my concern was with a writer's willingness to scrutinize how Mormon belief and practice shaped her ideas and experiences of marriage, regardless of whether she remained active and devout. Admittedly, this skewed the perspective; several orthodox women who were initially interested in contributing to the project dropped out when they learned that there would be sympathetic discussions of same-sex relationships and of loss of faith.

All of that is context to explain why, even though there are few explicit affirmations here of a writer's faith in correlated Mormon doctrine, I still think it appropriate to consider these essays a form of testimony and therefore fundamentally inflected by Mormonism in that they are thoughtful statements about what an individual finds meaningful, true, and worth sharing in her experiences. I hope the collection will help people, especially Mormon women, understand and articulate more about marriage and its crucial role in Mormon belief, culture, and experience.

Notes

1. I became an advocate of gay marriage when I first attended a gay commitment ceremony in 1992. In 2007, I published an article on Mormon mixed-orientation marriages titled "Clean-shaven: No More Beards," arguing that gay men would be better off marrying each other instead of straight women (see *Sunstone* 147 [2007]: 44–50). But that was before the church and many of its members devoted so many resources to passing Prop 8, and I needed to articulate to my own satisfaction the motivation behind that campaign. An article I wrote on the topic was published by *Religion Dispatches.* See "From Here to Eternity: Of Mormons and Celestial Marriage," religiondispatches.org, 6 October 2010. Some of the ideas presented there are developed more fully in this introduction.

2. The two main branches of the Latter-day Saint movement splintered after the assassination of Joseph Smith in Illinois in 1844. Major issues in the split were polygamy, which the RLDS rejected, and Joseph Smith's successor. The RLDS accepted Smith's son as their new prophet, while what became the Utah branch chose Brigham Young.

3. When we buried my mother, I insisted that we not put an engraving of the temple on her headstone. Instead, the headstone is decorated with a few bars of music carved into the granite—she was an excellent musician—and a photograph of Mount Graham in southern Arizona, the location of our summer cabin and one of her favorite places on earth.

4. The Doctrine and Covenants, often abbreviated D&C, is a collection of 138 "revelations" given primarily to Joseph Smith, establishing LDS doctrines, procedures, and policies.

5. An anonymous, undated essay published in October 2014 on the church's official website states that "Latter-day Saints believe that monogamy—the marriage of one man and one woman—is the Lord's standing law of marriage," although "the Lord commanded the adoption—and later the cessation—of plural marriage in the latter days." See "Plural Marriage in Kirtland and Nauvoo."

For an excellent discussion of the church's discontinuation of polygamy, see Kathleen Flake, *The Politics of American Religious Identity: The Seating of Senator Reed Smoot, Mormon Apostle* (Chapel Hill: University of North Carolina Press, 2004), print.

6. A man who wants to be sealed to an additional woman or women after the end of one marriage must get permission in the form of something called a sealing clearance, which leaves any previous sealings intact. See the *Church Handbook of Instructions* for details. This text is not made available by the church to anyone but the specific individuals—almost always men—who will use it. However, recent editions can be found on sites like Wikileaks.

7. Mormons believe that the dead rely on the living to manage the legalistic business of religion—i.e., the performance of ordinances necessary for salvation, such as being properly baptized into God's true church. Mormons do genealogy work in order to collect the names of everyone who has ever lived so that salvific ordinances can be performed by proxy in the temple for the dead: people who were not LDS in this life will have the opportunity in the next life to accept or reject the ordinances performed for them. Although Mormons see this as generous, it often feels anything but generous to people who learn that their deceased loved ones have been baptized into the LDS church, as in the cases when the church has had to apologize for baptizing victims of the Holocaust.

8. A pdf suitable for framing is available on the church's website: lds.org/bc/content/shared/content/english/pdf/36035_000_24_family.pdf.

9. For an officially sanctioned discussion of Heavenly Mother, see David L. Paulsen and Martin Pulido, "'A Mother There': A Survey of Historical Teachings about Heavenly Mother," *BYU Studies*, 50.1 (2011): 71–97. A brief, undated, unattributed essay about Heavenly Mother was published on the church's website in October 2015, shortly before this book went to press; see "Mother in Heaven," *lds.org/topics*, The Church of Jesus Christ of Latter-day Saints. For feminist discussions of Heavenly Mother, see for example Janice Allred, "The One Who Never Left Us," *Sunstone* 166 (2012): 62–69; Margaret Toscano, "Heavenly Motherhood: Silences, Disturbances, and Consolations," *Sunstone* 166 (2012): 70–78; and Holly Welker, "In Our Prayers and In Our Lives," *Sunstone* 166 (2012): 79–80.

10. This speech by President Eza Taft Benson, first delivered in February 1987, was printed as a pamphlet in March 1987. Although the church has subsequently acknowledged, as in "The Family: A Proclamation to the World," that "disability, death, or other circumstances may necessitate individual adaptation" to the expectation that couples have large families and mothers will not work outside the home, Benson's speech was quoted in October 2007 by General Relief Society President Julie B. Beck as advice that would be heeded by "Mothers Who Know."

11. See for instance "When He Stopped Believing." The anonymous author recounts her heartbreak and confusion when her husband announces that he no longer believes the LDS gospel:

> The one desire I had maintained stronger than any other in my life was to have an eternal marriage with a man dedicated to living the gospel. I had done everything I could in my life to live worthily, to marry with unmistakable surety, to keep my covenants, to attend the temple, and to dedicate my life and my home to the Lord. Would Heavenly Father really deny me the righteous desire I longed for the most, when I had done everything He asked to attain it?

Note that her greatest desire was not to have a successful relationship with the specific man she has already married; her greatest desire was that her husband, whoever he was, be a certain type of man. Furthermore, she believed that the righteousness of her desires and actions entitled her to the husband she wanted.

Strikingly, the article does not advocate divorce or suggest that the woman's marriage could not possibly be happy, as previous discourse often did. Instead, in answer to prayers, the wife is told to "Just love him!" She strives to do so and to remain happy in her marriage and her life.

12. See Lehrer and Chiswick, "Religion as a Determinant of Marital Stability." The study claims that couples where both spouses are active members of the LDS church divorce at a significantly lower rate than other couples, with an estimated fifth-year dissolution possibility rate of 13 percent, compared to 19 percent for couples in which both spouses are exclusivist Protestants, the next lowest rate; this compares dramatically to an estimated fifth-year dissolution possibility rate of 40 percent for intermarriages involving Mormons and a rate of 42 percent, the highest rate the study documents, for intermarriages involving Jews (Lehrer and Chiswick 393). The authors stress that the religious affiliations of both spouses must be considered in studies of divorce rates, a factor typically neglected in previous studies, which focused primarily on the wife's religion.

13. Her characterization of her essay is from a personal email to me. For examples of her scholarship, see the July 2015 issue of the *Journal of Mormon History* (41.3). Devoted to interrogating and complicating the question of race in relationship to Mormonism, it is coedited and introduced by Colvin.

14. See, for example, David Knowlton, "Belief, Metaphor, and Rhetoric: The Mormon Practice of Testimony Bearing," *Sunstone* 81 (1991): 20–27.

Works Cited List

Aristotle. *The Poetics.* Ed. Richard McKeon. New York: Modern Library, 1947. Print.

Austen, Jane. *Pride and Prejudice.* 1813. Ed. Donald Gray. 3rd ed. New York: W. W. Norton and Company, 2001. Print.

Beck, Julie B. "Mothers Who Know." *lds.org.general-conference.* The Church of Jesus Christ of Latter-day Saints, 7 October 2007. Web. 19 July 2013.

Benson, Ezra Taft. "To the Mothers in Zion." *fc.byu.edu.* Brigham Young University, 22 February 1987. Web. 18 July 2013.

Callister, Douglas L. "Our Refined Heavenly Home." *lds.org. Ensign,* June 2009. Web. 22 February 2015.

Cherlin, Andrew J. *The Marriage-Go-Round: The State of Marriage and the Family in America Today.* New York: Vintage House, 2009. Print.

Church Handbook of Instructions 1 Stake Presidents and Bishops. ge.tt. 26 October 2012. Web. 21 July 2013.

"College Students More Eager for Marriage than Their Parents." *news.byu.edu.* Brigham Young University, 28 November 2012. Web. 18 July 2013.

Coontz, Stephanie. *Marriage, a History: How Love Conquered Marriage.* 2005. New York: Penguin Books, 2006. Print.

"The Family: A Proclamation to the World." *lds.org*. The Church of Jesus Christ of Latter-day Saints, 23 September 1995. Web. 15 July 2013.

Hanauer, Cathi. *The Bitch in the House*. New York: William Morrow and Company, 2002. Print.

Hunter, Howard. W. *The Teachings of Howard W. Hunter*. Ed. Clyde J. Williams. Salt Lake City: Bookcraft, 1997. Print.

Johnson, Jeffrey Odgen. "Determining and Defining 'Wife'—The Brigham Young Households." *Dialogue: A Journal of Mormon Thought* 20.3 (1987): 57–70. Print.

Kimball, Spencer W. "Oneness in Marriage." *lds.org*. *Ensign*, March 1977. Web. 20 July 2013.

"LDS Young Women Survey Results." *LDS Young Women Survey*, N. pag., 30 June 2013. Web. 18 July 2013.

Lehrer, Evelyn L., and Carmel U. Chiswick. "Religion as a Determinant of Marital Stability." *Demography* 30.3 (1993): 385–404. Print.

McKay, David O. "Structure of the Home Threatened by Irresponsibility and Divorce." *scriptures.byu.edu*. Brigham Young University, April 1969. Web. 20 July 2013.

Packer, Boyd K. "The Plan of Happiness." *lds.org*. *Ensign*, May 2015. Web. 13 June 2015.

"Plural Marriage in Kirtland and Nauvoo." *lds.org*. The Church of Jesus Christ of Latter-day Saints, n.d. Web. 12 December 2014.

Snow, Eliza R. "Oh My Father." *Hymns of The Church of Jesus Christ of Latter-day Saints*. Salt Lake City: The Church of Jesus Christ of Latter-day Saints, 1985. 292. Print.

Stegner, Wallace. *Mormon Country*. 1942. Lincoln: University of Nebraska Press, 1981.

Tingey, Earl C. "Three Messages to Young Adults." *lds.org*. The Church of Jesus Christ of Latter-day Saints, 2 May 2004. Web. 19 July 2013.

"When He Stopped Believing." *lds.org*. *Ensign*, July 2012. Web. 20 July 2013.

PART I

For Better or for Worse

Figure 3. Brent and Heather K. Olson Beal, December 1992, Huntsville, Texas

Heather writes: "Like many BYU couples, we were married between fall semester finals and Christmas break, on December 19—an especially busy time of year not well suited to weddings outside of Mormonism. If you look closely, you can see the drab brown industrial carpet of the gym floor in the ward building where the reception was held. My mother, who did all the reception planning while I focused on my studies, decided that a December wedding meant Christmas trees, poinsettias, and a Santa hat for Brent. When I look at this picture, in light of the essay included in this book, I like to think that our young marriage was one big joint project that we have continued to work on together for all these twenty-three years. I marvel that our naiveté resulted, improbably, in so much joy, laughter, and growth."

Projects

HEATHER K. OLSON BEAL

For years I believed my marriage was bulletproof. Brent and I genuinely preferred each other's company to anyone else's and rarely fought. Girls' nights out baffled me: I had zero interest in getting away from my husband (though the kids were another story). We did stuff together—big things. We got two undergraduate degrees (one each), one master's degree (me), and two PhDs (one apiece). We bought our first house and renovated every inch of it. We had three kids.

More importantly, with Brent as instigator, we did crazy stuff, like buy fifty big desks at an auction, resell them piecemeal, and use the profits to fund six delicious weeks in Spain. We sold magnetic toys imported from Italy on eBay, netting about $10,000 one Christmas—a huge windfall at the time. We opened and managed six Subway restaurants and two wildly unsuccessful taco joints.

My parents are risk-averse professors who would never dream of jumping on such bandwagons. Brent grew up in a family of seven supported by two teachers' salaries, so his parents cycled through entrepreneurial endeavors—partly to make ends meet, but also for the fun and challenge involved. For Brent, working together on big projects is what makes life worth living. And having a partner who jumps happily into big projects with you? That's what Brent calls "love."

We spent years planning our biggest project yet: I would finish my PhD and find an academic position; he would be the trailing spouse. I was eager to enjoy the fruits of my doctoral labors. He was anxious to get out of academia, the "safe" career he'd chosen as a young Mormon guy looking to support a future family, rather than pursuing entrepreneurial fantasies. I would be the primary breadwinner; he would work from home and do more kid-duty. By the time I defended my dissertation, we felt we pretty much had it licked. I got a faculty position in Texas. We sold our house, packed our belongings, bid farewell to Brent's academic career in Baton Rouge, and bought a more modest home in backwoods East Texas.

Then Brent hit the wall. It was so cliché. He was thirty-nine. Although happy to be out of academia, he disliked the isolation of working from home. Our new town—more than two hours from a major metropolitan area—lacked the sort of business opportunities he had planned to make his professional focus. His Baton Rouge business ventures—difficult to manage from a distance—began to falter and then founder. The specter of bankruptcy loomed over us. He also lost his faith, though it was more a slow bleed than a sudden fracture. He became frighteningly depressed, but couldn't see the depression for what it was.

I felt he took every aspect of his life and dumped it into a huge junk pile. He studied the mound of rubble that was his life up to that point. I imagine him cocking his head ever so slightly to one side, his thumb on his cheek while his forefinger rubbed his prominent brow, the way he does when contemplating how to tackle a thorny problem. Then he picked up each piece—"belief in the afterlife," for example—and examined it as a toddler might examine an acorn or a piece of glass he'd picked up off the ground. He'd shake it, press it to his ear, maybe scratch it against something—before holding it up to the light to see what it *really* held. And then he'd either throw it in the trash or put it on a "To Keep" table. He went through this process with just about everything: belief in God, belief in Mormon temple worship, belief in latter-day revelation, belief in eternal families, belief in the Word of Wisdom, his ambitions, his professional relationships—you get the picture. I thought I could handle everything being scrutinized this way. There was no item in his junk pile labeled "Heather," after all. We'd been sealed in the temple. I was safe.

Then, late one night, he started talking. And talking. Lying beside him in bed, listening to him, I realized, the way I imagine someone might realize that an intruder was in her home: there is an item in his life junk pile labeled "Heather." And he is picking me up even as we speak, holding me to the light and asking himself: What is this curious thing? Why do I have it? Where did I get it? How long have I been carrying it around in my pocket? Would I miss it if it were gone? Might I be happier without it?

He was weighing our life together in the balance. And for the first time, I understood that my marriage was not bulletproof. He might not want to stay married to me. My throat swelled as if I were having an allergic reaction. I opened my mouth to say the words I never thought I would say, but nothing came out. I tried again: "Do you want to get divorced?"

It felt like a mostly rhetorical question. The foundation of our relationship—its eternal potential—hadn't changed. This was just a bump in our otherwise happy eternal marriage. We were a forever family. So I said the words, but didn't really mean them. I fully expected him to roll over immediately, face me, his familiar features still obvious though I couldn't see them clearly in the dark, and reassure me, "Oh, no, no, no. That's not what I want at all." And we'd go from there.

But he didn't. He didn't say anything. I felt deeply ashamed at my presumption that our relationship, unlike anything else in his life, was automatically reserved for the To Keep table. Looking back, I assumed that our temple covenants to each other would trump everything else. In my mind, they did.

A few moments passed. I pressed, the words coming out more slowly, as if to honor the weight I now realized they had. "Well? Do you want to get divorced?"

He sighed but kept his back to me, which felt like a slap in the face since we always fell asleep somehow intertwined. Finally, his voice hollow with defeat, he said, "I don't know."

I felt I had been unceremoniously kicked to the curb. I resisted the urge to burst into tears, focusing instead on thinking of something I might say to soothe him—or myself. Something to mitigate the pain his response inflicted on me. Nothing came to mind.

I had my dignity to preserve and a problem to work through. It wasn't a choice, really, what I did next: I got out of bed, went into the office, and stared at the computer screen while I thought through the possible consequences of our conversation.

*   *   *

So what does a good Mormon woman—humiliatingly smug in her together-forever-marriage—do when her husband loses his faith and considers discarding his marriage as well? I cried, but not as fervidly as I might have predicted. Mostly I bottled it up. I'm not the type who responds to a casual inquiry from a coworker like, "Hey, Heather, how's it going?" with "Oh, hey, my life's in the shitter. How 'bout you?" I found it similarly difficult, when visiting teachers dropped by and asked, "Anything we can do for you?" to respond, "Well, yes. Could you please hire a private investigator to find out what the hell my husband is up to? The man I married has been AWOL for about a year." Truth be told, I avoided talking about it with even my closest friends. I knew I'd either have to lie and say, "Oh, we're great. Just great," or tell the truth, but I didn't even know what "the truth" was at that point. Only one friend—whose own marriage was circling the drain—was a sounding board for me. And she was pretty busy with her own troubles.

I considered my options. I asked Brent if it would help if I lost some weight. (I hate that this idea even occurred to me.) I was relieved when he scoffed at the suggestion and remember thinking, "Hey, maybe the guy I married is still in there somewhere." I tried Dr. Laura's men-only-want-sex-or-a-sandwich approach. I started with sex. Sadly, he wasn't interested, which was a pretty serious red flag. I googled things like "mid-life crisis" and "libido + depression." I created a spreadsheet with columns for his overall mood each day (ranked from 0 to 10), whether we had sex, and notes about weird things he said or did.

I thought the spreadsheet might either persuade me that things weren't as bad as I thought—or serve as documentation in the event of the divorce I feared was imminent. Then I tried the sandwich approach, finding a recipe for banana pudding (his favorite) and making it from scratch, even though I never make anything. He liked the pudding. But it couldn't save our marriage.

I begged him to see a doctor and at least try antidepressants. He was clearly in a very bad place. I came home sometimes and found him in bed, in a fetal position, at 1:00 in the afternoon. He took lots of naps and couldn't sleep at night. He drove six hundred miles to Baton Rouge several times a month in an attempt to maintain a few faltering businesses. Every time he left, I watched him pull out of the driveway and wondered if I would see him again. Once, on his way home, he cussed out a cop who pulled him over for speeding. The cop threatened to arrest him. (Is it against the law to tell a police officer to fuck off?) On another drive home, he texted that he was thinking of finding the first hotel room possible, washing down a handful of pills with alcohol, and just seeing what would happen.

I wondered whether a confession like that was enough to get a person admitted to the hospital under police or medical supervision. I thought for a fleeting moment of calling his parents—maybe they could talk sense into him? But I knew Brent would see that as an epic betrayal, as we had never taken our problems to our parents. Since he refused to see a doctor, I asked whether he would see a marriage therapist and was relieved when he grudgingly agreed. I closed my office door one day and called my insurance company to ask what kind of benefits they provided for . . . I didn't even know the name of it . . . mental health problems? Armed with the names and numbers of in-network providers, I found one who sounded nice and scheduled an appointment. I hung up the phone, cried for about five minutes, then left to teach my class.

It was humbling to sit on the couch in the therapist's office and report on the state of our marriage. I was ashamed to be in counseling and blamed Brent for our being there. It was Brent, after all, who had changed the terms of our agreement. I discounted the fact that our agreement (read = marriage) had been made fifteen years before by two people we scarcely recognized. We sat next to each other on the couch and held hands. The therapist wasn't much help. She belonged to a local conservative Christian church, so we spent much of our meetings explaining weird aspects of Mormonism. Still, the process felt like both a knife in the gut and a balm to my soul. It was eye-opening to hear Brent's responses to her questions and have to articulate mine—knowing that a third party was listening.

Brent took a no-holds-barred approach to our predicament. He said whatever he thought, which was very painful on many occasions. I think now is as good a time as any to share a few gems we discussed in therapy. There was the

Father's Day when, after opening a thoughtful card, Brent looked me squarely in the eye and said: "If all I had in my life were you and the kids, I would drive my car off the nearest bridge." (He now claims to have no recollection of saying it, or says if he did, I must be forgetting some of the context. I know he said it, but now that nearly six years have passed, and the kids affectionately call that time period "Dad's Sad Time," I see his comment for the aberration it was. And in some ways I empathize with his sentiment—I also chafe at being reduced to the fixed roles of mother and wife and actively nurture other dimensions of my personhood.) There was the time that I confessed to him that I felt lonely. He said: "I'm lonely, too. It's ridiculous for both of us to be lonely in this relationship. We have nothing in common and don't want any of the same things." The saddest one (actually, it's hard to pick the saddest one) was the time when he said: "Heather, if we weren't married and met each other right now, we wouldn't even want to date each other." He was adamant that if I had met him right then, in his quasi-apostate state, I would have immediately written him off. I assured him that I hadn't married him because of his religious affiliation (although to be honest, it hadn't hurt). That gave him pause.

I swallowed hard and bit the inside of my lip to hold back tears as he unloaded on me, but I wasn't always successful. We started an unfortunate loop like the ones that pop up on a web browser sometimes. No matter how many times you click on the X to close it, a new window pops up. He would say whatever he felt in the moment, I would feel sad and (sometimes) cry, he would complain that he couldn't speak his mind, and I would assure him (unconvincingly) that he could. Rinse and repeat.

We talked a lot about what it means to "love" a spouse. He was certain that he didn't, in fact, *couldn't*, love me the way I wanted to be loved. To this day, I'm not entirely clear on what he meant by that, and maybe in his depressed state, it was the truth. Although "love" for me didn't imply finding my one true love or soulmate, there was a part of me that needed to know that when he contemplated our relationship, he felt lucky, the way I did when I looked at him, even in his worst moments. Even though it was difficult to love the despairingly unhappy man Brent was at the time, I loved who he'd been and was pretty sure I could love whoever he became next. I knew my life was infinitely happier and more fun with him by my side. At times, I felt like a used car salesperson—trying to convince him that I was the make and model he needed, reminding him of all the amazing things we'd done together. In a way, this scary thing, whatever else it was, felt like another of our "projects." We would tackle it together. But I didn't want our marriage to feel like a project; I wanted him to feel lucky on his own, when I smiled at him or he dropped off to sleep beside me. He was supposed to love me forever, after all. That's a long time. He couldn't very well do it if he didn't like me, and he seemed not to.

We finally got ourselves out of the loop through some combination of modern-day miracles and dumb luck. The first step was that he started feeling better. We don't know why. (Apparently that just happens sometimes; Google *spontaneous recovery from depression* and you get about two million hits.) I gave up on the marriage counselor when she implied that Satan was persuading Brent to do evil and suggested that I read *The Power of a Praying Wife*. Uhh, not exactly the right advice for someone whose spouse was losing his religion. Brent continued to pick through his rubble pile.

As his fortieth birthday approached, I stewed over how to handle it, worrying that it would add to his sense of failure. Should I plan a party? Buy a special gift? I knew the kids would expect a celebration. I even prayed about it though I've never been the praying type (Mormon upbringing be damned). I knew it was considered poor form to ask God to help me think of good birthday gifts, but our situation seemed dire enough to warrant unusual divine petitions. One night, late, I had an epiphany. Call it divine inspiration. I decided to make him a list of the forty coolest things he'd ever done—both individually and with me. It was a fun list. It included things he'd done in elementary school, high school, and college. It included all the weird projects we'd worked on and all the businesses he had started (even the duds). It included private things to which only we two were privy. I uttered a prayer to the god I was no longer sure existed, asking that the list be well received.

His birthday arrived. In our family, the birthday person gets to pick where we go out to eat. Brent chose Barnhill's Buffet—a terrible, greasy Texas buffet chain that he doesn't even like. His choice seemed to be his way of flipping the bird at the whole fortieth birthday event. Still, we had a nice meal; the kids were satisfied. After putting them to bed, I tiptoed his way and handed him a sealed envelope containing the list. I willed myself to remain silent (rather than engage in my customary interjections) as he opened it and began to read. He seemed to take longer than necessary to read through it; I was relieved when he chuckled a few times. When he reached the end, his eyes welled with tears and he thanked me.

I printed my own copy of the list and kept it in my purse. Every couple of days, I texted him one of the forty projects. The list was a gift that kept on giving. Later, he told me the list was "life-altering, the perfect therapy." It helped him see his life through a different lens—one that honored all his—and our—quirky achievements.

The birthday list didn't halt the examination of Brent's life junk pile, though it may have affected a few decisions about what made the cut. After about eighteen months, Brent's throw-away pile had long exceeded its container and only a few lonely items remained on the To Keep table. Most of the pieces of his Mormon life ended up either in the throw-away pile or the recycle pile (which meant that he was either withholding judgment or that his understanding of them had changed significantly). Being a dad was probably the only thing that remained safely on the To Keep table throughout the decluttering process. It makes sense—you can't unhave children—but Brent's a stand-up guy, and it mattered to me both that Brent loved our kids and that he never considered shirking his obligations as a father.

Oddly, one piece that made it onto the To Keep table was church attendance—although this time, on his terms. For Brent, that meant getting dressed up on Sunday mornings, driving to church, and sitting on the pew together during sacrament meeting. It also meant that he brought things to occupy him when he got bored: the *Paris Review*, a Scrabble dictionary, the *New Yorker*, a notebook. He would attend Sunday school and priesthood meeting until he simply couldn't abide it anymore, at which point he'd slip out to a convenience store for a Diet Coke.

Luckily for me, the piece labeled "Heather" also made the cut—although he sees our relationship much differently now than he did premeltdown. I'm happy to say that he likes me again, and I think he feels lucky and happy to be with me. Furthermore, instead of valuing our relationship primarily because of its eternal potential, he values it because of our shared history and because of the things we have done, are doing, and will do together. He derives life satisfaction from doing things. It's all about the projects—preferably joint projects (we've got three beautiful kids to raise, he says, how's that for a project?)—but it's also great that we support each other in our individual endeavors. Discussing our personal projects with each other, strategizing about how to do them well, is almost as rewarding as doing projects together.

So once Brent was on the mend, all that was left was for me to (A) go back to business as usual, or (B) subject my stuff to the same scrutiny as Brent's. To be fair, option A wasn't really a possibility. Go back to what? My former life as Semi-Grumpy Feminist Mormon wife (because truth be told, I had plenty of issues of my own—particularly when "women" and "the church" are found in the same sentence) married to Rising-up-the-Priesthood-Ranks husband? That guy had taken a permanent leave of absence. Not only that, it was unsettling to look down my nose at Brent's messy piles while smugly leaving the pieces in my life junk pile ("family," "church culture," "church doctrine," "Christianity," "career") undisturbed.

That left me with option B. As I held each of my own items up to the light, I had to consider them within the context of what I knew Brent had decided to do with his corresponding piece. For instance, take the idea of hauling the family up to the church building for eight hours of general conference satellite broadcasts to hear God's words as revealed through modern-day prophets. Well, Brent had put the "belief in latter-day revelation" piece in the "Throw-Away" pile.

So in order for me to put it in the To Keep pile, it had to be really important to me. I had to want to keep that piece enough to possibly take the kids to watch the boring broadcasts by myself. That was a no-brainer: it was out. I will add, however, that for several years afterward, we still went to the Sunday morning session of general conference. We got dressed up, drove to the church, and sat on the pew together for 120 long minutes. And then we went out to lunch. (The ban on eating out on Sundays was an easy toss into the Throw-Away pile for both of us. We like it too much.)

The most painful piece to find a place for was the one labeled "eternal marriage." This was possibly my favorite piece—the piece I had clung to almost like slimy Gollum from *The Lord of the Rings* clung to his ring. I'd held that piece in my pocket for years, rubbing its edges to reassure myself. Gollum referred to the ring—an object which unnaturally extended his life while corrupting his soul—as his "precious" and his "birthday present." My belief in the power of our eternal marriage had become more than just a belief; it had become an object I prized much as Gollum prized his ring. That naïve (though not conscious) belief allowed me to take our marriage for granted—to believe that it was something I possessed or, worse, something I had *earned* by virtue of our righteous choice to get married in the temple—rather than a process that required presence and vigilance and, perhaps most importantly, negotiation.

But Brent had ditched his "eternal marriage" piece and replaced it with the "we're staying married because we like doing projects together" piece. So I held my "eternal marriage" piece up to the light, knowing that Brent's matching piece hadn't made the cut. It looked tarnished. I hefted it and it felt tinny—kinda like a slug nickel. My piece actually wasn't any good without his. Oh, sure—I could have dug in my heels and gone with option A, flashing my solitary "eternal marriage" piece in front of Brent every once in a while. I could have used it as a bargaining chip or to manipulate him and the kids somehow.

But I couldn't bring myself do that—not to him or to the kids. Or to myself. The idea left a bitter taste in my mouth. So I asked myself the same questions I imagined Brent had asked himself as he held his "eternal marriage" piece up to the light: What is this curious thing? Why do I have it? Where did I get it? How long have I been carrying it around in my pocket? Would I miss it if it were gone? Might I be happier without it?

It was a major breakthrough for me when I asked myself, "Can I live without this piece?" and the answer was "yes." I shared that epiphany with Brent, unceremoniously announcing that I could live without him, even though I didn't want to. I could even take care of our kids without him—although I hoped he wouldn't make me. Releasing the idea that I couldn't be happy without him was a big step. It allowed me to release a lot of other things—both big and small—that I had held onto as well. For starters, I released the notion that temple garments were significant to my salvation. I still wore them for years afterward, probably due more to laziness and lack of interest in finding an alternative than to belief in their eternal importance. I decided to stop attending the temple indefinitely and to stop feeling guilty about it. I released my years-long attempt to reconcile patriarchal church teachings and practices as having divine origins. I also released a long list of behavioral expectations I had about our family's Mormonism that suddenly seemed petty: my obsession with arriving to church on time, my worry that other people might see Brent reading the *New Yorker* or one of the kids reading the latest kid fiction during sacrament meeting, the expectation that my children would graduate from early morning seminary, the fear that someone from church would see us walk into a restaurant after church on Sunday—you get the picture.

I ended up making a new pile of my own just for the "eternal marriage" piece. I still like the idea that whatever Brent and I have going on in this life will continue—in some form or fashion—simply because I don't want it to end. I just don't think we're the only ones who might get to do that. And I don't think that the reason we might get to do that is because we got married in a special building. I think Brent and I might get to do that because we're a good team. I like him better than anybody else. And hey—I can't forget: we work on projects together.

Make It Up Every Day

HEIDI BERNHARD-BUBB

My trajectory toward seminary graduation, Brigham Young University, temple marriage, and motherhood always felt so certain that I took it for granted. It was like the heavy gray sky that hung overhead during the long winters in Michigan where I spent most of my childhood: inescapable and ever-present, but form- less. My imagination, so vivid in other areas, never created a substantial picture of my future spouse. The man of my dreams was a hazy creature: sometimes bookish and dreamy, my male doppelganger; other times like the gentle college professors or theatrical salesmen of my family. I believed, rather unconsciously, that choosing a Mormon mate was about salvation, a way of shoring up that picture-perfect life of financial security, a row of kids in crisp matching outfits, and a spot in the celestial kingdom. The man I married was supposed to make me a better Mormon.

When I met Jared during my second year at BYU, I felt I had found a kindred spirit. In a sea of conformity, where testimony-bearing was a competitive sport and a way to show off your spiritual plumage to the opposite sex, he was refresh- ingly sane about our shared faith. In fact, a large part of our initial attraction was that we were Mormon in similar ways. Observing the Word of Wisdom, remaining chaste, and generally trying to be Christ-like were nonnegotiable. Regular attendance at all the meetings Mormonism involved, temple-going, and tithing were things we struggled with, but thought we should do. Without too much guilt, we ignored bans on tattoos, R-rated movies, and eating out on Sundays. In other words, we both liked the spirit of the law better than the letter.

Jared had grown up in a rural Pennsylvania community where most of his classmates went to work in factories or on family farms. A bright but average student, he wasn't considered university material, and people were surprised when he headed to BYU on an Army officer training scholarship. Jared loved the Army but struggled with authority figures. At BYU, he quickly got on the bad side of a succession of bishops, elders quorum presidents, and religion professors. But his questioning of authority didn't translate into questioning his membership; he remained essentially loyal to the church.

I wasn't physically attracted to Jared at first. Unlike the dark, androgynous boys I'd dated in high school, Jared was blond and blue-eyed. The high cheekbones and full lips of his delicate, boyish face contrasted with his slightly brutish, masculine presence. Still, the first time we touched, when my roommate asked us to move closer for a photograph, I felt a surprising but undeniable electric frisson. Six weeks later, when he confessed his feelings for me with an odd but appealing mixture of shyness and defiance, I kissed him.

After my formless childhood dreams of marriage, Jared's solid reality, with all his contradictions and particularity, delighted me. He played guitar and piano. He loved to read but preferred Nietzsche and Herodotus to the fiction I devoured. An unfailing romantic champion of lost causes and forgotten technology, Jared still surprises me after seventeen years of marriage. I've driven all over England looking for obscure Anglo-Saxon burial mounds with him and watched him take up woodcarving, spend countless hours trying to replicate Bronze-Age smelting techniques, form bands, write Byronic poetry, learn to make guitar effects pedals from the tubes of old televisions, and restore vintage cars and analog synthesizers.

When Jared asked me to marry him, only a few months after we met, I didn't hesitate or even pray for an answer. We might have looked like many couples at BYU, another blonde Heidi and Jared announcing their engagement at ward prayer, but I felt we were different. I chose Jared instinctually, without the characteristic anxiety I had over every other decision in my life. I could put this down to being young and romantic, but I don't think that was entirely true. I already saw that he was both flexible and fiercely loyal. More significantly, he made me feel relaxed and spacious, at home with myself.

I had grown up surrounded by faithful but open-minded and loving adults. My parents followed traditional gender roles, but are both strong individuals who maintained their own interests and spoke with an equal voice in our home. They taught my brothers and me that their marriage was a partnership based on friendship, sexual compatibility, and hard work. As parents, they gave me little to rebel against and, in return, I gave them little to worry about. I was a good girl—a good girl with an artsy, rebellious streak, but an honest, dutiful, straight-A, scripture-reading good girl nonetheless. "You were always so spiritual and wise," my mother would say, telling stories about finding me on my knees in fervent prayer at age three. Another family story is that I sat my parents down when I was four to tell them what I was planning to study in college. In high school, I tearfully confessed every minor infraction. "You were so upset, I thought you were going to tell us you were pregnant," my mom said after I told her and my father that I had tried smoking.

But there were things I didn't confess, stories that didn't make it into the family narrative. I never told anyone about the nights I stayed up, my seven-year-old self plagued with anxiety over where God came from. If God had created me, who had created God? I didn't know why, but asking felt like it would break my whole world apart. Increasingly frightened, I decided that I couldn't think about where God came from; I had to put it out of my mind. I figured that God would explain it to me later, in the next life. I wanted to keep being a good girl, one who didn't stay up late thinking about scary questions, so I stuffed my first crisis of faith down deep.

Despite my childhood skepticism and my attraction to a man who offered spontaneity and space rather than security, I panicked when we were engaged and Jared wanted to go for a drive in Provo Canyon instead of watching the second Sunday session of general conference because "one session's enough, and conference is boring."

"It's not boring," I said automatically, my whole body tensing. "It's modern revelation. They're telling us things we need to hear for our time."

"When was the last time you actually heard something new?" he asked. "They pretty much always say the same stuff."

"OK, but it isn't supposed to be entertaining. It's up to us to make it meaningful. I always find something that I can learn from, even if it's just a scripture or a small piece of advice," I said, parroting my mother and a lifetime of seminary and Sunday school teachers.

Jared shrugged and smiled. "Church would be so much better if it was videotaped and you could fast-forward through the boring parts."

I thought of the sleepiness that always overtook me during conference and how I stayed awake by thinking of books I was reading. I knew conference was boring, but didn't want to admit it. It was a relief, and weirdly thrilling, to hear someone say it out loud. I made him promise to read the second session when it came out in the *Ensign*—and then we went for the drive.

One night Jared tasted rum and Coke with a friend while watching a band play at a bar. A pragmatist, he reasoned that tasting the alcohol without having a whole drink was a suitable way to satisfy his curiosity without really breaking the Word of Wisdom. I was horrified when he told me. "Why would you risk our eternal salvation over a small drink?" I demanded tearfully. I made him promise to never do it again, and he, not seeing it as a big deal, agreed.

And then, a year after we got married, Jared said he wasn't ready to have a family. Having known since childhood that motherhood was my destiny, I laughed away his suggestions that we should finish college first, have only one child, or that I should keep working after we had kids. (Blithely underestimating the difficulty of balancing childrearing and a career, I assumed that I could do that later, when my kids were in school.) My husband was struggling at the time, unable to figure out what he wanted to do after an injury got him discharged from the Army. Whenever he called in sick to his part-time job because he didn't feel like going, I worried that he would never be a good provider. Fearful, I pressed him even harder, believing tough love could force him into fulfilling his priesthood duties of providing and presiding—a fake-it-'till-you-make-it shortcut to proper manhood. He responded by spending a month in bed, too depressed to attend class or go to work. Not knowing what else to do, I backed off and gave him space. In time, he decided to get a degree in history education, went back to class, and returned to work. Despite my misgivings, I accepted where Jared was at and we ignored church counsel not to delay having children: we waited for five years, until he was well established in his career as a teacher and I'd begun working as a freelance reporter.

With so many expectations for happiness and fulfillment pinned on my roles as wife and mother, it's perhaps unsurprising that my long, gradual slide away from full belief and activity in the Mormon church really started with motherhood. When we began our family, I adored my son, but motherhood wasn't the spiritually fulfilling bliss I was promised. It was a complicated emotional rollercoaster, and I was lost. Needing spiritual guidance more than ever, I turned to the church for counsel. The scriptures are largely silent about women's lives, but conference talk after conference talk told me that being a mother was the most important thing I would ever do and, even though it could be hard, it was selfish to put my needs ahead of my husband or children.

Unsatisfied, I began reading every childcare book I could get my hands on, thinking that if I just got the formula right, motherhood would become the spiritual bliss I'd been promised. Devouring book after book, I found tremendous comfort in parenting memoirs by a single-mother and former alcoholic and a bisexual riot grrl who parented with equal parts feminism and Buddhism. Their experiences were different from mine, but I thrived on their message that I didn't have to parent in one particular way. As I loosened my grip on being the kind of mother I thought I was supposed to be, I began to find my footing without compromising the delicate balance between my testimony and my deepening feminism.

Still, the crack in my testimony was there. As I held various callings, long suppressed doubts began to mount a rebellion. They constantly rose to the surface, troubling the equilibrium I had managed since that dark night of my seven-year-old soul. Doubts multiplied and divided until every prayer I gave or lesson I prepared left me feeling torn in half.

Our home life had never been overtly orthodox: we had no copy of the Proclamation on the Family hanging on the wall, our family scripture reading was haphazard at best, and our version of family home evening was Fun Friday where we got treats and watched a movie together. Consequently, I was able to hide the seriousness of my doubts for a time. I tentatively brought up unanswerable questions and listened to Jared's usually kind and open-minded responses while keeping my darker, more skeptical thoughts to myself. Despite my deepening doubt, I didn't know who I was without the church, and I couldn't begin to imagine our marriage as separate from the church.

In 2006, Jared got a job in the United Kingdom, far away from the expectations of our families, giving me literal space and time to come to terms with the doubts I had harbored since childhood. Two years later, as the world turned its attention toward California's Proposition 8 banning gay marriage, I realized that I had come to a fundamentally different understanding of marriage and identity. I had always believed that people were born homosexual, and I no longer viewed marriage as a means for salvation. I believed it was about love and partnership and could work in many different ways.

As I began to process and understand my own feelings, I eventually confessed the full extent of my doubts to Jared. Despite his complaints that church was boring and too concerned with conformity, he was devastated and his early reactions were harsh. He was as loyal to the church as he had always been to me. He saw the same problems I did, but accepted them as the way things were.

Days would pass without any mention of the church or the issues we faced, and then something would come up, a criticism from me or a passive-aggressive joke from him, and we would find ourselves arguing bitterly with little of the catharsis or common ground we'd always managed to find in the past. "You can't drink the Kool-Aid," he said late one night, picking up the thread of an argument that started at dinner. "That's how I've always managed in the church. I keep the big rules, but I ignore the stupid stuff."

For Jared, the "stupid stuff" was all cultural and human—it was Jell-O and funeral potatoes, the holiness ascribed to white shirts and members who were judgmental or unkind. But the issues that troubled me were more systemic, entangled in culture and doctrine. I worried about sexism and homophobia, the nature of God, and what it really meant to say, "I know the church is true."

"It's hard for me to ignore the culture, because the culture is most of our experience at church. Besides, I'm not even sure about the big rules," I said, feeling marooned and weary on my side of the bed.

"I think you expect God to be loving and cool all the time, but he's not like that. He's vengeful and wrathful at times; sometimes he's Old Testament," Jared said, growing more heated. "I follow the gospel because it's true and that's what God is telling us to do, not because I always like it."

"How do we know it's really God telling us and not just men, influenced by the culture and time they were raised in?" I said. "And why wouldn't God be loving, representative of the ideal, of what we're supposed to be?"

And so it went, round and round again, ending with me in tears.

"I don't think you're being prideful: I can see you're trying to do the right thing," he said, softening. "But I think you're taking a huge risk."

His fear was palpable and primal. He was worried about my soul, but more importantly, my rejection of the church felt like a rejection of our marriage. Jared said he worried that if I could change my mind about something as big as the church, I could change my mind about him too. I said he would have to have faith in me and in our marriage, in the same ways I had learned to do. I wanted to be with him because I loved him, not because of my duty to our temple marriage.

Jared became tormented by the thought that his lack of orthodoxy and presiding had led to our calamity. If only he had dutifully attended the temple and worn white shirts, he thought, we would have been safe. I knew in my heart that had he been that person, I would have been desperately unhappy and our marriage would be over. There were no threats of divorce, no slammed doors or nights with one of us on the couch, just a deadening silence that lasted well over a year. There was no way to fix this. Any solution would require one of us to sacrifice what they believed and neither of us could ask the other to do that.

Over a period of years, I had pulled further and further away from leadership and teaching callings. For a time, Primary seemed like a safe haven, a place to focus on basic morality. However, even my participation there began to feel more and more like a lie. Earlier and earlier in the week, I began to dread going to church; by Sunday morning, I was tearful and spoiling for a fight. Eventually, Jared said he thought I should give up my calling as Primary chorister and take a break from attending church. He was concerned about my well-being, but I also think he longed for more clarity. I had been willing to continue attending church to help with the children, sitting on my hands in Sunday school so I wouldn't be tempted to raise them and offer a comment. Somehow I thought that it would lessen Jared's feeling of abandonment. Maybe I thought I deserved some kind of penance. However, Jared didn't want to pretend; he wanted to be honest about where we were. I had thought that I would know when and how to leave the church, that I would come upon some graceful exit, but in the end, I just couldn't do it anymore. I grabbed at his offer like a drowning woman.

It was a crucial moment in our marriage. The moment when we stopped reaching for an ideal that no longer existed and instead turned toward the reality of who and where we were. I'd like to say that we've subsequently set upon some brilliant formula to make our mixed-faith marriage work, but that's not true. We're always negotiating, figuring out ways to make us both feel safe. Jared has been to counseling to work through some of his feelings of betrayal and fear. I've written and cried my way through a host of contradictory and confusing feelings. We peer into our children's faces like tea leaves, looking for signs to predict their future paths. Jared worries that he will be the last active Mormon in his line; I worry that I will find myself waiting outside the walls of the temple with the other nonmembers when my children get married.

I try not to take it personally when the children look at my coffee cup disapprovingly or be too smug when they call the church out on sexism or racism. When they ask tough questions about morality, or those cups of coffee, I answer honestly and then I say, "Your dad may believe something different; you should ask him too." This is what we both say, over and over again: "When you are older, you will decide for yourself about the church; everyone must decide for themselves. We will love you no matter what you decide." And we say it to each other, too: I love you, no matter what you have decided about the church.

In many ways our religious differences have simplified everything—our common ground is kindness and tolerance. We have chosen to accept certain seemingly paradoxical truths about the other. Despite my belief that the church is fundamentally sexist and wrong about many things, I believe that Jared is not sexist or foolish. Despite hearing a lifetime of teachings that those who doubt are prideful or sinful, Jared believes I am openhearted. I was raised to seek a "firm foundation," to believe that holding fast to my ideals would keep me safe and that peace comes through certainty. Our marriage isn't like that, a hard wall against the world. It is fluid and soft. We make it up every day as we turn toward each other, as we really are, instead of turning away.

The Language of Marriage

AMY SORENSEN

When we lie in bed, his leg over my legs and our feet hooked together, our torsos angling away from each other, we make the shape of a child's clumsy construction-paper heart. It's the comfort of the long-wed that comes from knowing how to orient our bodies to allow for what hurts, the pressure point on my thigh that he avoids so my knee doesn't twinge, the tilt of my body that relieves his aching hip. We adjust to diminish each other's pains and we stay like that until sleep rolls us apart.

But don't be fooled by that tranquil image: my husband and I are fighters. We have, in fact, argued this entire Saturday. Quite often in my marriage, what passes for normal is the spark to a fracas: our teenage daughter needs the car, I want to go for a run, the bathrooms are messy, there are five pairs of shoes under the kitchen table, and the TV's too loud—and then I drop the knife I'm cutting a bagel with. I drop a knife and now there's a small, thumbnail-shaped dent in the kitchen floor and a small dent of silence; an argument explodes. It's never fists or open palms we toss at each other, but words, chosen carefully even at the height of fury, for their ability to wound, deeply. We recriminate, we guilt, we scoff, we deride. The argument moves from kitchen to bedroom to family room to the car; it calms and then rises again. There are moments when hatred for this person I chose to marry fills me with blackness and others when no word but *weep* can describe the sound I make when I realize again that I also love him. The argument ends only when we finally remember that the other is just a hurting person, with wounds that originated long before we met. This scraping the other raw is how we get, finally, to the nakedness that allows us each to stop. Then we can talk instead of argue, can explain, and forgive, but part of the stilled conversation always forces us to ask: how do we arrive here so often?

Perhaps the more piercing question is *Why do we stay together?* It's one I ask myself every time we are caught up in argument. In a larger sense, this war we fight never really ends; the time we spend not arguing is simply a pause, sometimes weeks or even months long, between battles. During peaceful times, we are careful to follow the grammar of our marriage, the rules we've devised without explication that keep us from sparking up again. Our careful peace inspires me to become a watcher of married people. In the grocery store, at the movie theater, at the mall, and in church, I study the language they speak together. I see how they touch each other, the small courtesies they make. Also the seemingly invisible slights. I imagine the couple at the table next to us in the small Thai restaurant has never screamed like we do. But I only know my marriage. My own damaged, dramatic union.

Newly wed, one of our first arguments was over spilled milk—literally. I was just learning that my new husband's penchant for clean counters and vacuumed carpets has a darker side than all that tidiness suggests: messes are triggers. I spilled milk and he was angry and I was defensive because really? Spilled milk? Hadn't he heard the cliché? Listening to him yell about a spill was an entirely alien experience for me, as I hadn't ever imagined someone being mad about messes. It was like listening to someone speak a foreign language, Urdu or Bambara. That moment over the spilled milk is when I started to learn the true nature of marriage. It isn't romance. It isn't sweetness and light and always having someone to hold your hand. It's messy and complicated. Sometimes it's downright ugly. Marriage is, in fact, a language, one that only the two of you speak. No one else has the same dialect as you, unless it's your kids, who will take a portion of it and speak it in their own marriages where their spouses will at first find it utterly incomprehensible.

In the beginning, we hardly hear what the other person is saying. An argument over spilled milk seems to be just what it is, but really it's an anthology of unresolved issues. I came from a home where housecleaning was the way my parents emotionally manipulated each other, until the tension stopped anyone from cleaning up much of anything, even spilled milk. My husband came from a home where cleaning the house was a thing they could control in the face of the uncontrollable, which was his little brother's leukemia. In the battle of spilled milk, my apathy and his outrage are each a coded message we lob to the other, destined to explode in confusion. It will be years, decades even, before the language of our marriage can translate the message. Hours of conversation and argument and discussion; tiny syllables uttered mistakenly that finally and at last and only for seconds let us see the true person. The thousand million adjustments of self that occur as two people who were taught a language in their childhood make one of their own.

"I don't understand you," we say, or "How could you think that?" undertaking the semantics of our marriage. The language originates with those flighty days in the beginning, when simple nearness made your teeth ache with longing. When you couldn't imagine anything other than happiness with this person. Stories, laughter, the startling intimacy of the other are the protolanguage, the primordial forming of how you are with each other. The language starts with newness and evolves with shared experience: that time we hiked the waterfall together and were soaked in bliss; the vacation that was an endurance run of miscommunication. The night his mother died and the way grief was a thing that dissolved old bitterness is a phoneme. My father's slow descent into wordlessness is an allophone. The birth of children, yes, and the loss of them, either the abrupt miscarriage or the long, slow process of saying goodbye that is parenting; the first careful steps of our oldest daughter across spring grass, the confident first strokes of our youngest son on his bicycle. Also small things, burnt chicken, a tree ruined by pruning too fiercely, a scratch on the car. Shopping for shoes. Experience becomes history as single words become metaphor: "flannel," we say, by which we mean "thank you for understanding what I need."

But language, for all its propensity for meaning, is hard to understand. In marriage this is because we are bilingual. The person we were before we met the person we would marry had a way of being in the world, and that is our native tongue. Forget the student loans, the old TV, and the three brimming bookcases: what we bring to our marriage is this language of individuality, with its own history and permutations and aches and joys. The language the other person speaks is the reason we love them. But from it, conflict arises because it is so easy to misunderstand. We misconstrue, we misspeak, we stumble over words. We question whether we loved the language the other person spoke or if we were only intrigued by its exoticness. We come to discover that the real task of marriage is this language, is this trying to say the same word when we are each speaking in different tongues.

Much of the language of marriage is conversation using words in unfamiliar ways. We think we are saying a simple thing, but the unstated inflection is the real conversation. "What should we do on Saturday?" I ask, which really means, "I'd like to sit somewhere you can't see my face while you listen to my doubts about my parenting skills."

"I don't care; what sounds fun to you?" he responds, which means, "I've worked all week and really what I want is to veg out in front of the TV, but as some marriage rule book somewhere suggested that we should have a date once in a while, I'll go along."

In the language of marriage, conversations are more than words; they are shared history and thoughts kept in the dark and things we don't understand about ourselves; they are the curve of the neck, the arc of a shoulder shrug, the shape of an eyebrow. "Can you wash my socks, will you stop for a loaf of bread, could you hand me those scissors?" we ask, when really what we're asking is, "Do you love me, do you love me, do you love me?"

And these are just the small, easy conversations. The hard ones—not right and wrong, but opposing desires—become larger than the language we've invented. One person says *please*, the other says *no*. How to reconcile the conversations that speak from entirely different countries of desire? My husband and I talked for years over the same topic: I wanted another baby; he wanted to be finished. A discourse of pleading and guilt, it was the subject we couldn't get past, the plea I couldn't stop uttering, the *no* his body made over and over. I wanted the sweet neediness of infancy just one more time, wanted to give the holding and washing and watching that babies require. He wanted the freedom of older kids, the happy ability to decide to go somewhere and then just go; he wanted dialogue and a helper in the yard and kids who could feed themselves. "Tie me to that sweetness just once more," I said. "Free me from need," he replied. Someone has to compromise, and for me the waiting felt like sacrifice and for him the child in the end felt like sacrifice, and yes: we had one more baby, but we still have the conversation in our marriage's language. I speak it when I hold on to that box of baby clothes no one will ever use and he says it every time he's happy that that one last baby phase has ended.

*   *   *

"Conversation," we say, as if we aren't always on the edge of a skirmish. The subjunctive grammar of our marriage is designed to avoid fighting, but we speak it like infants. By now, we each know the rules. If I don't spend too much at the fabric store, we won't fight when we balance the checkbook. If he leaves me alone with a book for an hour, we won't argue about driving the kids to school in the morning. It's when we speak the words of our own wanting that speech becomes fierce. If he gets annoyed at the sight of me reading with messes at my feet, I'll put my book down. I'll straighten up the messes. But I'll let resentment grow in me—because reading isn't just reading, it's a tie to the person I was before I met him, and reading amid clutter isn't just ignoring, it is my way of stating what's important to me. Resentment simmers until salt is poured in, and then it boils over: the school is on his way, sort of; why doesn't he drive the car pool this morning? If we could only manage the grammar of this language, but the failure comes from need, the argument from the desire to live without constraint. These are primal forces we try to control.

Mostly argument is an ablaut: *dream, dreamt, dreamed*. We each try to say a word, often something similar, but not close enough to avoid conflagration. That's how this language that is marriage works. In trying to communicate, our voices are drowned by our need to be heard. We try to understand the other but there's always also the loud squall of our own desires. "Let's talk," we say, but rarely in the same words at the same time. Need goes unanswered as we bump around each other, perpetually in the dark. He asks for intimacy when I ask for rest. "Romance," I ask when he is saying "solitude." "Let's go," he says. "Let's stay," I reply. We are each, really, speaking only with ourselves, and in the clash of two soliloquies argument explodes. Happiness in my marriage happens on days that lack argument, which come when we manage to speak properly or by the random coincidence of us both wanting the same thing at the same moment. In unhappiness we shout our needs in our arterial language and at first we hear nothing the other says. Our feints and strikes are based on the knowledge of weakness: we rush to wound in order to protect our own and we strategize wisely because we also know the other's. This knowledge also brings us to the stripped places in ourselves that allow us to say the true thing and also, at last, to hear it. That space is where peace talks resume, where we find how to forgive and to move forward. Where we ask ourselves, *Why do we stay together when we can let it get this ugly?* And where the answer is only ever—finally, eventually—the one word we both can speak.

*   *   *

To an outsider, the language of our marriage must seem unbearably conflicted, our actions immature, our tempers selfish. Were there a peace negotiator in the mix—a marriage counselor, perhaps, a helpful friend, a concerned church leader—wondering why we are still married, he or she would have to translate our language before proffering wisdom, and that's a long story. A battle song, perhaps, but understanding my marriage's language means knowing that I'm not afraid to fight with my husband. He and I are not the speakers of a pastoral tongue. Much as I wanted a sonorous marriage, one full of trills and rolled R's and assonance, the language we created is a guttural thing, packed with abrupt silence and explosive consonance. In our language there is no gentle *around*, there is only ever *through*: the long uphill cant. Where we arrive at the end—at last, at last at *no*, at *yes*, at *try*, at *see*, at *love*, at the same word we have both been speaking without saying—is the answer to the question *why stay*.

My marriage is a diphthong, two vowels crammed into one structure, and it's the conflict in the blending that makes the sound we are together. Neither one of us was made to be a passive receiver of peace, and that is the thing that connects us. Like birth and cooking and living and art and death, it's messy. There is spilled milk, spilled breath, spilled blood. We argue, we say things we shouldn't, we are unnecessarily cruel. We also make it *through*. We find the way to say the word we need to have heard, despite the problems of translation. We forgive. Sometimes we surprise each other by finding the word without the argument; usually we settle on compromise and accept that neither one will be completely happy. Batting away help, holding hands, making fists, cupping our wounds, we speak and speak and speak this language until we find the angle that comforts one and assuages the other, until we find the place where we fit together like a clumsy heart, cut jagged but still one piece, falling quietly into dark.

The World We Share

MARILYN BUSHMAN-CARLTON

In the evening we came back
Into our yellow room,
For a moment taken aback
To find the light left on.
　　—May Sarton, "A Light Left On"

My husband and I fell in love like a faucet, one that dripped in the fourth grade, again in the seventh, until it rushed as a stream in the ninth. We had grown up together in Lehi, Utah, at the time a small town. We were in the same grade, took many of the same tests, and participated in common spelling bees. Both good students, we competed, in a relaxed way, with each other. My father was a dairy farmer, his, a Geneva Steel worker. Being told we "couldn't afford it" was a daily reminder in both our homes.

In January 1961, as high school students, Blaine and I had our first official date: his sister and her fiancé took us to Salt Lake City to a movie and dinner at a Japanese restaurant. While I declined to drink the tea served with the meal because it was against the Word of Wisdom, Blaine did not. He came from an inactive family; his parents seldom attended church, and they didn't have family prayers. Once when he was asked to give a Sunday school talk, he came to my house to browse through church books because there were none in his home.

We broke up after high school. He had never talked of serving a mission; his nineteenth birthday came and went. I heard rumors that as a university student, he didn't believe in God. I knew he was, by nature, a skeptic; I also knew that religion was something he wrestled with. He asked me out a few times at that point, but I declined. I had a testimony and knew he couldn't be for me what my devout father was to my believing mother. We would not have that unified glow of gospel light flooding the rooms of our home.

A couple of years behind schedule, he accepted a mission call. He phoned me a week before he left for Brazil, and we went out. A spark still ignited between us. At his farewell, I sat at the back of the overflow hall, crying afterward over what felt like a final goodbye. I was twenty-one; surely I would be married by the time he returned.

Instead, we were married in the Salt Lake Temple seven months after Blaine returned from his twenty-seven–month mission. By then he also had three years of college under his belt and plans to go to law school. Because my older sister hadn't been able to go to college—I had listened to her conversations with our parents who "couldn't afford it and didn't think it necessary"—I had dropped my own hope of further education like a broken pencil and spent five years after high school working menial jobs that still allowed me to buy things my family had never been able to afford.

Blaine and I began our marriage in 1969 as the second wave of feminism percolated. It didn't particularly interest me. I had always liked being a woman. My father was an involved and generous priesthood holder who watched out for his family. I had no desire for a "career" and liked the idea of having my own house, keeping it tidy and running smoothly. I wanted to be at home with my future children. Having "worked" for five years, I was ready to be a wife, a mother, and a homemaker. I was anxious to get pregnant, not only because I wanted a baby, but also because I wanted to quit my job.

Blaine and I agreed at least that women should earn equal wages for equal work. His position came purely from political ideology. In a town as Republican as it was Mormon, his family were Democrats. Equal pay, if women wanted a career, made sense to me, too. I believe in fairness. But that was that. I got pregnant, quit my dead-end job, had our first baby, Blaine changed his mind about law school, and we headed off to Florida where he would pursue a master's degree in political science with an emphasis in Latin American studies, a change motivated by the years he'd spent in Brazil. I was bursting with happiness as we drove across the country toward our new adventure.

And then reality set in. With a child who took two long naps a day, housework that could be done in short order, and a husband who was either at school or studying, I was bored. He suggested I go to the library. I bristled: he just wanted me to keep myself busy and out of his hair. But reading filled in some of the gaps in my days and before I knew it, I was pregnant with our second daughter. In the meantime, problems surfaced in our marriage: the University of Florida was the Berkeley of the East during the sexual revolution that accompanied the feminist and antiwar movements. While he roamed a campus clamoring with scantily clad single women, I was barefoot and pregnant. Although I hadn't voiced my disappointment when he decided against law school, I became convinced that coming to Florida had been a huge mistake. Not only was the atmosphere un-bearable for me, friends in our ward told him that jobs for college professors in his field were few and far between. In desperation, Blaine went to our bishop, certain that he would see our situation to his advantage—after all, our bishop was a college professor. To my husband's amazement (and mine; I'd refused to go with him), the taciturn bishop suggested, "Surely you can find a vocation that will make you both happy."

Back in Salt Lake, where Blaine entered law school, and where three little boys joined our family in quick succession, I understood that Florida hadn't been the core problem: I could see no happy future for myself. I don't remember what came first—was it reading feminist literature or sitting beside my husband, the brilliant law student, in gatherings where every time someone listed her credentials, the whole scene reaffirmed for me that I was nobody with nothing to show for my life? OK, I had children I loved, but so did all the other wives. The problem with no name described by Betty Friedan in *The Feminine Mystique* carved a gaping hole deep within me.

I had to do something. I went to a consciousness-raising group of women at the University of Utah. Speaking in public, particularly in small groups, made my heart pound, stole my breath and speech. So that everyone would be treated equally—after all, that's what the movement was about—each had a turn speaking for a designated period of time. Somehow I did it, and even though I wasn't like the others there, we all identified with that nameless problem. I attended a writing class at a local bookstore, but I was the only one there who wasn't already a writer. Wherever I went, I felt years and textbooks behind.

I was angry at women with careers, at women without careers who still had even a year or two of college, at men because they had it so easy, at the system that said that's how it's supposed to be. I was angry at my parents who couldn't send their daughters to college but could send two sons to college and on missions, too. I was angry at my husband, in particular, for having opportunities to study and learn. He could spend time preparing for his life's work and could put it first for the rest of his life. He could have children, but without getting mashed potatoes in his face or sour milk on his nice clothes. And he got the kudos that came with being an intelligent attorney. I was angry at the church and its glib assertion that women could be happy without intellectual stimulation or authentic praise. The patronizing speeches about the high calling of motherhood only fueled my anger.

I said so. Out loud. I said the church was wrong. I said I couldn't believe in a church that withheld opportunities from women, that fought against equal rights for women, that patronized me, that thought education for women was only "in case."

I loved my children, and, in between the times I resented my husband, I loved him. But I was not living happily ever after. And I said so. I said that and much, much more. And I said it for a long time. Three things happened. The first: nothing. Nothing happened when I said these things out loud to Blaine. I wasn't struck by the lightning rod of God's hand. Second, Blaine didn't offer to give me a priesthood blessing or tell me to repent. I hadn't disappointed him or broken his heart. I don't know why that surprised me, since he was still a struggling, active-in-the-church skeptic. He had told me that one reason he married me was that he knew he needed my faith; he could hold onto my skirt hem as he sought his own sure witness.

Third, my husband listened. He listened, and he talked. We talked. We began a conversation about religion that continues today. He understood, as much as he was able, why I felt cheated. As men too often do, he offered advice. He told me I was a "frustrated intellectual" and needed to go to college; in fact, he said he knew I'd never be happy until I did. At first I was insulted. Was he smarter than I because he was more educated? I was and am an avid reader, I'm street smart, I have an ability to understand people and grasp concepts. Nice observation, I thought, and no doubt true, but I had—correct that, *we* had—five dependent children, some of them not yet in school. Even if we had had the money, I wouldn't have considered leaving them with someone else. In the end, it was just talk.

Life went on in much the same way, although I read more, formed a book club, and taught Relief Society for many years, which, more than anything, saved my life. The curriculum was broader then than it is now, and topics I researched and taught challenged me. I found creative ways to present the material. At the same time, I tried to be the best mother I could. My children and I studied, worked, and laughed together. But deep in the fertile soil of my mind, I nurtured the seed of a dream Blaine had planted there, inspired by the early connection of the "deepest world we share," to use a line from May Sarton's poem "A Light Left On," the world that allows us to know each other from the roots up.

When my youngest son began kindergarten, I began as a freshman at the University of Utah. I had children in grade school, junior high, and high school; my oldest daughter and I overlapped my last year at the U. As a family, we made it work. So as not to deny them things I had provided in the past, I made homemade bread and desserts, wrapping them in individual cellophane packages to freeze. Mornings, the children made their beds and got themselves ready. Blaine put the children's lunches together and participated in the neighborhood car pool. I attended morning classes and studied before the kids got home. Blaine and I helped them with their homework. We all did housework on Saturdays. Not only did my going to college make my children independent, it modeled for my daughters, especially, the importance of education. Each family member was, in some way, responsible for my being able to graduate. They were proud that I, like them, went to school and studied. They understood that it was my right to be in school, and we shared our similar struggles, successes, and accomplishments. The house where we lived and cooperated then is a fond, still-lit memory.

My college experience and degree in English, emphasizing creative writing and women's studies, transformed my life. The advantages of learning cannot be overemphasized. I loved carrying my stacks of books from the bookstore each quarter thinking that, at the end of the quarter, I'd know everything in them! I no longer felt inadequate: family and friends acknowledged that I was "going to college"—and with five children! They cheered me on and celebrated my graduation. My degree led me from one opportunity to the next. I took a writing class and no longer felt dumb among the others. I got a poem published, then another. A book published, and then another. Today, as then, my husband and children respect the fact that I do something that fulfills me and makes me happy.

While I now have much more confidence and self-respect, I don't feel smarter now than I used to; going to college confirmed that I knew much more than I'd thought, though there is still so much to learn. And although our couple conversations did not change much, it's important that my husband, because of the "deepest world we share," understood what I so desperately needed. Just as in Sarton's poem, there was an "open book . . . found out" by the soft light left on even when a couple is away. In our case, that book is the outward symbol of our common love of learning and the trust and tolerance that remains even as he delves into orthodox Christianity, and as I write and continue battling to keep things fair.

Leave the Rest to Fairy Tales

MELISSA G.

I was fourteen weeks pregnant with my fourth child and in the throes of morning sickness when my husband walked out on me one weekday evening. For some reason I had decided to make homemade salsa that afternoon. Too nauseated and exhausted when I finally finished to think of eating anything myself, I still had to feed Mike and the kids, but I wanted to give myself a few moments to rest before I began dinner—or did anything about the counters strewn with dirty dishes and bits of tomato and onion. When Mike got home, he was clearly upset by the sight of a messy kitchen. I could tell he'd had a bad day at work by the way he sighed loudly and shoved dishes into the dishwasher so forcefully that I feared they would break. His long-suffering disapproval and disappointment, on top of everything else I had to deal with, was unbearable. "Just leave it," I said. "I'll do it. I was too tired right after I finished."

He didn't say a word or even look at me, just kept cramming dishes into the dishwasher. I don't remember what I said next, or what he said after that, but before I knew it, we were arguing.

Those days, it seemed all we did was argue. This time, fortunately, the kids were upstairs playing, out of earshot. A small disagreement over a dirty kitchen escalated quickly into a battle over anything and everything wrong in our marriage. Finally, Mike shouted, "That's it. I'm leaving!" He stormed from the kitchen and into our bedroom.

I followed close behind. He began packing, and I could tell by what he chose that he was serious. He wasn't just shoving random clothes into a suitcase for effect; he was gathering practical items: a cell phone, his medication, his toothbrush. I couldn't let myself admit what was going on. I tried to reason with him as he rushed around collecting his things. In desperation, I grabbed his shoulder, trying to turn him to look into my face. "Did you forget I'm *pregnant*?" I asked. "You're leaving me all alone with three small children?" Without responding, he finished packing and walked to the garage, slamming the kitchen door behind him.

He was gone. I listened to the garage door open, listened to the car start, listened to it back out, listened to the garage door close, and then, for several seconds, I listened to the silence that followed.

Those few moments took my breath away as the reality of my situation sunk in. He was gone. My husband really was gone. My kitchen was still a mess; dinner still needed to be served and cleaned up. Those were just the immediate tasks I had to address in the next hour. What about the hour after that, and the next day, and the next week?

By that point, my kids had come downstairs. *Where was Dad? Why had he gone so suddenly? When was he coming back?* These were the very questions I was asking, but what do you say to three small children who are anxious and afraid? "Daddy went on a business trip," I told them in the steadiest voice I could muster, willing myself to keep it together. Thankfully, they asked no more questions.

I had never felt so alone in my life. I lived 1,500 miles away from both of our families in a huge city I hated, where the only people I knew were other Latter-day Saints in a big ward stretched by urban sprawl. I was pregnant, hormonal, exhausted, and facing the very real possibility of being a single mom. Mike had given me no indication where he was going, or when—or even if—he might come back.

I felt a profound shame that my marriage was in such a terrible state. I couldn't imagine admitting to someone else what was happening. I felt like a complete failure. Had I been the one to leave, I could have told myself that I was withdrawing from a complicated situation to find perspective and insight. But to be left made me feel like I wasn't worth staying for. I didn't want to call a friend and hear concern in her voice as she asked questions about my situation. I knew that listening to a sympathetic, well-meaning voice would make the fact that my husband was gone seem all the more real, shameful, and terrifying.

I don't know if I even thought to ask myself if I'd seen this coming. Mike's leaving was both the biggest surprise and the most obvious of outcomes. Our marriage had become increasingly difficult over the previous years. A job change, a cross-country move, and a pregnancy were just the beginning. While Mike certainly had his share of problems, it hurt to admit that I was to blame for much of the recent stress: I was trying to cope with a vicious form of obsessive-compulsive disorder.

I don't think I had ever considered the possibility that one of us would actually decide to end the marriage. Divorce was so final. To me, an eternal marriage meant that you worked through your problems and disagreements, no matter what. With the exceptions of abuse or infidelity, I simply didn't see any valid reason to end a marriage. You can't just give up. That doesn't fit into the equation.

*   *   *

How exactly does a marriage go from happy and rewarding to desperate and miserable? My marriage declined gradually; the earliest signs of weakening and withdrawal were almost imperceptible. Mike and I were such a typical Mormon couple in many respects. We met in high school, married young, and pursued educations.

The first few years of my marriage were incredibly happy. I had married my best friend, and marriage seemed like everything I had hoped it would be. Mike encouraged me to work toward my goals and to push myself in new directions. I felt I supported him in professional, personal, and spiritual goals. We shared almost everything with each other; our goals seemed perfectly aligned. We were even better friends than before we married; we laughed and joked together constantly.

We made each other happy, both because we worked at it and because that's just how we felt when we were together. Although we were poor, we found ways to treat ourselves, even if it meant saving up coupons given out at school so we could get ice cream cones at the creamery after a difficult week. Every so often, Mike would plan little surprises. Once I came home from a really bad day at work to find a picnic set up in our living room, complete with a picnic blanket and our favorite meal. Mike was always thinking of me; I did my best to reciprocate his generosity and selflessness. I would leave him little love notes and make his favorite desserts. This was the fairy tale ending people were talking about. This was my happily ever after.

Not quite two years into our marriage, Mike asked if I wanted to start a family. I was about to begin a graduate program, along with the accompanying commitment of being a graduate instructor, so we agreed to wait another year. Our planning seemed responsible and reasonable, but a few months later we changed our minds on a whim and decided to try to get pregnant while I was still in graduate school. It worked so fast that we barely had time to let the news sink in before we learned that we were expecting twins. We were thrilled and did our best to finish up our schooling and prepare to be parents.

I want to say that things got hard after our kids were born, but that doesn't seem entirely fair. Children expanded our ability to love each other, but things certainly got more difficult when our girls were born shortly after our third anniversary. Our twins were very premature and spent months in the neonatal intensive care unit. Mike was trying to balance a career and take care of me after a frightening, life-threatening pregnancy and delivery. I was trying to recover from my medical ordeal and adjust to the reality of motherhood. When our twins finally came home from the hospital, I felt thoroughly unprepared to protect them. They were so fragile and small, at high risk for infection. The medical team instructed us not to take them out in public for six months, which isolated me in the home with two very demanding newborns.

Within a few short months, I had gone from being in graduate school and teaching university courses to being a full-time, stay-at-home mom. I struggled to adjust to my new role. There was no time to focus on our marriage: every waking moment was spent trying to care for our babies and maintain the house. I constantly had bottles to wash, babies to feed, and an endless pile of laundry to tackle. Mike had a full-time job, but did his best to help out not only with household tasks but also in caring for the twins. We had so little time to ourselves.

Gradually, the isolation and stress of parenting became all-consuming. I noticed, without being particularly alarmed initially, that I was starting to have obsessive-compulsive thoughts. I was convinced that it was my sole responsibility to keep my children healthy, so I cleaned constantly. I allowed few guests into our home; I was sure they posed a risk to our kids. Mike was at work most of the day, so I was in charge of the house, and by controlling all the details, I felt I had some semblance of control over my life, which had become uncertain and frightening.

My obsessive-compulsive disorder only worsened after we had another child about two years later. By this time, Mike and I were more like roommates than spouses. We shared a household, managed the finances together, and divided up the chores. On those rare occasions when we had time together, we were both so tired that we typically just watched a movie together. We didn't have friends over, and we seldom went out together. Our relationship was put on the back burner so we could deal with the details of keeping the household together.

We could see and feel ourselves becoming emotionally distant, though we intended it as a kindness to the other. I knew Mike was tired from working and trying to help out at home, so I didn't want to burden him with my own struggles. He knew that I was dealing with small children all day, as well as holding down an adjunct teaching job and trying to keep the house clean and the meals prepared, so he thought that staying out of my way was the best way to help. If our conversations weren't geared toward our children or mundane tasks around the house, we had almost nothing to talk about.

My obsessive-compulsive disorder wasn't the only issue, though. Mike became severely depressed and was seeking counseling and trying to find a medication to ease his symptoms. I didn't know what to say or how to help. I had never dealt with depression and detached myself from a situation that was both foreign and frustrating. I tried to find support from the church, but realized that depression isn't widely discussed and in some cases is viewed as a spiritual failing. I didn't know where to seek help or who to talk to, and neither did Mike.

While we were busy trying to sort through these difficulties, Mike's job offered him an opportunity to move from our small town in Utah, to Houston, Texas. I didn't want to go and pleaded with Mike to either keep his old job or find a new job closer to family and our support system. I told him repeatedly that I wanted our families nearby and had no desire to take a higher paying job in another state. But this promotion was Mike's dream job, and he wanted very much to accept it. We argued for weeks. Eventually I felt there was no other option, so I reluctantly agreed to give it a try.

As soon as we moved, Mike cheered up immensely and his depression eased, but I felt more sad and anxious by the day. I dislike big cities, and we were living in one of the largest cities in the country. I made friends in the ward, but everything in my life seemed like it had turned upside down. I missed my family fiercely. I felt like all my dreams and goals had been tossed in the trash, and I had no idea how to salvage them. I had worked hard and deliberately pursued an education in order to ensure that I would always have options and never feel trapped or unable to change my situation.

But my education and planning offered no help in dealing with the circumstances I found myself in. I had never felt like I had so little influence over my situation, and I didn't know how to integrate my new reality into who I was. I was so miserable that all I could think about was how to move back home. Of course I knew we wouldn't be moving back anytime soon. Mike was happy in a stable job and the economy was beginning to plummet. The only financially viable decision was to stay.

This meant, effectively, that I was trapped, and I felt it. Walls felt too close; the awful humidity of Houston meant that every time I went outside, even the sky felt too close. The tall, thin trees that abound in Houston made me feel constantly closed in. As a result, my obsessive-compulsive disorder manifested itself in devastating ways.

Being trapped is an experience that causes panic. When you're trapped, you don't think, "Oh, OK: since I'm not going anywhere, I might as well relax." No, you think, "I have to escape. That's the only option to pursue because an imminent danger will hurt me and people I love." Soon after settling in, I began feeling very unsafe. Even sitting in my house caused me great anxiety, and I began playing "what if" scenarios in my head so often that they kept me up at night. I started out afraid of general risks, such as someone breaking into our home or kidnapping my children. These fears eventually fed into more specific anxieties that involved my role in preventing or eliminating some danger or threat. For instance, I was convinced that someone would break into my house if I wasn't vigilant enough in checking that every lock in the house was bolted tight. I spent hours checking and rechecking every latch and lock on all the windows and doors, only to start over and do it all again.

My OCD affected my ability to function in the role of a wife and mother. Grocery shopping was incredibly stressful because I was afraid the food was unsafe. A discoloration on an apple would make it unsuitable to purchase, so grocery shopping took hours because I sorted through so much food trying to find products that seemed safe. Once I got items into the cart, I had a specific organization system. Meat had to be on the opposite side of the cart from produce. If a produce bag touched the meat bag, the produce was no longer safe to eat. There were an infinite number of things that could go wrong from the moment I left home to the point I returned home with groceries. It got to where I couldn't feasibly do the grocery shopping, so that was one more thing Mike had to do. Not only did it make me feel like a terrible wife, but I realized I was creating an additional burden on Mike, and I had no idea how to stop it.

It goes without saying that Mike was increasingly frustrated with my inability to calm down and act "normal," both because of the hardship my OCD created for him and because he missed the happy, fun person I had once been. I missed her, too, but I didn't know how to get her back. I felt so desperate and sought help everywhere I could think of. I had Mike give me a blessing. I prayed constantly for an understanding of how to help myself. I went to church faithfully and attended the temple. None of it seemed to help. I sought a mental health counselor and attended counseling weekly, but that didn't seem to help either. I tried one medication after another to regulate my obsessive-compulsive disorder through chemical means, an arduous and disheartening process that involved gradually acclimating up to an appropriate dosage, staying on the dosage long enough to see if it worked, and when it didn't, gradually withdrawing from it so it didn't further disrupt my brain chemistry, then giving my system a rest before trying something else. Each attempt took weeks and caused serious side effects. Finally, on the sixth try, I found a medication that seemed to ease my anxiety slightly, but it was still a struggle to get up every day and go through normal routines.

My medication may have helped my personal well-being, but my marriage was collapsing. Mike blamed himself for moving me despite my reservations. He felt frustrated that I was so impaired by my OCD, frustrated by the additional burdens that he faced as a result, and frustrated by his resentment of me. He didn't know how to connect with this new version of who I was and distanced himself even further.

Resentful, hurt, and frightened of how difficult my life had become, I blamed Mike far more than he deserved. I felt like my real self was buried somewhere that I couldn't access. I was so emotionally exhausted from simply trying to get through each day that I had no energy left to give to anyone—including myself. I was giving everything I had—and it wasn't enough. My best wasn't good enough to manage my obsessive-compulsive disorder; it wasn't good enough to bridge the growing rift in my marriage. Discovering that your best isn't good enough is devastating: it means that you can't just work harder at something to make it improve. It means you have no way to influence the situation for the better.

Mike and I found a marriage counselor, hoping she could help us work through some of our issues. During the first session, as we explained why we were there, I felt so much hatred toward Mike that I couldn't even look at him. Sitting beside him on the couch in the counselor's office, I felt my face grow so hot with rage that it seemed my skin was burning. Over and over I asked myself, "Why did you marry this man?" I loathed him. In my mind, he had sacrificed all my dreams and hopes and values to satisfy his own selfish desires. Why hadn't he just kept his old job in Utah or tried harder to find a new job closer to home? It could only be because what he wanted was more important than what I wanted. I know now this was unfair and wrong, but at the time, those feelings were overpowering. I didn't know how or even if I could ever love someone so selfish and disloyal, someone I despised.

Because our progress with the first counselor seemed so slow, we sought out another marriage counselor after a few months, and then another. After three years in our new area, I realized that we had been in counseling for nearly all of it, and we were both still miserable. Mike didn't understand the causes or depths of my misery, and I didn't know how to help him see it. I remember thinking that I didn't want to be married to him for another day, let alone eternity. How had I made such a mistake? Why had I dragged three children into this mess? I clearly remember thinking that this wasn't how marriage was supposed to be. All marriages have challenges, but mine didn't seem to have any bliss to balance out the challenges. All we were left with was one big, wretched wreck.

During a few moments of stability and hopefulness, we decided to have another child, only to realize shortly after the pregnancy began that things were not improving. During pregnancy I had to stop taking my medication, and any progress I had previously made in managing my OCD was quickly replaced by obsessions even more overpowering than I had experienced before. *Everything* seemed an insurmountable problem; every perception I had was colored by my obsessive-compulsive disorder. I began thinking of all the potential hazards I had to watch out for so I could protect my baby. I was terrified of potential harm to my growing child, so even cooking a meal became an exacting process. I threw out all of our plastic dishes and utensils, because it seemed like plastic could leach toxins into the food I ingested and damage my baby's development. Nothing seemed safe enough to eat, and I didn't have an appetite anyway. Eventually, I would end up anxiously forcing myself to eat something, anything, all the while thinking with despair about how my child would be deformed because I had given in and eaten contaminated food.

I was beside myself, as was Mike. How do you stay committed to a relationship that is clearly broken and making the people in it miserable? Sometimes I would remember hazily how much I once loved Mike. I would think about how great we were together, how forgiving and supportive we were. I ached for what I remembered as the "old Mike." He would never have judged me or made me feel inadequate. He would love me unconditionally and never threaten to leave. He would stand by me and see me through any trial, because he would know that this would make us stronger in the long run. He would remember that we were sealed for eternity.

In general, we hear little in church about problematic marriages unless the discussions focus on issues such as infidelity, abuse, or pornography. What about all of the other problems that can be equally damaging but fall under the radar? There is so much pressure to get married, so many talks about the blessings of an eternal marriage, so much focus on our belief that the marriage covenant is key to obtaining celestial glory. For such an important concept, it's perplexing that there's so little discussion about what to do when marriages are in crisis. When I looked around at church, it seemed I was surrounded by happily married couples. Even if the topic of marital conflict came up in a lesson, no one ever said anything specific or concrete about their struggles or what they did to help alleviate them. How could they, when no one would admit in public that they even had marital struggles or conflict in the first place? Everything I heard in lessons on marriage was vague and full of platitudes; the advice typically offered to couples in distress was to seek counsel from their bishop. I was searching for tangible information, information about the experiences of my ward members. What did they struggle with? How did they resolve it? Who could I turn to for help and guidance?

I realize now that Mike was just as desperate, confused, and terrified as I was. He didn't know how to reach out to me when I was so mentally unstable. He didn't know what to say, what to do, or how to make the situation right. Mike didn't know if things would ever get better, or if it was healthy to stay, so he simply left that evening early in my pregnancy.

Mike did come back. In fact, he called me two hours after he left. He didn't apologize, or ask how I was, but he left the number where he was staying. I think that was as much as he could do to reach out to me at that point. The next morning, Mike told his boss that within a year he needed to move back to Utah. In our collective history, Utah was home, where our family was. Mike knew I was incredibly homesick and yearned to move back to what I remembered as a safe, comfortable environment. This was Mike's last effort to keep our marriage together. His boss graciously offered to let him work remotely after we moved back to Utah so he could keep his job. Mike came home that night and told me his plan, making it clear that if our marriage didn't improve after the move, he would leave for good.

Part of me was incredibly relieved to be moving back to an area that felt comfortable and familiar to me: it carried with it the possibility that I might actually be able to lead a normal life. But another part of me remained wary and resentful. I was still processing the fact that Mike had left. Yes, he had come back, but it didn't change the fact that he had left and might leave again. The hurt and betrayal he caused by giving up on our marriage, even if only for one night, made me feel that his commitment to our marriage was conditional. I also thought of how I had supported Mike not only through depression but also through some incredibly difficult personal issues. I had never left or threatened to leave, and I was still processing what felt like a double standard.

It's been several years since that night Mike left. In the meantime, he came back; we had a baby; we sold our house, moved back to Utah, and have settled into a new life. Things are much better, and my marriage has vacillated from truly awful to happy and fulfilling. I still don't know which factors combined to pull us out of a miserable relationship and create enough stability and trust that we could decide to stay together. What makes our situation different from some of my friends who have divorced? I wish I could articulate what changed for us; I wish it were tangible so I could hold it in my hands, stare it in the face, give it to someone else.

I'm very open about my experience with marital unhappiness. I think hiding my struggles and pretending they didn't happen or couldn't happen again is a disservice to both my own experience and the experience of others. I don't want anyone else to feel the shame and loneliness of conflict without feeling validated in their struggle. Being in an unhealthy and miserable marriage colors how we view ourselves. When I was struggling, it seemed that all my accomplishments were diminished by my failure to sustain a vibrant, healthy marriage. It was like I had one standard of measuring myself, and if I fell short, it had sweeping significance for all areas of my life. These feelings are hard to forget and even more difficult to cope with on your own.

A few weeks before I began writing this account, Mike and I sat on our deck shortly after we had put our children to bed and watched the dusk gather. A cool breeze stirred as the light faded, the sky deepening into purple. It was a summer evening as perfect as the ones I cherished in my memories from childhood. Mike and I sat together, listening to the crickets, sharing a few tranquil moments, and not saying a thing. It was not an awkward silence, but the silence between two people completely at ease. A few years back, I hadn't known if I would ever be in this place with Mike—a place where we were content, peaceful, calm.

In some ways, I feel like the fairy tale of my life has come full circle. What started out looking like "happily ever after" was just the beginning of our story and has morphed into many things and been redefined many times. I suppose it's a fallacy to expect the happy ending without progressing through the journey of marriage. Now, I'm tempted to think that a continual, steady feeling of "happily ever after" in this life happens only "once upon a time." For now, I am content and happy in a rewarding marriage. I truly hope it stays that way, but I'm the first to admit that life is full of unexpected trials and struggles that impact marriages. Now, I have more realistic expectations of what a fulfilling marriage is and what it isn't. A fulfilling marriage is an experience full of beauty, introspection, struggle, and sacrifice; it's earned. There are no shortcuts to get a "happily ever after" ending. Today, I have readjusted my expectations based on the reality of sharing a life with someone and decided that I'll take my "happy enough" and leave the rest to the fairy tales.

I Am Never Without It

STEPHANIE LAURITZEN

Like those of countless ancestors, including two grandmothers and a mother, my wedding didn't involve walking down a church aisle. No flower girls tossed rose petals, no familiar wedding march echoed in the background. Instead, like my mother and my grandmothers, I knelt across an altar in the Salt Lake Temple and said "yes" when a man I didn't know asked if I promised to give myself to my husband. Daniel didn't promise himself back, but my grip on his hand proved strong enough to crush any cognitive dissonance about the inequity of our arrangement. Maybe it was an honor for my grandmother to give and not receive. Maybe my mother answered "yes" with the hope that her daughters would answer different questions and receive different answers. I answered "yes" with plans in my head for more. Our unequal marriage vows necessitated mental gymnastics worthy of an Olympic sport, but somehow we would manage to give each other the equality our wedding ceremony lacked.

That night, I stood before family and friends at our ring ceremony. The sun was setting on the Ides of March (beware!), and I knew that this hastily as-sembled "ceremony" represented my one chance to speak. To promise to do more than just give, to be more than a hearkening ear, a promise of a more I didn't fully know I wanted yet. I let go of Daniel long enough to unfold the e. e. cummings poem I'd printed off the night earlier, and I "revealed the deepest secret nobody knows . . . i carry your heart (i carry it in my heart)." If Daniel couldn't promise himself to me in the temple, I would simply take what I felt to be mine. I would carry his heart with me, the strange man in the temple be damned. Promising to carry Daniel's heart felt greedy. It felt greedy in the way the first breath of oxygen feels in your lungs after swimming across a pool. But no one should promise herself without at least something, a strong beating heart, to help her mourn the loss of personhood. With one word, I belonged to somebody else. Maybe a heart in return was enough?

At age twenty, I trusted two things: my testimony in the LDS church and my marriage to Daniel. Not only did I trust both entities, but like Siamese twins sharing vital internal organs, they seemed inextricably bound together; I couldn't imagine one existing without the other. My faith led me to seek out a funny, unusually soft-hearted man who didn't mind that I occasionally questioned the brethren on issues like gay marriage and gender roles. My spouse led me to strive to increase my faith, to work toward the celestial marriage that meant my promise to love Daniel "higher than the soul can hope or mind can hide" wouldn't stop with death.

With so much at stake, with my grip so tight on Daniel's hand, I could forget the flash of panic I felt the day I took out my temple endowments, a ceremony in which I promised to hearken unto my husband as he hearkened unto God and promised to serve my husband as a priestess while his soul went on to grander things: acting as a priest unto God himself. I promised to remain a second-class citizen in Mormonism, terrified as my temple covenants took away my birthright: my right to speak to God without an intermediary, my right to listen to my own soul, and trust that God loved me enough to speak to my spirit, regardless of marital status. Walking out of the temple, knuckles white, I told myself that I could work through this. Just as Daniel and I occasionally fought but made up, I believed in compromising with and forgiving my church.

Compromising and forgiving one another allowed Daniel and me to survive our first three and a half years or marriage. However, I found myself unable to work things out with the church. Despite once viewing my relationships with the church and my spouse as perfectly inseparable Siamese twins, I started to resent the third presence lingering in our marriage.

Increasingly angered by the language of LDS patriarchy, I felt myself stiffen each time a talk reinforcing rigid gender roles echoed through a chapel. I felt powerless in an organization that demanded my money, my time, and my faith, but refused to grant me equal status with my partner. Could this truly be God's will? I felt forgotten by a Heavenly Father who, prior to my marriage covenants, seemed to know me as an individual: a sometimes sarcastic, secretly optimistic, career-driven individual. Did God still see me this way? Or did my answer of "yes" over the marriage altar somehow transform me into a woman who somehow "knew" that LDS women "should be the best homemakers in the world"?

Like any mature twenty-four-year-old, I engaged in a series of unhealthy behaviors in an attempt to repair my increasingly damaged relationship with Mormonism. I justified, I ignored, I passive-aggressively blogged. Delicately wielding an invisible scalpel, I performed secret surgery on the Siamese twin responsible for the language of patriarchy and homophobia, hoping the other twin, my marriage to my funny, kind, computer-genius husband, could somehow survive.

In 2010, Elder Boyd K. Packer declared in the October General Conference that Heavenly Father wouldn't make someone gay, and not one but two men in suits reminded us that "the prophet is the only man who speaks for the Lord in everything." I remembered the terror I felt when I promised to hearken unto a man (even a good man) instead of God; I felt the scalpel slip from my hand, hitting a major artery. I watched the pulse of my faith skip and falter. How could I carry Daniel's heart in mine if I had broken it by destroying the faith that brought us together?

For months, our relationship struggled. Daniel felt betrayed by my loss of faith. I felt angry that he couldn't empathize with my feminist rage. I wondered if I could maintain my trust in Daniel while abandoning my trust in the church. I tested Daniel daily, trying to ignite his own flame of rage at gender inequality. Sometimes subconsciously, sometimes deliberately, I concentrated my efforts toward destroying the remains of our Siamese twin. I didn't understand why Daniel clung to ideas I wished to abandon, but I knew it made me angry.

Thus consumed, I didn't acknowledge the signs of his mourning. In my anger, I couldn't recognize the stages of Daniel's grief: the denial, anger, bargaining, and depression that came as a result of our loss. But we did lose something, something beyond faith or testimony. When I lost my faith, somehow we lost our ability to love each other fully. We stopped seeing one another as "whatever the sun will always sing." We stopped carrying each other's hearts.

Daniel mourned for our loss and my loss. Like me, he often turned to anger as a coping mechanism. Frequently, he compensated for my lack of faith with renewed devotion to the church. But mostly, he mourned. At first, he grieved for himself and for opportunities lost. (We would never be the couple who spends their golden years on a church mission.) He grieved for betrayal felt, and covenants seemingly broken. Over time, however, he started to grieve for me; he mourned my loss when I couldn't mourn myself.

I didn't know I needed to grieve. I didn't recognize the need to ceremonially bury my childhood belief system. Unbeknownst to me, when I performed the surgery separating my faith from my spouse, I cut out a piece of my soul as well. Eventually, though, when the initial anger and denial faded, I began my own cycle of grief. I mourned the loss of my relationship with a god, cried for the death of my innocent belief the day I took out endowments, and wished I could magically rejoin the world of the easily faithful. I felt the pain of a broken and wounded soul and wondered if I could ever feel whole without the stability of Mormonism. Despite wanting to eradicate any remnant of Mormonism from my life, I couldn't stop thinking of the words from my favorite hymn: "Where can I turn for peace, where is my solace? When other sources cease to make me whole?" Traditional Mormonism ceased to make me whole, but did another source exist?

Another source did exist, and after months of alternating anger and stony détente, managed to survive despite a "wounded heart, anger, or malice." Daniel knew before I did that our anger and frustration couldn't lead to a solution. So he began to mourn, waiting for me to mourn with him. When we stopped relying on anger, we found ourselves better equipped to mourn and comfort a spouse in mourning and pain. We mourned together the death of my testimony; we mourned the death of Daniel's dream for a traditional Mormon family. We cried over my feelings of betrayal when I first expressed my doubts to Daniel and he reacted with anger and judgment. All the same feelings I felt before, but different in one significant way: we felt these feelings together. We began to carry our hearts together, and we learned that hearts don't need to match one another perfectly. My skeptical heart could still carry Daniel's believing one. Daniel's faith and devotion for the church didn't impede his ability to hold my agnostic heart within his. We realized we never married because of a shared faith, but a shared devotion to each other, a devotion that saved our marriage when every talk on celestial marriage fell flat.

After a traumatic event, like a death or soul-shattering betrayal, psychologists often encourage the trauma victims to create a "New Normal" representing the reality of the present instead of the past. When our marriage improved, my quest for a New Normal included both my relationship with Daniel and my relationship with God. I could no longer use my spouse as the basis for my faith, but I knew I missed many aspects of Mormonism. Slowly, I investigated ways to reconcile my belief in feminism and equality with a belief in God. I embraced the freedom to reclaim my Mormon heritage in ways I find meaningful.

Now, I pray to a divinity that transcends gender. I see saviors in the way people treat others, so I honor the legacy of Jesus by practicing kindness. Sometimes my faith journey finds me back in church, but frequently it finds me in conversations with friends, or within the pages of books extending far beyond LDS scriptures. Today, my spouse doesn't represent my faith. There's no Siamese twin. I love my spouse and my faith enough to let them stand individually, not bound in ways that weaken them both. As I grow in my journey, Daniel travels with me occasionally. As I reunite with some aspects of Mormonism, and when I don't figuratively beat him over the head with the bat of feminism (and even when I do bring out the bat), Daniel remains the funny, soft-spoken man who doesn't mind that I constantly question the brethren on gay marriage and gender roles. I'm always surprised to realize that I still believe in some aspects of Mormonism. I'm even more surprised when I see my husband let go of orthodoxy in favor of balance and change. I'm surprised, but happy we survived, and continue to survive, as equal partners. Recently, I asked Daniel when our relationship started to heal, what made things better. Always the minimalist, he responded, "Things changed when I realized that 'truth' means sharing."

Daniel and I believe in different "truths." However, though our "truths" differ, the ways we share them don't. We started sharing our "truth" when we decided to mourn my loss of faith together. When we share "truth" in ways that are kind, loving, and accepting, we thrive. In the future, if we dedicate ourselves to teaching our children our different truths in a manner of sharing instead of demanding, our kids will probably be OK. While life seemed simpler with a shared faith, our life is better now with our different, but still shared, truths.

When I married Daniel, I never considered a future where the trials came from within our relationship. I expected external trials: financial struggles, health problems, stress from work and children, but not a trial where we mourned the death of our first relationship, and faced the challenge of rebuilding a new one. Even now, the idea that Daniel and I will spend the rest of our marriage navigating our beliefs and nonbeliefs occasionally exhausts and overwhelms me. But

> here is the deepest secret nobody knows . . .
> and this is the wonder that's keeping the stars apart
>
> i carry your heart (i carry it in my heart).
> —e. e. cummings, "i carry your heart with me"

Long, Tall, Square Peg

KIRA OLSON

He didn't know me. But somehow he knew it was time to decide: are we headed toward marriage? I liked him; we had a great time together. My roommates thought he was perfect and constantly reminded me that the prophet said we should not delay marriage; any two righteous people can make a marriage work. Years earlier, in a Young Women's class, I had made a list of what I required in a husband, and he fit the first four items: have a testimony, be a worthy priesthood holder, be a returned missionary, be taller than me. He barely made that last one, but it still counted. He was nice looking, and I really did like him. But he didn't know me. Later, after I told him, *No, I'm not coming back for another semester to "see where this goes,"* my roommate related the long talks she had with him on my behalf. He doesn't understand, she said, and he even cried. No, I thought with dry eyes, no, he does not understand.

I walked onto the campus of Ricks College (now BYU-Idaho) at age seventeen eager to embark on the adventure of obtaining my "Mrs." degree. I had grown up in a small town in northern British Columbia where our tiny LDS branch was held together by a few families and a constant stream of bright young missionaries. The elders who preached at our pulpit, ate at our tables, hiked our mountains, and weeded our gardens were revered. In them I saw my future husband, a man dedicated to God, a priesthood holder, someone to take my hand and lead me into eternity. I befriended them decorously—no flirting—and took silent notes on how righteous young men behave.

At Ricks I took a class called "Dating and Marriage." I made cookies with my roommates and delivered them to good-looking boys we knew. We went on group dates in the science building, shooting Nerf guns at each other and eating pizza on campus lawns. One night my roommate came home from a date with a well-regarded leader in our student congregation. During dinner, the young man had pulled out a piece of paper, from which he read a list of questions: *Did you graduate from seminary? Do you have your Young Women's medallion?* A gold-toned necklace featuring a young woman in a long billowing dress, the medallion was an award for completing a program centered on developing talents and gospel knowledge. I was very faithful growing up, but our fledgling branch couldn't provide the same structure and guidance as bigger congregations, so I neither graduated seminary nor completed the Young Women's program.

As my roommate related her story, I felt both shame and indignation. She should read him her own list, I said, starting with: *Do you intend to continue balding?* I railed against him for turning their second date into a worthiness interview. But really, we were all being evaluated, all the time, and it wasn't enough to just be a good Mormon. It seemed that only certain girls got asked out, only certain guys were sought-after, all of them perfect pictures of 1950s beauty and tradition. I was tall and gangly, not petite and girlish. I didn't spend a lot of time in front of a mirror. I didn't do a lot of crafting. I worried that my hopes for finding the boy of my list would be hampered by my failure to meet all the items on *his* list.

The love, courtship, and marriage part of being Mormon wasn't the same as just being a Mormon. And I got lost in it. It became harder to differentiate between spiritual and emotional experiences. I couldn't tell if I actually liked the drippy LDS soft rock my roommates played Sunday mornings while we primped before church. I continued to bake for boys and even started sewing, but it wasn't enjoyable anymore, and it didn't help me get dates. I had more fun sneaking out at 2 A.M. to play basketball with my roommate and a bunch of guys, one of whom had keys to a church building in a neighboring town. I liked the boys better on the basketball court than at church. The returned missionaries I once admired held their scriptures like badges and spoke from the pulpit with a dramatic flair that didn't quite seem sincere.

After two years at Ricks, I got a summer job in the wilds of northern British Columbia that introduced me to Jim. He was beautiful, with an easy smile, and wore ripped cutoffs over his tanned muscular legs. Jim met the fourth requirement from my list: he was taller than me. But he wasn't Mormon; he didn't hold the priesthood; and he hadn't spent two years in a suit praying every day.

We spent every day together, and they were some of the happiest of my life. We loved to talk and talk and look at each other; he didn't care if I wore make-up, he didn't care if I had graduated from seminary. But he did care that I wouldn't have sex. Jim felt he understood my faith, for the most part, but he couldn't understand why I would restrict myself to marrying only someone who went to my church. Every time we talked about it, I would feel more convinced that he was right. How could I limit love? But I was Mormon all the way through, even if I felt out of place finding a partner of my faith. And so we parted. I suffered sorely, as I saw no alternative from my past or foreseeable future that seemed comparable to this man who loved me, who didn't expect things from me, who didn't pretend he was better than he was. Yet I couldn't sacrifice the life I wanted for myself and my future children, even if my vision was cloudy.

I transferred to BYU in Provo. Enter the man of my roommates' dreams for me. I tried to fall in love with him. He was a good guy who thought I was pretty great, even with my clumsiness and lack of baking prowess. But he didn't know me. I played the girlfriend role, but I hid my fears of marriage, my notebooks of poetry, my uncertainties about myself, and my surety that I would disappoint him eventually. I prayed. He met all the other requirements a Mormon girl could want, and how many chances would I get? I was already twenty, after all . . . I often felt like I *should* try harder to make it work. But every time I heard or felt *should*, I was ready to run. I missed what I had with Jim. I wanted so badly to be in love and not care about either of us having all those lists.

So, I ran. All the way to Thailand. It was such a relief to interrupt college and boys to spend eighteen months on a mission, sweating on my bicycle, forgoing makeup, and giving my life over to everyone I saw. But I couldn't escape for long. On the eve of my return home, the mission president's wife met with some of us sisters and read advice from a book intended to help women find husbands. There we were, sunburned and tired from days on our bikes, our heads full of scriptures, while she read suggestions that we pretend to be afraid of cows as an excuse to grab the arm of a male companion. She meant well, I'm sure, but it wasn't helpful. I came home determined to continue on a strong spiritual path and find the right partner who knew and loved me. Even if I wasn't afraid of cows.

Back at BYU, I dated an elder from my mission, someone I felt spiritually led to and with whom I shared a strong bond. It seemed perfect: we both spoke Thai, we loved spending time together, and we were still floating on a postmission spiritual high. In my prayers, I gave thanks for him and hoped that I had found my eternal companion.

We spent Thanksgiving with his family in Idaho. I remember washing dishes and chatting happily with his mother and sister in the kitchen, while he, his father, and brother watched football in the living room. My mind jumped to the future: If we got married, is this how it would be? Would I rub his feet after a long day at work? Hush the children, freshen my makeup, and put on a dress before pulling the roast from the oven, barely sweating? I was mad at myself for not looking forward to those possibilities. I wanted to be a wife and mother, didn't I? And I loved this man, right?

In the end, I didn't have to discover how I would handle the domestic duties. His attention drifted away, though he wanted badly to stay friends. He tried but could never explain why he loved me but didn't want to marry me. I think he figured it out when he met his future wife only months later. She was petite, pretty, and emotionally effusive, and although I have no proof, I'm pretty sure she made him dinner and did his laundry long before they were married. A cynical judgment from a jilted ex-girlfriend? Maybe. Yes. I was devastated.

I fled Utah. Philadelphia gave me independence and a happiness I hadn't felt for a long time. I attended a small singles ward where acting out the roles of proper Mormon boys and girls didn't seem as important a requirement for getting along. I loved having friends from varying backgrounds and religions. I waded through several relationships that each taught me something valuable, prepared me further, but seemed to break me a little more. As a serious boyfriend and I discussed marriage, sharing our hopes and concerns, he worried aloud that I wasn't the "scrapbooking type." To his credit, he apologized the next day, declaring that if it was really important for his kids to have scrapbooks, he could make them himself. He was right, and I hope he's happily pasting pictures right now. But it was further proof of my lack of marriageability.

I got ready to run again, this time to graduate school, when along came Brad. He took the church seriously, but could be a bit irreverent. He was faithful in his callings, with a strong testimony, but more liberal-minded than most guys. We were just friends at first, as he was several years younger than I. But we clicked in a way I hadn't previously thought possible. When he looked at me, it didn't feel like he was scrutinizing, wondering, hoping anything. He just saw me, and he knew who I was. He loved that I kept a basketball in my car trunk. He liked that I could polish off a plate of spicy chicken wings. We held hands in the van on our way back from a ward trip to Palmyra, New York, a week later we kissed in the church parking lot, and a few months later we got engaged spontaneously in his apartment. It was too easy. I waited for a car crash or an avalanche. But it was just me and him, no questions or lists or doubts. He didn't even ask if I knew how to sew.

I finally made it. Still me, still Mormon, and though I had long ago abandoned my "list," I managed to find someone who actually met my numbered adolescent hopes—all while being uniquely himself and loving imperfect me. I had freed myself from the expectations of Mormon perfection that I felt had oppressed me over the years!

Our first year of marriage was like playing house. We'd lounge in front of the TV with Chinese food and candy. We decorated our apartment with next to nothing and made spaghetti in our tiny strip of a kitchen. I worked and he went to school. It was good. Our roles were essentially equal, although I did a little more cleaning, which had more to do with my standards than his expectations.

Sometimes Brad played softball with other men in our ward, and at the games I would sit with the women. I watched them dig through their giant diaper bags and chase after their children. I would dream of the year before, when I was the one running around in a field, grabbing a Frisbee out of the air, laughing with friends later over waffles at IHOP. Instead I was talking about nothing with distracted women, watching my husband run after a ball, envying his grass-stained knees and flushed face. I started to worry.

I was quiet when Brad wanted to talk about our future. You can work, he said, even after we have children (not that you need my permission, he would qualify), you can do whatever you want. And he meant it. I loved being his partner, but wished I could somehow not be *married*. He could be as supportive and liberal as he wanted, but the fact remained: I was his wife and that meant I cleaned the bathrooms. That meant I was called Sister Olson, *his* last name; I would be the one asked to bring dinner to the sister who just had a baby. We could try to change; he could say I didn't have to clean the bathrooms, but then we would just have gross bathrooms. I tried to keep up some of my previous activities; I played basketball with a group of sisters in our ward until I was six months pregnant. But it was a lot of jumping.

I forced myself not to worry and looked forward to being a mother. I watched the women at church closely; so many seemed to fulfill their role naturally. I focused on how blessed I felt to be a woman and grow this baby in my own body! For a while I didn't care what was expected of me. I was going to be a mother. I could suspend my fears for a little while.

Shortly after the birth of our first child, Brad's job moved us to a new city. I stood outside one day with our six-month-old on my hip and helped her wave goodbye as Daddy backed out of the driveway. When he was gone, I scanned our quiet neighborhood: the houses all one-story brick of varying muted shades, the green blocks of lawn in front of each house, the straight gray sidewalks. I turned to walk into my perfect little box, its sides as high as the universe.

I gained twenty pounds over the next six months, sitting on my couch eating popcorn and red Twizzlers, watching HGTV and reruns of *Friends.* We ate out a lot because I didn't feel like cooking. I never painted the tiny corner of the living room wall where the previous owners ran out of paint. It took me months to put up curtains. I had everything: a beautiful house, a beautiful baby, and a loving husband who was a righteous priesthood holder. But I felt like nothing.

It was happening again. Now that I had managed to enter the coveted world I wanted and feared at the same time, I felt like I was starting all over again when I looked around me. I watched the families sitting in the pews at church. The mother with stylish clothes and makeup, the children dressed like magazine covers, all reverent and pleasant-faced. I felt frumpy and ill-prepared for everything. I dragged myself around, playing the role as best I could: I went to story-time and playgroups, pretending to enjoy conversations about crawling and baby food. I went into homes with impossibly perfect interior decorating and even more impossibly delicious smells wafting from their ovens. But I felt I wasn't like any of these women, who seemed to know what they were doing, smiling and perfectly creased. I questioned, again, how I fit; I wanted to be home raising my daughter, but I didn't want to be the cover of a 1950s women's magazine.

It would have been easy to blame it on the whole Mormon culture I had butted against since my Young Women's classes. I could say I was sure every husband had a list for what they wanted their wife to provide: dinner on the table at six, sex on demand, tear-inducing testimonies on Sunday. I could imagine the family sitting in the pew behind us shaking their heads at my toddler's messy hair and periodic high-pitched screeches during the passing of the sacrament. I could let these possibilities, these perceptions of other's expectations wall me in again, and then I could say *See? How am I supposed to live like this? It's not me.* I could let every Relief Society meeting leave me feeling that I wasn't good enough, I *should* be scrapbooking my child's every move, I *should* be making all our family's meals from scratch. Because at first, that's all I heard.

If my past relationships with Mormon men led me to the on-again-off-again battles with expectations throughout my life, it was Mormon women who pulled me out. I count it a great irony that one of the turning points in my perception was joining a group of women to scrapbook every week in the cultural hall of our church building. We would sit around a table, sharing polka-dot pages, puffy stickers, and flower-shaped hole punches. And while we taped and cut, we talked. I'm grateful for the shared supplies and ideas that led to a simple album of my wedding, but I am even more grateful for the shared lives. I learned about how one couple handled infertility, another a marriage of mixed religions, and another where the wife was thousands of miles away from her country and language of origin. One woman admitted she was a terrible cook and that her husband happily took over that role in their home.

A gradual shift occurred with every strip of glue and burst of laughter from these women I grew to love and admire week by week. Instead of beating my head against my interpretation of what I saw, I stepped past the Sunday smiles. I spent countless hours with a grandmother who raised five children in the church and told me *living the gospel isn't the same as going to church.* I had long talks on a living room floor with a mother who was preparing to go back to school, while our toddlers ran around the house in giddy play.

I saw *possibility* instead of walls, finally. I saw success, defined by me and God, not by a stray comment on homemaking. I finally saw that as much as Mormon culture appeared to push around those who entered at their own risk, it was *me* who kept trying to jam my square-peg self into the circle-shaped image of an apparition I had created out of stereotypes and offhand comments over the years. Gradually, I let go of any real or imagined pressure about how

I was supposed to act—hadn't I abandoned that already on my long trip to the altar? I went to playgroups with an open mind and tried to be the one to add some non-baby-related topics for discussion, in addition to helpful points on removing vomit stains. I brought my individuality back into my life instead of just half-heartedly playing a role. I joined a gym. I began running again. I taught my daughter to throw a ball through a hoop. I started a graduate program. My husband continued to exhibit the traits that attracted me to him in the first place—he encouraged and supported me; he let me be me as he always had.

Now, there are days when my marriage with Brad appears every bit as traditional as what I thought I feared. I still clean bathrooms; there are delicious smells coming from *my* oven; I stay home with the kids while Brad goes off to work every day. But I don't feel like anyone *made* me do it. I don't feel I am a doormat with the clumpy feet of *should*s walking all over me. I know I have a choice, and I choose my life. I acknowledge that the expectations or notions of good Mormon womanhood never really go away. But if they come up (*ooh, I love that gorgeous wreath, Sister Swanson*), I let it go much faster than I used to. If someone truly exhibits disappointment at my lack, I'm happy to let that go too. I'm happy to be me, progressing at my pace, my own little Mormon way. And that's all that matters.

This Great Happiness

TIFFANY MOSS

My freshman year of college, I met a boy named Drew who electrified my world. Our lives intersected at Brigham Young University in my hometown of Provo. I was distraught in just the way you'd expect an eighteen-year-old to be when the school year ended and he returned home to the East Coast, but two months later he was back—to serve a mission.

It was brutal having him so close, often just an hour away by car, while our interactions were relegated to the postal service—stringent mission rules forbade phone calls and visits. Young and lonely, I dated other guys during his absence. I also foolishly shared many details in my letters to Drew, so it isn't hard to understand why he eventually stopped responding. He finished his mission with plans to return to BYU in the fall. We talked on the phone a few times that summer and I hoped we would date again, but wasn't certain we would. However, the chemistry reignited the first time we got together, and our romance picked up right where we'd left off. This time, however, talk of marriage and a shared future was woven into our conversations. Over Christmas break, he took me to Massachusetts to meet his family. I fully imagined being his wife and the mother of his children.

The only thing impeding our marriage plans was that during Drew's absence I'd decided to serve a mission myself. When he returned to BYU, I was eight weeks shy of my twenty-first birthday, at which point I could submit mission papers. I could have scrapped those plans like so many other girls and gotten married, but part of me didn't want to settle down yet. I loved Drew and wanted to be with him, but I also wanted to see the world and experience a bit more of life. I figured if we were still so attracted to each other after his mission, our relationship would weather mine as well.

In many ways a mission was an odd choice for me. My parents deeply believed the teachings of LDS prophets, but I wrestled with existential questions in high

school and found it hard to accept certain LDS doctrines. I was particularly conflicted about the nature of God. I struggled to know when mercy could trump
justice and worried that I would fail to make it back into God's presence for
eternity. I didn't steal or drink or take drugs or do anything beyond kissing with
my boyfriend, but I drank Coke, watched R-rated movies, occasionally swore,
and let the kissing go on too long. Because I wasn't rigorously obedient, fear of
a lesser reward and divine disapproval nagged at my subconscious, exhausting
me mentally and spiritually.

By high school graduation, I'd grown apathetic. Without abandoning belief in
God, I wanted a spiritual reprieve from Mormonism's exacting nature. Accepted
to a small private college back East, I was ecstatic at the thought of getting out
of Provo. I suspect my parents lost sleep as they envisioned the fraternity parties
and atheist professors I was sure to encounter. Much to their relief, my partial
financial aid fell through at the last minute. I had just weeks to scramble for a
less-expensive alternative. I had decided to go to the University of Utah when
my dad persuaded me to talk to our neighbor, who was the dean of admissions
for BYU. Jim convinced me that BYU was the academically superior school, and
that was enough to entice me to enroll at the LDS university across the street
from my high school.

At BYU, although religion classes were mandatory and Mormon-think was
ubiquitous, I felt more freedom to make religious decisions than I had in high
school. I was spotty on my church attendance. By the middle of Drew's mission,
I was entirely inactive and living by myself in Salt Lake City, having dropped out
of BYU in order to write and discover the inner machinations of my soul. Not
that it panned out that way: I ended up spending my time working, making new
friends, and hanging out. But I never lost my romantic ideals of doing something
momentous that would lead to discovering life's deep meaning. Before he quit
writing to me, Drew kept telling me a mission was an experience so profound
he couldn't explain it; to understand, I would have to experience it myself. So I
decided to do just that.

I submitted my papers a few months after I turned twenty-one and was called
to serve in the Belgium Brussels mission. I entered the Missionary Training Center in March 1992. I rather enjoyed my time in the MTC, but after a few months
in Europe, the rigors of mission life caught up with me. The many, many rules
seemed impossible to keep. In addition, the relationships that had grounded
me for years were relegated to weekly letters and the new friendships I made
were transient: I might be assigned to work with someone I really liked, but it
was only a matter of time before one of us would be transferred. The instability
left me unmoored and vulnerable; I never got used to it.

But by far the most destabilizing factor was that Drew went silent when I left.
The weekly letters I anticipated rarely came. It was wrenching to go from seeing

him almost daily for six months, to having practically no contact—particularly since it was a more intense version of a pattern of separation I'd grown to hate during the preceding five years as friends left on missions. Why Drew barely communicated was a mystery I couldn't solve. After several months, I finally wrote and requested that he not contact me for the rest of my mission—it was too painful to wait week after week for news and be disappointed time and again. His response was essentially "Whatever you want." Well, what I wanted was regular letters, but that wasn't what I got.

Drew's final communication arrived in November, a few weeks after my twenty-second birthday, which he didn't acknowledge. I'd been in secular Western Europe roughly six months. Perhaps things might not have been so hard had I been busy teaching people. However, there was little interest in Mormonism among the locals. Most were contented cultural Catholics or agnostics or atheists quite happy without religion. I spent my days knocking on doors without much luck, trying to strike up conversations on public transit with even less luck, or visiting inactive members. We often hung out at members' homes for hours. It wasn't what we were supposed to do, but we had twelve work hours to fill each day and so few people to teach.

About the time Drew sent his final letter, I met Elder Daniel Singer in the Belgian town of Liege where I had gone for a few days on a work trade-off. My first image of him was his lanky 6-foot-4-inch frame towering over me, a plastic bag on his head as we scraped wallpaper off the ceiling of an investigator's apartment. It was a pretty goofy look for a first impression, not at all the impression I suspect he had hoped to make. He had told one of my former companions that he had seen my photocopied passport picture in the mission newsletter when I first arrived and had been overcome with the feeling that he would get to know me well—*very* well. Of course that companion promptly relayed this confession to me, so I was curious as to what this guy was like. It seemed his prophetic gifts were weak; we exchanged only a few brief pleasantries. I forgot him as soon as I left.

Two months later, at the start of a bitterly cold February, transfers were announced: Elder Singer would move into my district in Arras, France. It soon became a district where everyone—all four elders and both sisters—really liked each other. We spent time together whenever we could: church meetings and activities, sometimes even our preparation days. Toward the end of the nine weeks Elder Singer and I spent in the same town, we began to chat on the phone for longer than necessary when he called to gather weekly statistics. We'd talk about our plans for the future, scriptures or *Ensign* articles we'd found meaningful, what our lives had been like before our missions. Shortly before we both transferred out of Arras, Elder Singer hinted that he'd like to continue a friendship when we got home. I let him know that would be just fine with me.

Arras is also where I learned through the grapevine that Drew was seriously dating someone else. He had taken her home to meet his family for Christmas, just like he'd done the year before with me. As I still harbored intense feelings for Drew, this news was gut-wrenching. But it also made Elder Singer more appealing since it seemed Drew had moved on. By the time I transferred out of Arras, I had created a fantasy around the cute, charming elder with a vision of getting to know me well. I was flattered by his interest in me, and it gave me something happy to think about on days when my companion and I had absolutely no one to teach and nowhere to go.

I suppose it's not unusual for a college-aged girl to be interested in love, but it wasn't just romance I wanted. The nuclear family is everything in LDS theology: human beings come to earth to progress spiritually, and God's optimal design for spiritual growth is the family unit. Sharing this message was the reason I was thousands of miles away from home. I was perpetually immersed in ideas like this one from President Spencer W. Kimball: "If two people love the Lord more than their own lives and then love each other more than their own lives, working together in total harmony with the gospel program as their basic structure, they are sure to have this great happiness." There it was: marriage equaled great happiness. On those all too frequent days when I wasn't experiencing much happiness, I fantasized about the time when I would.

Mission rules prohibited any exchange of letters or phone calls between missionaries in the same mission except for official business. And yet, about three weeks into my sojourn in Amiens, a postcard arrived from Elder Singer. His justification: a postcard isn't a letter. I thought to myself, "Now that's some pretty fine logic." The card featured a picture of a funky 1970s couple meant to represent us. What delighted me was that Elder Singer had cut and pasted a piece of orange paper on the man's head to render him a redhead. Elder Singer had red hair and a quirky sense of humor, both of which I liked enormously.

A mission, with its innumerable rules, triggered all the feelings I still harbored from adolescence of not being good enough to merit divine approval. I wasn't prepared for the toll the rigors of conformity would exact on me. I struggled with obedience and discipline, and experienced profound guilt and shame over my failures. My misdeeds consisted of things like getting up late in the morning, staying up late at night, listening to unapproved music on occasion, not wearing nylons, wearing a knee-length skirt rather than one at my calf, or leaving my companion's side for an hour to be alone. But by far my biggest indiscretion was illicit communication. I sometimes called friends back in the States and wrote or called other missionaries in my same mission who weren't my leaders.

Once Elder Singer's postcard signaled that he too wasn't a strict rule-follower, we began corresponding, mostly about scriptures, theology, and missionary work. A few times, we even spoke on the phone. He was a kind friend and a most welcome listening ear. I always felt guilty, but not enough to stop; the weight of depression and loneliness was stronger than the guilt.

Month after month of teaching barely anyone when teaching is a proselytizing missionary's main purpose was devastating. Leaders intimated that if I just tried harder, was more rigidly obedient, was bolder in testifying on the subway, etc., etc., God would bless me with people to teach. The logical conclusion when I had no one to teach was therefore that it must be my fault. In my mind, the problem wasn't that most people weren't interested—I understood that Europeans are notoriously secular. No, I believed that because of my personal unrighteousness, I wasn't being led to those who were interested. Leaders assured me that somewhere in the cities where I served there lurked golden contacts, people prepared by the Lord to hear the fullness of the gospel. Their eternal welfare was partially my responsibility since I was already blessed with knowledge of the Lord's restored gospel. I felt an immense obligation to find these people and offer them a chance at salvation. But obviously I was failing miserably to find those who sought the truth.

Three months before the end of my mission, I was transferred to Saint Quentin, France. My new companion was good-natured but afflicted with seriously poor health; she lacked the stamina to meet the grueling work requirements. Those months with her were bittersweet: I enjoyed her relaxed company immensely, but it wasn't enough to relieve the crushing shame and loneliness I felt. And I broke. The ebullient girl who had entered the mission field was gone. All I knew those last three months was that I wanted the constant ache of failure to stop. I wanted someone to comfort me. And most of all, I wanted stability and permanence in my most profound relationships. And that's when I wrote a letter to Elder Singer that went something like this:

> Dear Elder Singer,
>   How's the work going? It's not? Yeah, same here. I've been listening to the new Sting album, *Ten Summoner's Tales*. I especially like the song "Shape of my Heart." How about getting married?
>
>   Love,
>   Sister Moss

One might guess I was nervous proposing to a man I'd known for only a few months, never been alone with, and never physically touched beyond a handshake. But I wasn't. Why? Because by that point I was partially insane. Evidently Elder Singer was about as insane as I. He responded:

> Dear Sister Moss,
>   Sure, I'll marry you. I've never really dated anyone in my life. I mean, I went to prom and all and I've been kissed by Sarah Staker on the way home from Mormon night at Disneyland. That counts, right? Glad you asked.
>
>   Love,
>   Elder Singer

So that was it. I was confident that Elder Singer and I both loved the Lord enough to make a good marriage and idealistic enough to think a few phone conversations and letters proved that we were a good match. I mean, we both wanted seven kids and weren't into traditional gender roles, plus I thought he was cute. What more was needed to determine our compatibility?

I told my parents our plan and asked my father to hire Daniel at his janitorial company in Provo after Daniel got home, a month before I did. Days after returning to California and giving his homecoming address, Daniel moved to Utah to live with his brother who attended BYU. My dad not only gave Daniel a job, he let Daniel drive my car.

I've often wondered why my parents aided and abetted this obvious insanity. Perhaps part of it was that they dated only a semester at BYU before marrying. Perhaps they also thought that a relationship forged during missionary service would ensure that my husband and I remained faithful Latter-day Saints. I will never fully know.

In any event, I stepped off the plane at the Salt Lake International Airport with an honorable release and, I see now, a case of full-blown clinical depression. Six and a half weeks later, a month after turning twenty-three, I married a mere acquaintance. It wasn't until my wedding night that I abruptly saw through the fog I'd been in. The reality of losing my virginity was nothing like I had imagined. I'm guessing first-time sexual encounters are frequently quick and awkward, but this felt tragic. The intimacy of sex made it abundantly clear that I didn't know Daniel well enough to marry him. I felt violated. Once the initial act was over, I locked myself in the bathroom and wept for hours, while my bewildered new husband lay in bed, listening to my sobs and wondering what was going on, until he finally drifted off to sleep.

In the years that followed, I often found myself wondering what sex would have been like if Daniel and I had dated longer—hell, if we'd dated at all. But that night I knew I had made a huge mistake in timing.

I wanted out of the marriage but couldn't see how to leave. Beyond embarrassment that my entire community had just come to my reception and wished me well and given us gifts, the solemn commitments I had made not only to Daniel but also to God weighed on me. I tried to find happiness in my situation but met with little success. Within months, I spiraled into a depression too dark for me to navigate. I asked my parents if I could move back home.

Being back at my parents' house provided space to think but no relief. Annulling the marriage was never a serious option because I was afraid to incur God's wrath. I decided what would solve all my problems was if Daniel and I could somehow create a strong sense of intimacy. Problem was, intimacy is usually the product of time, an accumulation of shared experiences and numerous incidents by which a person proves he or she can be trusted. Sure, we had the rest of our lives to create intimacy—but I needed a bond between us right then to feel anything but despair when I thought of our future together. So I decided on second best: great sex, something we hadn't managed so far. I wrote Daniel a letter and left it on the bed in our apartment when he wasn't home. Shortly thereafter, I stopped by to see how my letter had been received. We ended up making love and it was good enough to convince me the two of us could create the chemistry I longed for. I collected my bags from my parents' house and moved back to our apartment.

I had quit taking the pill when I moved back to my parents' house, figuring I didn't need it. Three months into the marriage, my period was late and I was gripped with a sense of certain doom. Days later, Daniel and I were at my parents' house doing laundry, a fight raging over my beige J. Crew shirt he had washed and tinted pink. I had specifically asked him not to wash my clothes. For whatever reason, I chose that point to go into the bathroom and take a pregnancy test.

When the plus sign indicated positive, I began howling like a tortured dog. No one knew how to console me, so everyone left me alone. When my crying finally ended, hours later, I descended into a black, oppressive depression. Abortion or adoption weren't options I entertained and the fleeting thoughts of leaving my marriage ended. The baby cemented the union.

After a few months, my despair abated simply because it had to: I lacked the strength to feel that awful indefinitely. So I settled into a constant dull ache periodically punctuated with acute despair. The beginning of our marriage knocked me off my feet; for a decade, I never got back on them. During that decade, we had four children. The intimacy issues remained and were compounded by the LDS church's stance on birth control. Certain methods were counseled against and there was pressure to have children soon and often, which I did. Raising kids is challenging in the best of circumstances, but the difficulty is greatly exacerbated by strained resources of time and money. Daniel was trying to work and go to school full-time. I worked until I got pregnant with our second child, then transitioned to being a stay-at-home mom. Before Daniel finished his bachelor's degree, we had three children. Those years were defined by stress and tension. We fought over finances, over how to spend our limited free time, over who was responsible for which chores, over who had it harder. Resentment and fatigue seemed to rule our lives. There were, however, brief periods where things felt fine. Those fleeting glimpses of an elusive happiness helped keep me in the marriage. I clung to hope that things could improve.

When I did contemplate divorce, I was terrified out of my mind of parenting alone. Daniel was an active parent and helped with the kids. I felt deep in my bones that I didn't have the bandwidth to hack it alone. I also knew the earning potential of a woman with small kids and no college degree. And I couldn't forget admonishments from LDS prophets that divorce is rarely justified before God. Incapable of leaving the marriage or changing it to my satisfaction, I settled into a stultifying stasis that was a far cry from the craving for stability and security that had led me to marry so quickly.

After sixteen years, I began to wonder if divorce was my best option after all. I still worried what the eternal repercussions might be—but I figured the ones for suicide were worse. When I confided this to a friend, she suggested I read a 2007 General Conference address by Dallin H. Oaks titled, simply, "Divorce."

I woke early one Sunday to study it. Elder Oaks made it clear that "modern prophets have warned that looking upon marriage 'as a mere contract that may be entered into at pleasure . . . and severed at the first difficulty . . . is an evil meriting severe condemnation,' especially where children are made to suffer." I mentally took inventory. There had been little pleasure in the marriage and I had hung on year after year. Plus, my children were already suffering. They had grown up in a home where the roiling tension between their parents often boiled over. It was the condemnation that hung me up. At what point could I terminate the promise I had made and not be divinely condemned?

And then I read this: "Now I speak to married members, especially to any who may be considering divorce. I strongly urge you and those who advise you to face up to the reality that for most marriage problems, the remedy is not divorce but repentance. Often the cause is not incompatibility but selfishness."

"AAAAHHHHH!!!!" A primal scream of molten rage spewed past my lips, reverberating around the room. I fiercely crumpled the pages I held and pitched them at the farthest wall. "It's not fair! It's just not fair!" I snarled, pounding my mattress with my fists.

I was taken aback at the ferocity that erupted from me. But I couldn't abide one more pious, facile admonition that wanting out of my marriage was a sign of sinfulness. The implication that I was solely to blame for my circumstances, and that the LDS leaders whose messages had shaped my desires and decisions had no responsibility, was too much to bear. While I'm sure my adolescent self had misconstrued some things, the fact remains that the church has explicitly encouraged quick courtships, early marriages, and large families as both righteous and the best way to be happy. Call me gullible, but I had believed Spencer Kimball when he promised that if I just loved God, the church, and my spouse, everything would be puppies and roses. Well, I guess that was pretty accurate. I had proverbial shit on the carpet and a thorn in my side.

Eventually I felt shame for my outburst. I felt guilty that I was so angry with God's chosen servant, but I did allow myself the subversive pleasure of relegating that talk to the recycling bin. Unfortunately I didn't do it before reading this: "A couple with serious marriage problems should see their bishop. As the Lord's judge, he will give counsel and perhaps even discipline that will lead toward healing." That line nagged at me until I scheduled an appointment to see my bishop, even though our personalities clashed. He saw God as a punisher, and more than once, I fled the church in tears over counsel from the "Lord's judge." The one good thing to come of it was that he agreed to help pay for professional counseling, since we couldn't afford it ourselves.

My counselor was a lovely LDS man in his early sixties. He stood at a cross-roads in my life and mercifully pointed me down a path of personal empowerment I hadn't known existed.

"I don't give a damn what Elder Oaks says in that talk or what your bishop says, either," he told me one spring evening about six months later. "What do you think you should do? Do you want to get divorced? Do you want to stay married and work on the relationship? Is there enough there to salvage? You tell me. What do you want to do?"

"I d-d-don't know," I stammered. "I just don't know."

"Well, that's not good enough. You need to know. And I think you do know."

"I don't know. If I leave him I don't know how I'll support the kids. I . . ."

He interrupted me, leaning forward and asking me a direct question: "Do you or do you not want to stay married to Daniel?"

All the learned dysfunction from our families of origin had come into play in our marriage. Misery begat misery: years of criticism, selfishness, stonewalling, and depression had trained us to act from the darkest, ugliest parts of ourselves. I couldn't live like that anymore.

"No. No, I do not," I said. "I've tried for years to make it work. I've been to countless therapists with him and alone. I've read a mountain of self-help books. I'm sick of trying. I don't know how to fix this and I'm miserable. We all are. I do *not* want to be in my marriage anymore." It felt powerful to allow myself to speak that truth in defiance of the teachings of the leaders of my church.

I was sick to my stomach the day I met with a lawyer. It was scary but ex-hilarating to finally take action. I had threatened divorce before, but this time I meant it. I had lost my fear of defying priesthood authority and gained the confidence to trust my intuition. I didn't care if I lost my comfortable house or endured poverty; anything was better than staying in a soul-sucking marriage. The overwhelming fear of eternal condemnation was gone. I would no longer allow anyone to guilt me into staying married. After the lawyer reviewed all possible options, I went home and laid them out for my husband.

Daniel's response? He didn't want the marriage to end. He asked if I would consider staying.

On some level, I still wanted to be married to Daniel. After sixteen years of shared life, he was no longer a mere acquaintance. We had conceived four children together, shared their pregnancies and births. We'd changed diapers and cleaned house and lost jobs together. We'd bought two different homes and vacationed together. We'd celebrated birthdays and holidays, mourned deaths and tragedies—together. I didn't want to throw all that away if I didn't have to.

I said I would give it another shot, but going forward I had some nonnegotiable absolutes. First, the specter of LDS hierarchical and patriarchal authority that had loomed over our marriage, infiltrating everything, was banished. I told Daniel I would no longer defer my life's choices to the counsel of LDS leaders, relying instead on the counsel of my own heart. I also made it clear that the LDS idea of a patriarchal order, in which men preside and rule over everything, would not work for me. In our marriage, we would be equals, true equals, or we were done.

That was several years ago. I eventually quit participating in the LDS church. Daniel later followed suit. There was so much damage done, so much promised to us by religious leaders whose authority I came to doubt and whose counsel I now mistrust. I still believe in and long for this great happiness: a partner who is my best friend, trusted confidant, and passionate lover. Perhaps Daniel and I will eventually achieve it. Perhaps not. But I'm convinced that if we do, it will be in spite of our temple marriage and acquiescing to LDS authority, not because of it.

PART II

Complicated Paths to the Temple
(Or Not Getting There at All)

Figure 4. Katrina Barker and Jared Anderson, March 2008, Bountiful, Utah

Katrina writes: "I had waited a lifetime for this moment coming out of the temple hand in hand with my eternal companion, but having to wait an additional year after our wedding to finally be sealed makes this photo bittersweet. Instead of basking in the joy of a new bride, I was five months pregnant, and mostly just felt relief to finally have my eternal marriage recognized by the church."

Plan A

NAOMI WATKINS

Growing up, I didn't sing or dance in the glee club; I didn't do crafts or play a musical instrument. Instead, I enjoyed camping and hiking with my family, reading books, excelling in school, and competitive swimming. My interests drew criticism from some ward members who told my parents that if I didn't participate in more "feminine" activities, I would grow up too strong-willed and independent for men to want me. When these comments got back to me, I looked to my mother, a convert to the church. She was one of the most strong-willed, independent women I knew, and she married. I figured I was OK.

At church, I learned what to expect from a Plan A life: meet a returned missionary, date, fall in love, get married, have a basketball team of babies, and live happily ever after. To make Plan A happen, I needed to be sweet and kind. I needed to cook and sew. I needed to be pretty. So I learned to do and be many of those things, yet my efforts didn't yield romantic attention from boys. I don't recall a contingency plan in case Plan A didn't work out. No one ever told us as young women that we might marry later in life or not at all. And while I knew even as a child that I didn't want to be one of those girls who married young, which I then defined as earlier than age twenty-three, I most certainly did *not* want to be one of those women who never married at all.

At home, our focus was on striving to be one's best. Yes, marriage was something my parents advocated, but never with the insistence I heard at church. While my parents married young, they always stressed that they were guided by the Spirit in that decision. They taught me that all my life decisions should be based on study, prayer, and seeking and following spiritual answers and promptings. Their attitude was that when marriage was to happen, it would happen. In the meantime, I should live life, get an education, and establish a career.

After high school, I enrolled in a small, private liberal arts university not far from my home in California. One of only five Mormons on campus, I was surrounded by classmates who rarely if ever spoke of marriage. Sure, I dated and my friends and I talked about boys, but if we discussed marriage, it was in the context of someone's parents' failed marriage or something we would do far in the future—definitely after we finished our educations.

After three semesters, I wanted a larger university experience, so I transferred to BYU. Despite all the lessons in Young Women's about preparing for marriage and finding a worthy priesthood holder, I was shocked by my new environment. Dating and marriage were the focus of many conversations in and between classes, at the library, in line to buy books or pay for a snack, and at church. Bishops and stake presidents bragged about the number of engagements each semester in their wards and stakes. Wedding magazines covered the coffee tables in many apartments. Friends got engaged and married after quick courtships.

My journals from that time reflect a tug in two directions. On one end, I was no different from my peers. I wanted and sought attention from the opposite sex and was pleased when I got it. One summer, I dated and had my heart broken for the first time by an all-American, just-home-from-his-mission boy. And then, I dated some more. But while I certainly enjoyed dating, I specifically wrote about wanting to wait to marry after I graduated. And so, without regret or worry for the future, I graduated from BYU sans diamond on my ring finger and moved to the Phoenix area for a job teaching English to seventh graders.

One evening, I sat across a picnic table from a strawberry-blond boy, enjoying the coolness at the park as night came to the Arizona desert. I'd met him on a setup; we rendezvoused in the fish department of the local big-box pet store before heading to the Mesa Temple to see the Christmas lights display. Having always had a thing for dark-haired guys, I was surprised when I looked at him one day and decided that I could marry him. It was the first time I had felt this way. And yet, when I said "I love you," he didn't feel the same. "I just don't like you the way you love me," he said. We tried to remain friends, but such a relationship was impossible for me. Soon, he married another girl.

So I continued to date. As I started each new relationship, I was hopeful that it would be my last. They all began so positively, but something crept up eventually—a guy whose wit equaled my own, but who kissed like a rotor rooter; another whose untreated bipolar disorder when I finally encountered it meant I never knew whether I'd get the sweet or swearing-like-a-sailor version that day; a ward acquaintance with whom my relationship began on a cruise ship so that my friends termed it "the boatmance." It was as short-lived and as intense at the cruise itself.

Fast forward many years and dates and relationships later. I still felt confident that I would marry. I just had to find the right guy. I thought a reserved guy in my ward with beautiful hazel eyes and a kind heart might be him. Late one night, he haltingly and tearfully confessed to me his almost two-decade-long porn addiction. I was speechless and stunned, yet we dated for a few more months. Eventually, I decided that I couldn't do it—I would rather be single than take on his burden. Getting married just to get married was not the Plan A life that I wanted. And so, I broke his heart and mine.

Now in my thirties, I'm no longer as resilient as I was in my twenties. It's much more difficult to hear "I like you, just not enough to do anything about it" and bounce back when a relationship ends—especially given that there's not much to bounce onto. I used to console myself after a breakup with the idea that this painful ending offered the chance of adventure and good things to come despite the heartbreak. But now, a relationship's end signifies failure and the prospect of starting over with very few serious options.

Plenty of well-intentioned people speculate: I'm too picky; I'm too intimidating; I should date online; I should date nonmembers; I should move again; I should speed date; I should grow my hair long; I should attend another conference; I should tell men I'm a teacher instead of a professor of education; I should lower my expectations; I should go on thirty dates in thirty days with thirty different guys; I should agree to another setup; I should be more patient; I should pray more; I should take what has been offered me.

Yet, when I am alone, my speculations go a different direction, and I whisper to myself: *It will never happen to me. I'm not good enough. I'm unlovable. There are no good men left. It's impossible. I will always be alone.* And I believe the speculations of others and sometimes even follow their advice. But after years of dashed hopes and heartbreak, it's difficult to foresee that doing the same things over and over and over again will ever yield a different result.

And then, listening to another leader in a singles ward joke over the pulpit about our lack of a spouse; attending another activity that treats us more like late teens than adults with advanced degrees, established careers, well-stamped passports, and mortgages; reflecting on one more Sunday where the focus has been on getting married instead of on Christ, I wonder: what's so wrong with being single?

I wonder if marriage is something I really want or something I've just been told to want. I've spent enough time on my own to know that if I chose to, I could live the rest of my life alone, and I would be OK. I have a good life: an educational path that led me to a solid career, travel adventures that have allowed me to hike the peaks of Machu Picchu or snorkel with sea turtles in the azure blue water of Hawaii and the Caribbean, and friends and family whom I love and who love me.

But I see what marriage adds to the lives of my loved ones, and I also know that I would much rather share this life I've built with someone who is my equal partner. And that's part of the sticking point: I really do want an equal partner, someone who shares my values and interests, someone who loves me as much as I love him, someone with whom I share mutual respect and commitment to our relationship, someone who believes my dreams and passions and work are as valuable as his own and who supports me in these endeavors, someone who inspires me to be better as I do the same for him. I'm not willing to just marry anyone. If I were going to settle for less than I desire and deserve, I would have done it many years ago.

When I silence the thoughts trying to convince me that the Lord has forgotten me, that I'm unlovable, or that marriage won't happen for me in this life, I remember the Plan A my parents taught me: study, pray, seek answers to prayers, and follow spiritual promptings. I remember that the best things about my life have come from following this plan.

And so, I continue the cycle. I agree to another blind date. I create another dating profile. I attend church meetings and activities. I half-listen to my married friends' advice. I cry into my pillow. I open my heart again. I try to push the fear and loneliness aside. I vent my frustrations to the Lord. I feel his love and reassurance that I will marry. And I repeat.

Pull a Handcart Without Giving Up in Missouri

CHRISTMAS JONES

I love love.

And I am probably never getting married.

Hello, you may have met me. I'm a late-twenty-something with a professional degree, a house, great friends, a 401(k), and other than that mortgage, no debt.

I've come to terms with the fact that I am almost certainly going to be single for the rest of my life. In fact, it's getting to the point where, between my age and lack of suitable suitors, the clarifiers (*probably* not getting married, *almost certainly* staying single) are unnecessary. But my church, my friends, and my family can't accept the idea. They reject it the way a patient in kidney failure rejects an incompatible donor organ, apparently unaware that acceptance is what sets me free. I try to help them understand that, *No, really, it's OK*. Still they resist.

"You'll find the right guy soon," reassures my aunt.

"You're so fun!" says one friend. "Just keep putting yourself out there."

"You've still got hope in the eternities," intones every church leader, ever.

But the problem isn't my single status.

It's living in a culture that wants to pat my hand like I'm some elderly maiden aunt and tell me it's OK that I'm single. When all I want is to talk about *anything* but that.

* * *

In January 2013, I went to a Sundance screening with my roommate and my cousin. After the film, the director, Stuart Zicherman, stepped onto the stage to answer questions—but first, he posed one: *Who here is an ACOD?*

ACOD stands for "adult child of divorce." I first heard of ACODs when my parents divorced. Psychologists coined the term to address the phenomenon of middle-aged or elderly couples dissolving their marriages and involving their adult children intimately in the details.

Minor children are often pawns in divorces. They may hear dirty laundry here and there—*your mother is selfish, your father is irresponsible*—but it's generally understood that kiddies should be shielded from the bloodiest battles.

This layer of protection falls away in adulthood. ACODs are often active, albeit unwilling, players in the drama. I found my mother her real estate agent. I helped my father pick his attorney. My sister closed their joint bank accounts. My brother got the locks changed on the doors. All of us spent a weekend packing our mother's things and hauling them to her new house.

A year of my twenty-something life was spent not flirting, traveling the world, or anything as mundane as refinancing my mortgage, but reviewing the appraisal of my childhood home and attempting the mediation over Grandma's silver.

As soon as I heard *ACOD* was coming to Sundance, I knew I had to see it, and not just because I adore its stars: Jane Lynch, Amy Poehler, Adam Scott. The storyline spoke to me, in ways I suspect it spoke to most of the four hundred–plus people in the audience.

In the film, the term *ACOD* is broadened to include any adult whose parents divorced, no matter how old the child was when it happened, as long as the parents remained acrimonious in the decades that followed. I was a traditional ACOD—my parents separated when I was twenty-seven. My roommate was this new type of ACOD—his parents split when he was a toddler. My lucky cousin fit both categories—her parents began divorcing when she was seven and finished after she turned ten (it was one hell of a divorce), then her father ended his second marriage when she was twenty-four.

When the director of *ACOD* asked the audience to raise their hands if they were an ACOD, over half of those in attendance waved at him.

He held up his iPhone and took a picture of us.

                              *   *   *

The first time I announced I wasn't getting married, I was nine. It was in Sunday school, and I was ignored, aside from the stern, "*Yes, you are! Everyone gets married!*" from the teacher before he resumed his lesson.

My mother (bless her dysfunctional heart) sowed the seeds of marital dissatisfaction in me from a young age. I was her oldest child and from kindergarten on, she would drive me to school early so she could talk to me, uninterrupted, about how unhappy she was.

She hated being married, hated staying at home, and I suspect (though if I were to ask, she'd deny it) she hated motherhood. She took her unhappiness out on my father, refusing to clean house and collecting more clutter with every passing year, which led to weekly screaming matches. She refused to stay within the family budget, which meant another verbal battle each time a credit card bill arrived. And she spent my childhood, and my siblings,' using us as soldiers in her trench war.

Despite—or maybe because of—my mother's best efforts to turn me against him, I remained a steadfast daddy's girl. Unlike my younger siblings, who wouldn't recognize what was going on until years later, I couldn't be persuaded that our father was some bully who hated fun and loved being mean. At the same time, I lacked an adult's understanding of my mother's depression and dearth of social outlets. This left me with one conclusion: *If my father was good, and my mother was so bitterly unhappy, then marriage itself must be awful.*

A tomboy by nature, I had equal numbers of boy and girl friends as a child. But as we moved into junior high, the land of sweaty, awkward crushes, I found myself crippled by fear at the prospect of hand-holding, much less dating. In seventh grade, I burst into tears in the middle of class when a boy asked me to the winter dance. (Without any evidence, I was convinced his invitation was a cruel joke in disguise.) In eighth grade, my best guy friend revealed he had a crush on me, and I retreated behind a shy Mormon tween's best line of defense: *The prophet says I can't date until I'm sixteen.*

No amount of Young Women's lessons ever managed to convince me that marriage was my destiny. I spent most Sundays squirming in my seat, wondering who these teachers thought they were kidding. The first time a Beehive teacher suggested that we, as twelve- and thirteen-year-olds, might be married in a mere six or seven years, I thought I might throw up.

High school was no better. After my first date, I literally jumped out of a moving vehicle so I could avoid the inevitable doorstep scene. I faked nausea on the drive home after prom for the same reason. Let it never be said that I blame the male gender for my current lack of a husband—I dealt out a fair amount of dating trauma myself, in my day.

It wasn't until halfway through college that I got it together. At twenty, I met a cute boy at a fraternity party. He was smart and sarcastic, blue-eyed with an East Coast accent, and when we kissed, I found that I didn't mind the taste of beer as much as I'd thought I would.

Yes, that's right. I got over my fear of dating . . . by dating a nice Catholic-turned-atheist boy.

It didn't work out between us, that cute premed with a penchant for rum and Cokes, but he helped me discover something strange: I may be terrible at dating, but I am an excellent girlfriend. Making someone happy *makes me happy.*

As with many an ACOD before me, that information came as quite a surprise.

Soon after that I asked (I asked!) a coworker to my sorority formal. He was technically Mormon, and when I say "technically Mormon," I mean he claimed Mormonism but never went to church. We ended up dating for a few months before he broke up with me so he could spend more time at work. Really.

If there was ever a reason to encourage teenagers to date, it's to get that first heartache out of the way early. Twenty-one is too old to experience it for the first time.

After my coworker, I dated my first BYU grad. He was smart and sweet, funny, and endearingly chubby. My biggest concern in our relationship was that he seemed so *certain* of his testimony in the LDS faith, while mine was a hope at best. He assured me that wasn't a problem. Then he dumped me over the phone, two days after he told me he loved me. He had a feeling it "wasn't right," whatever that meant. I was crushed for about a month.

Despite these romances, I occasionally found myself struck with that same dread that once led me to jump from a moving vehicle. There was no pattern, no logical reason why some guys triggered my fight-or-flight response and others didn't. They fell into Mormon and not-Mormon camps, both upstanding gentlemen and (as I sometimes found out later) scoundrels in disguise. I was still self-sabotaging, but for no real reason. The only difference was that now I was trying not to.

By grad school, I was determined that my parents' marriage wouldn't define my future happiness. At the same time, I felt more and more isolated at church. Despite growing up in a heavily LDS community, I'd never been able to befriend people at church. My best friends were always the Baptist and Catholic kids, the agnostics and dabblers in Wicca. College did nothing to reverse this trend. I went to church, I accepted callings, and then I went home and watched *South Park* with my sorority sisters.

As a semi-inactive friend said once, I just wasn't born with a sweet spirit. I was fun and loyal and willing to help friends move, but I liked Quentin Tarantino movies and gay rights, and that seemed (to me, at least—maybe I didn't give people enough credit) an insurmountable friendship obstacle at most singles ward activities.

Young Women's General President Margaret D. Nadauld once said (and then countless other LDS leaders echoed), "The world has enough women who are coarse. We need women who are soft." This never made sense to me, as "we" seemed to have *oodles* of soft women. We had just a few women who seemed like they could, as my dad put it, "pull a handcart without giving up in Missouri."

I was one of those coarse, tough, *unsoft* women. And I did not fit in.

And just like Mormon girls didn't seem terribly interested in befriending me, Mormon guys, by and large, weren't interested in dating me. Whether it was due to ambition, awkwardness, an off-kilter sense of humor, that aforementioned lack of a sweet spirit, or simply a wide array of girls prettier and more accommodating than I to choose from, only a handful of Mormon guys asked me out. Fewer still wanted a second date.

So I got proactive. I set up online dating profiles and asked friends to schedule blind dates. I went out with an attorney, a doctor, a slew of students, and even more entrepreneurs. (The term *entrepreneur* should be interpreted loosely as "returned missionary with a strong desire to not have a boss.") I attended church and encountered guys both gallant and condescending (like one who asked whether I was studying "teaching or nursing"). Nothing went particularly wrong, but nothing clicked.

After watching my parents' spectacularly bad marriage, I didn't really care about temple marriage. If I married a Mormon guy, I'd be happy to have one. If not, I didn't care. All I wanted was someone I liked, who liked me, and with whom I could maintain low-conflict, mutual liking in perpetuity.

And then I met Jack. He was perfect for me in every way, except all the big ones. He didn't want kids—I suspected I did. He didn't want to get married—I knew, despite my parents' awful example, that I would. He had left the church, which wasn't a problem for me, but, as it turned out, was a big problem for him.

But we could talk for hours and it seemed like no time had passed. Or we could sit in silence for just as long without it ever getting uncomfortable. Arguing with him was more fun than agreeing with anyone else. And our biggest point of contention was always the church.

You might wonder why, if I felt adrift within the Mormon community, I wouldn't just leave for Jack. I wondered that myself. It was partly stubbornness. I didn't think Jack should ask me to change when I accepted him as he was. It was partly that I couldn't, and still can't, make a guarantee about how I will feel about the church in the future. I might become more devout, I might become less. And I can't be in a relationship predicated on one unwavering opinion, with the threat of breakup or divorce depending not on external behavior like fidelity or selflessness, but on internal belief.

But the biggest reason, I think, is that for me, Mormonism is like an uncle I spent a lot of time with as a child. Occasionally he was overly strict, but mostly he was fun. He influenced how I see the world—usually for the better. Now that I'm an adult and have distanced myself somewhat from his (at times) embarrassing antics, there is one thing being raised by my parents taught me: your family is family, no matter how they complicate your life.

Jack and I dated for a year, partly long-distance, never officially committing. In Jack's mind, my Mormonism was an insurmountable obstacle. In my mind, if I continued to be loving and supportive, he would realize that a connection like ours didn't happen every day—that a funny, smart, thoughtful girlfriend didn't just appear under your pillow like a gift from the tooth fairy.

But then there was the biggest issue. The sex elephant in the room.

For better or worse, Mormonism and that early fear of boys guaranteed I entered my mid-twenties as sexually inexperienced as possible. The longer I dated Jack, the more obvious it was that we couldn't just make out forever. I loved him and I wanted our relationship to work. He said he would reconsider the marriage thing, but couldn't move forward until we'd taken the next step physically. I said I was willing to consider sex before marriage, but only if he was willing to give us a real chance.

No more seeing other people. No more declaring our relationship "casual," despite speaking every day and spending hundreds of dollars to see each other when we were apart. He would be my boyfriend, I would be his girlfriend, and then we would have sex.

Truth be told, I wanted to take that step. If I'd ever had any doubts about my sexuality during those years when I was terrified of dating, they were put to rest by how badly I wanted to have sex with that boyfriend.

But.

He didn't believe me. What's more, he thought that even if we did have sex, our relationship was still doomed because I wasn't willing to leave the church.

It was an impasse we never got over.

To this day, whenever I discuss my dating life with friends, the sex elephant will raise his trunk and silently wave it at me, like some sort of asshole Babar. *You didn't forget about me, did you?* One friend—my roommate's boyfriend— actually said it out loud: "I hate to be honest, kiddo, but I wouldn't ever date a Mormon girl unless I knew she was going to put out. I'm not in junior high anymore."

There's that elephant. *You think you can date a nice atheist boy again? A Catholic? Buddhist? A Jew? Good luck, honey! Make sure you keep going to Zumba, just in case you get a chance for another sex audition!*

Because that's what it would be—an audition. Unlike the rest of the adult American population, I didn't lose my virginity in my teens or early twenties. And now, if I wanted to take that step, I'd have to get over the socially awkward hurdle of never having done it before. Of wanting it to be special and accepting that it might not be. Of remembering that I declined chances to experience that rite of passage with guys I loved, and now being presented with the option of just getting it over with a guy I kinda-sorta-barely-like.

Being a single, progressive, late-twenty-something Mormon woman is like having your foot stuck in a bear trap. I can wait around for a Mormon guy who also loves college football and doesn't want to preside any more than I want to be presided over . . . or I can move on. But only if I cut off my leg.

I don't know which option is less appealing. One thing is sure, though.

The longer I wait to decide, the worse it's going to be.

*   *   *

Since breaking up with Jack, I have come to a realization: the older you get in Mormondom, the weirder your dating prospects become.

I dated a single dad. When I mentioned this to a friend, he was surprised. "Him? He's gay."

Really? How do you know?

"Because I saw him at a gay club, where he stuck his hands down my pants."

I dated an LDS guy who accused me of being needy and marriage-hungry after I told him I didn't want to text so much.

I went on a first date with a guy who got engaged to someone else three days after he kissed me goodnight.

I had my first NCMO—that's a "noncommittal makeout," for those who grew up outside the Mormon Corridor—at twenty-seven. He was thirty-six. I didn't know it was a NCMO until after the third time we hung-out-without-going-out. I made the grave error of thinking a Mormon bachelor of his age was too old for those sort of shenanigans and had been giddy that a handsome, successful guy was interested in me after a long dating drought. Things became clear when I asked him if he wanted to attend a party with me, and he confessed that he had just started dating someone. It took a second to realize that, no, he didn't mean me.

And then, finally, blessedly, my parents divorced, turning me into an ACOD at last. I watched my parents, shackled for three decades by marriage to the wrong person, discover that life didn't have to be an endless series of conflicts.

In the middle of the divorce, my bishop asked me if the dissolution of my parents' relationship had soured me on temple marriage. I couldn't help it—I actually laughed.

No, bishop. Divorce is the best thing that ever happened to our family. Everything that happened before that soured me on the idea of temple marriage.

At twenty-eight, I went on a blind date with a guy who was divorced, living with his parents, and still working on his undergraduate degree. He told me that, at my age, prospects were dwindling.

He was also twenty-eight. In his words, "Guys just have more time than girls."

With every one-word email from a guy too lazy to express a complete thought, every weird setup, every visit to a singles ward where hardly anyone spoke to me, I got more and more depressed about dating.

Not about the prospect of dying alone, mind you. No. The thought of *opening an Internet browser one more time* to see which young chap had sent me a pithy "Hey" on OKCupid or LDS Singles became overwhelming. The prospect of putting on a cute outfit and doing my hair for yet another disappointing date held as much appeal as ripping out my fingernails.

Why can't I just do what I love? And while I love being in a relationship, I do not love dating. I actively *hate* dating.

But I love throwing dinner parties for my friends and watching movies with my roommates. I love skiing and geeking out over my favorite books. I love hiking and playing with my dog. I love writing and a good *West Wing* marathon.

I think the revelation came when a friend was griping over the cover of some gossip magazine. "Would they step off Jennifer Aniston's ass already?

That woman has millions of dollars and shiny, shiny hair. She can do whatever she wants, whenever she wants, for the rest of her life. And we're supposed to believe that she's sad and lonely? What a joke."

And suddenly, it clicked for me.

Yes, I wanted to find a guy who hates Ayn Rand and loves zombie movies as much as I do, but *at least I can vacation whenever I want.*

I can keep throwing dinner parties. I can keep buying ski passes. I will always—*always*—be free to do the things I love. Even if I never find someone to do them with.

And better yet, as long as I am single, I will always—*always*—have the option of avoiding things I don't want to do.

For Mormon girls, that exchange (husband over freedom, family over fun) is supposed to be a given. *Of course you choose husband and family! What else are you here for?*

But for perpetually single Mormon girls—like me—it becomes so obvious that the clearest benefit to singledom is the avoidance of everything married people complain about *constantly.*

From that point on, I started making a note whenever my single, child-free status was a bonus, not a detriment. Whenever I was at dinner with my sorority sisters (now moved on from *South Park* to the *Blues Clues* stage of life) and someone mentioned *membranes stripping* or *vaginas ripping* or (horror of horrors) *NIPPLES DETACHING*, I would thank my lucky stars that, *No sir, not me!* My house is vomit-free.

I may not find that special someone, but I hit the snooze button as often as I want and if I want to use up all the hot water, no one will complain.

And whenever that doesn't seem like enough, I just have to repeat the mantra in passive voice Thomas S. Monson–speak: *Membranes were stripped. Vaginas were ripped. Nipples were detached.*

And I feel better about myself all over again.

*   *   *

My younger sister got engaged. Her fiancé is a good egg if there ever was one, and I am delighted for her—though less excited about the bridesmaid dresses she picked. A guy I know asked me if I was jealous.

I don't understand that, this idea that single women are jealous when friends pair off. If anything, it gives me hope.

My Ivy League–educated cousin got married at twenty-seven.

One of my few Mormon female friends—a PhD!—got engaged at twenty-nine.

A coworker got engaged at thirty-two.

Another one at thirty-three.

There's still a chance for me.

Hope.

Except, sometimes hope isn't welcome. There's something about that sort of thinking that feels self-defeating. The more I hold on to hope, the more depressed I get. The more I accept that my life might really be sleeping in on weekends and breakfast-for-dinner whenever I want, the more relieved I am about my light left ring finger.

*   *   *

After the director of *ACOD* took a picture of all the ACODs in the audience, he said something that I thought was kind of beautiful. "I didn't want to make a movie that was just about divorce. I wanted to make a movie about how our lives are not dictated by our parents' choices."

I spent my childhood scared of marriage, in a culture that worships at the altar of fairy-tale endings.

I spent my early twenties discovering that I did want to be in love, but with no idea how to get it right.

In my late twenties, I attacked dating like a numbers game where the stats would eventually tilt in my favor. But at some point in the year when I made my first Thanksgiving dinner, not because I had a family of my own, but because I had a single father who needed the help, I realized my choices might not be so simple. I had been thinking the right guy would be the right guy, regardless of religion—but most non-LDS guys will not want the girl with her foot caught in a bear trap.

And then, not too long before I went to go see a Sundance film, I realized . . . *I can just let all of this go.*

I want to fall in love and get married. I'm (probably) not going to.

That is not a contradiction. That is not a tragedy.

That's fine.

*   *   *

Like most LDS girls, I once wrote out, at the insistence of a Young Women's leader, a list of the attributes I wanted in my future husband. Like most LDS girls, I lied. (We all saw the public shaming delivered to the girl who dared put "hot" on her list. I certainly wasn't going to admit that I didn't even want to make a list.)

Returned missionary. (That was a lie. I couldn't have cared less.)

Kind. (Ah, the bare minimum for humans: kindness. Guys wonder why girls don't go for "nice guys"—it's because if "nice" is all you have going for you, you might as well be saying, "I won't cheat on you or hit you." It's not nearly enough, fellas.)

Smart. (True)

Funny. (True)

Fifteen-year-old me didn't know what else to write, so I ended the list.

But here's my grown-up, almost-thirty list. If I find this guy, I will make the leap with him and never look back. And if I don't meet him, giving up bathroom space won't be worth settling for anything less than someone who:

Wants to email me when he's at work. Reads the news. Listens when I talk. Has something interesting to say. Likes animals. Is able to help with home improvement projects. Is willing to help throw (or at least vacuum after) parties. Loves, or is at least benignly indifferent to, the outdoors. Helps carry in groceries. Is financially conservative. Is socially liberal. Has gay friends, or can easily befriend my gay friends. Loves travel. Brings breakfast-in-bed. Accepts breakfast-in-bed. Holds my hand in scary movies. Wants to have sex with me. Likes that I want to have sex with him. Is open to kids. Doesn't want me to do all the work if we do have kids. Has good dental hygiene. Is pronapping. Is proservice. Is probarbecue. Is willing to be silly. Is capable of being serious.

Is tough enough to pull a handcart without giving up in Missouri.

Dinner and a Movie

MARIE BRIAN

I grew up in Utah County, home of Brigham Young University and Osmond Studios. In fact, I live in Utah County still. Its nickname is Happy Valley—and you'd be surprised how many people don't mean that ironically. As a teen, I was blissfully naive and thrived in a protective bubble of zealous, perky innocence. At high school graduation, most of my friends weren't just virgins—they were lip virgins, unlike me. I had my first kiss at age seventeen. On stage. In a play. I and the boy in question didn't know what we were doing and didn't want to be doing it. It was about as erotic as two fish dying together on the same hooked line.

In our spare time, my friends and I would play racquetball, ring doorbells and run away before anyone could answer, or steal portable flashing street signs and leave them on the front porches of boys we had crushes on. (We liked that for its subtlety.) Also, some of my friends were devotees of a super-secret ritual called blatting. I never managed to blat, but a friend who betrayed her blatting vow of secrecy told me about it: initiates were required to buy a Hostess pie, place it on the road still in the wrapper, wait for it to be run over by a car, then crawl to it on their knees and lap up the resulting pie spatter like a dog. The act involved (1) pointless zaniness, (2) making a public spectacle of yourself, (3) sloppy eating, and (4) bad desserts, so it was pretty much perfect fun for most Utah County teens—and good training for more important endeavors.

The very best thing—or so I thought at the time—about growing up in Utah County was dating. It wasn't just ordinary *blah* dating. It was *creative* dating. It relied on pointless zaniness and making a public spectacle of yourself, it often involved sloppy eating, and bad desserts were highly encouraged. There was also often the added element of matching outfits, because sometimes the mere fact that you were interacting with a group of people in silly ways wasn't enough to alert complete strangers to the fact that you were on a creative date. And for some reason, you *really* wanted strangers to notice you and know what you were doing—or at least wonder really hard.

The first step in the creative dating process is: Ask Someone Out. Heaven forbid you just phone the person and ask them to spend time with you! You need to ask them out *creatively*. Like this, for instance:

Will You Go On A Creative Date With Me?
Yes _____
No _____
You Are Crazy ___X___

You then slip it into something tricky like a balloon or the mouth of a rotting fish. (You think I'm kidding. I'm not. My brother totally did that.) Other popular ask-someone-out methods include: scavenger hunts, so that only after considerable effort does someone learn that they've been asked out; puzzles, preferably homemade (glue a photo of yourself to a piece of cardboard, then cut it into puzzle shapes), with the message written on the back and decipherable only after the puzzle is assembled; and singing telegrams (ideally delivered in public for maximum spectacle).

Keep in mind—that's just the asking; the answering must be creative too. I once informed a guy on his doorstep that he had to pour a bucket of ice water over his head to tell me that, "Yes," he wanted to go to some dance with me. Doorstep interactions like this of course required an audience—usually a group of giggling teenage girls, congregating on the front lawn while the boy's mother watched with a conspiratorial gleam in her eye.

The actual date must of course be creative and should involve at least four people. The point, you see, is not to get to know one person. You don't want to spend time discussing your ideas or values or hopes and dreams, or telling stories about the experiences that have made you the people you are, or generally having the kinds of conversations that most people think help you determine whether you (A) are compatible or (B) actually like each other.

Instead, you want to find out how your date behaves in group situations. Does s/he play along, cheerfully? Do anything the group requires, no matter how embarrassing, uncomfortable, or ridiculous? Maintain enthusiasm and encourage it in others? Enjoy looking as much as possible like everyone else? Pitch in to help clean up the tremendous mess that having fun invariably creates? Those are the traits that creative dating encourages and helps one assess, because those are the traits that make one a desirable mate in Utah County.

A popular creative date—a classic, really—is the messy spaghetti dinner. Couples don black garbage bags over their clothes, are tied together at the wrist (when I did this at age sixteen, it was the closest I'd ever been to a boy), then eat spaghetti not with forks, knives, or spoons, but with spatulas or tongs or wire whisks or even a garlic press (if you knew one of the few people in Utah County who actually cooked with fresh garlic). You get to laugh at how hard it is to get spaghetti in your mouth with a spatula while tied to another person at the wrist, and you get to laugh at how messy everyone gets. Isn't that *hilarious*? Isn't that *creative*?

One Saturday afternoon, half a dozen of us took a blanket and a picnic basket and enjoyed a lunch not on some grassy park ground with a beautiful view of the mountains (Utah has lots of those), but in the middle of foot traffic at a mall. We wore matching shirts and took photos. Even though there were three guys and three girls, for some reason, many of the photos involved all three girls and only one guy at a time—*way* too polygamous-looking. I remember thinking that this was the most fun that teenagers could possibly have, but having since learned about other options—like, for example, heavy petting—I feel robbed.

As juniors in high school, my girlfriends and I decided that for the girls' choice Sadie Hawkins dance, we wouldn't just ask our own dates; we would *make* them. So we dressed dummies in outfits that matched ours and attached balloons for heads.

At the time, I didn't know there was anything risqué about dating something you inflated with your own breath. We thought we were being cute and clever, brilliantly one-upping the whole system. We even took our Balloon Men out to dinner (they didn't eat much), then danced with them, twirling them around the gym floor. (But not letting them get too close. That's evil.)

Happy Valley boys were just as enthusiastic about creative dating as the girls. Some guys I know once hiked up a steep mountain and created a picnic table and chairs out of logs. My lady pals and I climbed up said steep mountain, then all of us ate Chinese take-out on the manly-hewn furniture. I called it Xtreme Picnicking. Afterward, we hiked back down the mountain and played racquetball, because one way to increase the creativity of a date is to increase the number of activities it involves.

For years I accepted creative dating simply as the way the world was and should be, but eventually I grew tired of all the goofiness and theatrics. By my first semester at BYU, I had devolved into an angsty grunge stage. Normally, I sat in the back of the class in my baseball hat, looking surly and unapproachable. But one day I noticed the back of this red-haired guy's head. I have always had a thing for redheads. So instead of the back row, I parked my baggy-denimed butt next to the ginger on the second row—next to Danny. And then I retreated into my sullen self and never spoke to him.

Until one day, several weeks into the class, when Danny started up a conversation about movies. "Have you seen *Schindler's List*?" he asked.

"Yes," I said.

"*Silence of the Lambs*?"

"Yes."

"*Thelma and Louise*?"

"*Loved* it." I sensed a theme: they were all R-rated movies, which good Mormons aren't supposed to watch. He was quizzing me.

"Would you like to see *Crimson Tide* with me?" he asked. It was a Jerry Bruckheimer blockbuster about a submarine, and it was rated R. And that was when he had me. No weirdness. Just a simple "Will you see this possibly inappropriate movie with me?"

I said yes. Not many girls at BYU were willing to see an R-rated movie on a date. I'd passed his test. And he'd passed mine.

The date was noncreative and glorious. We ate at Chili's. I had the chicken tacos. He had the chicken crispers. Over dinner, we talked not about how messy we were getting or how hard it was to eat with tongs (we actually used regular table utensils!), but about our ideas and values. We told stories about experiences that made us who we are. We discovered that we were pretty compatible. We realized we liked each other.

The movie was enjoyably suspenseful, with no nudity or sex and not as much profanity as you might expect considering its R-rating. Rather than tying our wrists together, Danny simply held my hand. Afterward, we talked about the movie. He liked Gene Hackman. I liked Denzel Washington.

That night, before I went to sleep, I knelt by my bed in prayer. "Dear Heavenly Father," I said, "thank you for sending me a man who rescued me from the misery of creative dating. Never again will I have to go for a ride in a horse-drawn carriage around Temple Square while wearing pajamas and a wig. Amen."

Which is how I ended up engaged at nineteen and married at nineteen. There weren't many men who understood the delights of dinner and a movie, and I wasn't about to let the one I'd found get away.

Sure, there were trade-offs to marrying so young. I dropped out of college, for starters. Deprived of a prestigious education that would help me acquire a prestigious job, I now find myself engaging in pursuits I have a natural affinity for (embroidery, crochet, writing) for both leisure and a wage.

I also had my first baby at twenty-one. But due to a defective womb, I was sadly unable to have as many kids as most married-at-nineteen Mormon girls generally bear: I reproduced only three times, a sure sign that my husband and I were not as righteous as we should be.

There was another sign that we were insufficiently righteous in the eyes of our Utah County neighbors: we refused to creative date. Because here's the thing: that stuff doesn't automatically end when you get married.

No, to keep the magic and the interest alive after you tie the knot, you're supposed to creative-date as a married couple. People "have testimonies of creative dating," which in Mormon-speak means that it's *true*, or ordained by God.

You might think I'm kidding, in which case you should check out TheDating Divas.com, a group of Utah County ladies who claim they're "strengthening marriage, one date at a time." They'll tell you how to engineer a scavenger hunt for a group of thirty-something adults all dressed alike that's supposedly the most fun anyone ever had in their whole lives. They'll tell you how to turn shopping for a minivan into a super fun all-day date with your best friend! ("Best friend" is a Utah County euphemism for "spouse.") Make sure you have a good printer: almost all their date ideas involve printing information on card stock and gluing it to another piece of card stock in a complementary color, because that's one way your husband knows you are on a creative date and not just accidentally spending time together.

Matching outfits, as mentioned, are another way to alert both your date and random strangers that you're on a creative date. Merely dressing up isn't enough to signify that you are on a creative date—because women in Utah County are supposed to be well-dressed every day. At the time of this writing, sparkly butt jeans are all the rage. Ideally, your butt should have more bling than Beyoncé's whole entourage. Bumpits are also encouraged, being a piece of plastic you stick to your head and then comb your (bottle blonde) hair over, giving it more volume. Many girls rely on Bumpits for prom hair, but Utah County ladies want prom hair every day.

This emphasis on looking good while having many kids is one reason Utah has one of the highest rates of plastic surgery in the entire United States: six pregnancies in rapid succession can do a lot of damage. A few years ago, I went to dinner with some lady friends. Of the six women there, four had had boob jobs. No, I wasn't one of them, but I understand the need for reparative cosmetic surgery. I myself had a not-very-elective hysterectomy in my mid-thirties. (Bye-bye, defective womb!) Heck, I even get why some women just want to look better. We all do things to keep ourselves from falling apart. I sometimes wear ChapStick and control top pantyhose.

I think, and shudder, sometimes, about how I could have had a different life. I could have been a woman in sparkly butt jeans—OK, no, I couldn't; I really, honestly *couldn't*. But I could have ended up with a guy who loved creative dating and wanted to do it for the rest of our lives. I'm grateful to be with a man who doesn't expect me to buy us matching costumes and adopt a theme every time we want an evening away from the kids.

And guess what: he still takes me out for dinner and a movie, and holds my hand instead of tying us together at the wrist. Even without scavenger hunts, silicone breast implants, or sparkles on my ass, we've kept the magic alive.

I, Katherine, Having Been Born
of Goodly Parents . . .

KATHERINE TAYLOR ALLRED

I loved the liberal town of Davis, California, where my family lived before moving to Provo, Utah, when I was eleven. It was a bitter change to go from long summers and mild, rainy winters to the extremes of Utah. Even more bitter was the submersion into a wealthy, homogenous, Mormon neighborhood east of the Provo Temple, where those who were different paid a high price for their individuality.

I asked too many difficult questions to fit in well at Sunday school, but I loved Mormonism, which I had been raised to believe was Jesus Christ's one true gospel. I recommitted myself to it as I grew out of adolescence, trying hard to be faithful after a period of skepticism and wildness in my mid-teens. In high school, I had dated boys who starred in school plays, wore letterman jackets, and earned Eagle Scout awards; I also dated boys who smoked pot, hacked computer networks, and vandalized railroad cars. While I was raised with certain feminist ideals, I always assumed that I would marry and have children, and I knew I could only marry a man who would understand both the traditionalism and liberalism in my blood. I needed someone who could intimately understand my Mormon heritage—and my devotion to and frustration with it.

When our mothers arranged a shared family home evening at his family's house, Nephi was twenty-five, having moved back home after college. He already despaired of ever finding a soulmate. I was twenty and involved in a rocky relationship with someone else. I didn't believe in love at first sight—at least not until I walked into his parents' kitchen and saw Nephi leaning against the stove, eating popcorn. I could feel him watching me closely, so I slipped into a mode of what I hoped was cool disregard while I closely watched him back. I couldn't tell if he was into me, though others who witnessed it said he was obviously smitten. In any case, he cracked a dirty joke and I was charmed.

I went home and broke up with the other guy.

The first eight words of the Book of Mormon are "I, Nephi, having been born of goodly parents." In high school, I had known a few boys named Nephi, and I'd sworn that I would never date one. Such a man was guaranteed to have at least a hint of fundamentalism about him—at best, he would be neither intellectually curious nor eager to explore religious or philosophical nuance. But *this* Nephi challenged every one of those assumptions. This Nephi was nothing like the stern, muscle-bound Nephi who rebuked his disobedient brothers in Arnold Friberg's illustrations of the Book of Mormon. This Nephi had a red beard, tousled auburn hair that fell to his shoulders, an easy smile, a sharp wit, a dark sense of humor, and a deep sense of curiosity.

Three weeks after we met, we sat on the couch in his parents' library late one night, talking about how we saw our separate lives unfolding. I couldn't escape the image of us standing together, facing the world side by side. "Do you want to get married?" he asked.

"Of course," I replied. "It feels like we already are." Growing up Mormon means when you know, you *know*. It's called "trusting the Spirit," and it's been an excuse for rash decisions since the New Testament was inked on lambskin. In any event, we saw no point in denying that we felt destined to share our lives.

After announcing the engagement to our families, talk turned to when and where to have the wedding. Normally this conversation for LDS couples centers on which temple they'll be married in, but ours was an odd situation. Nephi and I had both been raised by that rare creature, the Mormon feminist. His mother had been excommunicated for apostasy, and mine was in the process of leaving on her own terms before church leadership could excommunicate her as well. Their crime was writing and speaking about a longing to connect with a Mother in Heaven, counterpart to the Father in Heaven so central to Mormon doctrine. Unable to get temple recommends, our mothers couldn't attend any wedding held there.

We were both close to our mothers and wanted them present at our wedding. But Nephi and I also believed devoutly in the covenant of eternal marriage, and we knew that if we didn't get married in the temple, people would assume we'd had premarital sex and therefore weren't spiritually pure enough to get temple recommends. This decision, choosing between our mothers' presence at our wedding or a temple wedding in which we would be "sealed for time and all eternity," weighed heavily on us.

We were both descended from Mormon pioneers, and our extended families expected us to honor that heritage by obeying Mormon commandments and customs. But our parents taught their children to engage in the gospel with questions, believing faithfully that every question had an answer that would bring us closer to eternal truths. Probing the gospel through scripture study, prayer, and meditation was a sacred part of my own spiritual struggle, and I recognized the same struggle in Nephi.

Nephi, being a returned missionary, had attended several temple sealings. I hadn't taken out my endowments or been ceremonially initiated into the secrets of the temple yet, so I asked Nephi to verbally walk me through the ceremony, even though I knew he was supposed to keep the details secret. I don't remember the particulars of his explanation until he said, "Then the wife gives herself to her husband, and the husband gives himself to God."

"*What?*" I exclaimed. We looked at each other in silence.

I had latched onto feminism from the first time I watched *Mary Poppins* as an eight-year-old. "Votes for women?" I wondered as Mrs. Banks told her housemaids in song to "cast off the shackles of yesterday, march shoulder to shoulder into the fray," waving her signs and sashes about her grand foyer. I had seen my two older brothers go to Scouts every week for years, racing Pinewood Derby cars, going on campouts, learning to tie knots, identifying animal tracks, practicing archery. I longed to do the same, and the sole reason I couldn't was because I was a girl. It made no sense.

Mrs. Banks inspired me to do more research in my small-town public library. I was a suffragette for Halloween that year, wearing an old velvet skirt and fitted peplum jacket left over from my mother's bohemian days. I carried a homemade poster taped to a yardstick with VOTES FOR WOMEN written on it. At the church Halloween party, several boys cornered me in the foyer, away from the supervised gymnasium. They pushed me down and shouted that boys are better than girls. They tore up my sign and stepped on the pieces as they ran back into the party. I was left in tears.

That experience marked me, and as I grew older, I searched for ways to reconcile my Mormon beliefs with my personal sense of equality and justice. For years, reading the words of prophets and apostles about the role of women in the church, I assumed I would be able to make it work. Eliza R. Snow, my favorite early Mormon, had, with the approval of Joseph Smith, laid her hands upon the heads of fellow Mormons and given them blessings, a privilege reserved for those who hold the priesthood. Surely women's role in the church would move back to that reality when the members were ready for it. Mormonism was a church that had evolved, with revelations from God guiding the prophets through the social changes of ending polygamy and, a century or so later, giving the priesthood to black men, a group previously denied it. But the more I explored the issue, the more I realized that I was never going to be seen as equal to my spiritual brethren. If church leaders were to be believed, my eternal fate rested on hitching my wagon to a man who could get us both to the celestial kingdom. And if I didn't find the right priesthood-holder in this life, I would be sealed to a righteous, priesthood-holding man in heaven, probably as a second or third wife.

A feminist himself, Nephi knew what I was thinking when he said, "The wife gives herself to her husband, and the husband gives himself to God."

I couldn't believe in a God who would deny me an eternal marriage simply because I wasn't married in the correct building by the correct old man. I believed in a merciful God who knew my heart. And in my heart, I knew that I would be undoing myself if I made a commitment to the man who would be my eternal partner in a way that denied our eternal equality. My relationship with God was no different from his, and I knew I had access to God that required no mediation.

"I can't do that," I said to Nephi.

"I don't want to either," he replied.

So we decided to be married in the Springville Museum of Art, a beautiful Spanish colonial–style building in a small town south of Provo. The late Reverend Canon Dr. Alan Conde Tull, a friend of Nephi's family and the venerated rector of St. Mary's Episcopal Church, agreed to do the ceremony. He even bent the rules a little and wore ornate gold brocade vestments not usually worn outside the cathedral in Salt Lake City. Our wedding mass began with "Come Thou Fount of Every Blessing," a beloved old hymn not included in the most recent Mormon hymnal. My mother walked me down the aisle, and Nephi's mother read the wedding mass scripture. Though the faces of some of the wedding guests were as somber as if at a funeral, broadcasting their disappointment in our "gentile" wedding, the faces of family and friends who knew us well were radiant, sharing our obvious joy.

Bucking family, cultural, and spiritual expectations was terrifying. But it was also exhilarating to forge our own path together. That was in the fall and winter of 1998. Since then, our marriage has evolved in ways that have brought us to greater levels of partnership and equality, though we've had to fight for it. We privately renewed our vows in 2010, just the two of us, pledging ourselves to each other all over again with a deeper understanding of what that choice means. Part of that choice is knowing that we can make a different choice at any time. That knowledge gives us the opportunity to commit to each other anew every day, a powerful act of freedom that confers sacredness on our daily interactions. It forces us to think about why we are together and banishes carelessness in the way we regard each other.

The choice we made the day we wed is remade every day and has nothing to do with where we were married. It has only to do with us.

The Law of the Harvest

LIA HADLEY

"We need to plan your wedding, Lia," my mother said, for perhaps the thirtieth time.

"Not now. After I've defended my thesis. I need to finish this first," I replied, scribbling notes on my research. I had been working hard on my thesis for months, probably too hard, now that I look back. But I wanted to get it done and do it right.

I felt the same way about my marriage to Tim: I wanted to do it *right*. By right, I mean that I wanted to do it on my terms. Or, rather, as things evolved, on our terms.

My mother wanted to do it right, too. For her, *right* had to do with the event. My younger sister married several years before me with a gorgeous dress, amazing photographs at the Salt Lake Temple, rigged-out reception center, rented bridesmaids dresses—the works. My older brother Adam, who married a few months before her, had an equally big wedding. Actually, it was probably bigger (maybe because they got married in a reception hall instead of the temple).

My eldest brother, Reuben, had married within months of returning from his mission. After the sealing in the Salt Lake Temple and brunch at the Lion House, the reception was held in the cultural hall of the ward building near my parents' house. We girls wore bridesmaids dresses sewn from a floral poly-cotton fabric picked by the bride, and there were mints in little cups and slushy punch.

My younger brother, Joseph, married while I was on my mission, so I missed it. The wedding was a pulled-together affair after his girlfriend ended up pregnant. He was very sincere when the vows were spoken, a sincerity he stuck to as his wife descended into her family's pattern of mental instability and emotional abuse. He held on much longer than any of us expected. Eventually we all pitched in to help him pay for his divorce.

So, there I was, the eldest daughter, left high and dry amid four married siblings. At every occasion, my extended family asked when it was my turn.

My mother had despaired of me ever marrying. Truthfully, I didn't think I would either. I wasn't interested in men or marriage. From what I saw growing up in Utah, marriage wasn't an institution I wanted to confine myself to. It didn't look like any fun. It looked like "duty" and "obligation" and "multiply and replenish" and "support and honor" and "hearken unto your husband" and . . . well, live out the Mormon narrative of a temple marriage to a worthy priesthood holder who had served a faithful mission, then have lots of kids, fulfill all your ward and stake callings and support your husband without complaining while he fulfills his, be the perfect Mormon wife and mother, and then . . . well, wait until your kids grow up and repeat the pattern while you dote on the grandkids for a moment before using your savings to serve a mission or three with your husband. Then, with any luck, you die and get to rest.

Oh, and did I mention that I didn't want a Mormon husband-wife relationship? Yeah. That, too. From what I could see around me, these relationships were dutifully affectionate and dutifully endured. The spouses in these marriages didn't seem to crave each other's company or have fun together. Instead, they grimly went about the divinely mandated task of loving and honoring each other while they bore children. I looked for variations on this relationship, hoping to see something better, but no matter how carefully I attended, all I saw was endless futility.

Even my friend who had a wonderful relationship with her fiancé—in less than five years of marriage, they were doing all the things I dreaded. Invariably, simply by following the doctrinal and cultural guideposts that marked the path down the road of eternal marriage, couples seemed to doom themselves to being resigned to their commitment rather than renewed by it. Mormon marriage, it seemed to me, was a surefire way to ruin any good relationship.

And then there was the problem of finding a good relationship with a Mormon man in the first place.

I knew only one guy who, if my life and eternal salvation depended on it, I thought maybe I could marry. But only because we had been friends since childhood. I didn't particularly want to marry him, but he was my best bet. I knew him; I trusted him; I even cared for him. Just not like *that*.

Then he was in a violent accident the summer I finished my associate's degree. His head was smashed in, a large chunk of his brain turned to mush. He was found dead, and although he was miraculously revived, he was never the same.

While I was terribly, terribly sad about what had happened to my friend, I also felt I'd been let off the hook. There wasn't anyone else I could possibly marry, right?

The young men around me lined up to prove otherwise. As it turned out, I was a "good fit" for eternal companion criteria. I was obedient, intelligent, active in the church, came from a good family . . . and I had long dark hair, fair skin, and hazel blue eyes. It probably would have been easier if I hadn't caught their attention so much, but all their attention never seemed to involve trying to get to know *me*. I often wished I were invisible.

If I didn't want marriage, what did I want? Mostly, I wanted to go to school. I thrived as a student. I wanted to be a student as long as possible. I explained all this in a "get to know you" interview with my singles ward bishop when a new semester started. Our conversation went something like this:

"Well, hello, dear sister. How are you?" Extending a hearty handshake.

"Fine, thank you." Sitting down demurely.

"And what are your plans for the future?" Leaning back and smiling at me, sure he already knew my answers.

"I would like to finish my bachelor's degree and then serve a mission. Then I would like to get a master's degree." Spoken quietly and matter-of-factly.

A long pause while he raises his eyebrows and leans forward. "But right now you should be meeting young men who have returned from their missions and trying to find your eternal companion." As though explaining something terribly important that I must have somehow missed.

"I would like to serve a mission." Still very quiet, sitting stiffly in my chair.

"You can serve a mission with your husband after your children are grown." His voice growing louder, more insistent.

"I would like to finish my degree and serve a mission, bishop." Voice low and intense.

Another long pause, while he gathers all his commanding force into his finger, which he points at me, as he calls me by name and proclaims: "I promise you that if you serve a mission, the Law of the Harvest will be in effect, and all the young men that you might have married will be taken, and you will be left alone. There will be no one for you to marry." His voice booming out, resonating in the corners of the office.

Despite feeling intimidated, I found myself thinking, "That doesn't sound too bad. That means I really *am* off the hook and can avoid the whole 'marriage and babies' thing." His prophecy didn't disturb me; instead, it was a relief. I thanked him and left his office.

As the semester progressed, the bishop tried to set me up with young men in the ward, even asking one of them to hold my hand to warm it, after the bishop had shaken my hand and found my fingers "too cold." I declined the offered hand-warming and quietly set about making myself scarce in that ward.

*   *   *

I did serve a mission, and when I returned, I started a master's program. Everything was going according to plan. But, alas, the bishop's prophecy was wrong. As a graduate student, I still encountered plenty of fellows who thought I would make the right kind of spouse. One even told me earnestly that he thought I was "perfect." Needless to say, this scared the hell out of me. Perfect for what? Not selfhood, I'm guessing.

Then I met a guy who kept hanging around and wanted to be friends. Actual friends.

This hadn't happened since childhood. Every other guy was after a *relationship,* meaning marriage, not a friendship. But this guy was different. When we talked, I could tell he was listening to hear what I was saying. The others I had known to that point only listened enough to form a calculated response to "win them points." Tim, on the other hand, wanted to engage fully and wasn't afraid to disagree with me. He told me once that just because I could argue better didn't mean I was right. He spoke not as a critic, but as a friend. It was so different from the ready-to-preside attitude of his peers.

He was also brave enough to make me laugh. I was so serious at that point in my life that I don't think I even smiled very often, but he was always ready with his motley humor and quirky take on life. This was enhanced by his unicycling, juggling, and balloon-twisting. One day I called him a Philosopher Clown (in company with the Philosopher Gypsy and the Philosopher King), because I so enjoyed his mix of theories and ideas alongside his circus talents. He loved this title, as he felt that others saw him as a clown and nothing more. This reciprocity was the foundation for a friendship where we each saw the other as a complex person rather than as roles or pieces in a puzzle.

Slowly, hesitantly, we cultivated a friendship. When he asked me to date him, I said no. I didn't want to ruin our connection. He said he was willing to forgo dating, but he wanted some kind of assurance that our friendship would continue. From there we created what we named a "committed friendship," which was basically our friendship with one addendum: if either of us wanted to run away, we would talk to the other first. The beautiful thing about this new relationship was that it was a risk for both of us.

And so things went for a couple of years.

We learned to talk to each other; we learned to listen to each other. And we both changed.

The first time he brought up the topic of marriage, I said I didn't want to talk about it. He countered, "So, we're friends who can talk about anything except one subject? I'm not asking you to marry me. I just want to talk about the concept of marriage."

He had me there. I told him it was a very large can of worms he was opening. He said he had his can-opener at the ready.

Thus began some of the most intense conversations of my life. For the first time, someone listened fully as I poured out my fears about Mormon marriage and all it entailed. Yes, he had opinions that pushed directly against mine, and sometimes we had to back off for a bit, but the longer we talked, the more we created a new idea, a new concept of marriage that didn't rely on the Mormon narrative. Instead it relied on the friendship of the people involved.

This marked the beginning of me thinking that maybe I could marry. No, wait. Marriage still sounded like a bad idea. But marriage to *him*—that might work.

When we got engaged, we both proposed and exchanged rings after a hike to a waterfall. Ready to plan the wedding, his parents asked us that night when we intended to get hitched, offering to send us to Hawaii on our honeymoon. But truly, we had no idea when we would get married. We hadn't gotten that far yet. All we knew was that we wanted to commit our souls to each other.

Later, my parents, Tim, and I sat on the couch together, looking at photos of the waterfall. One of the pictures was of our hands, each with a matching silver ring. "Oh yeah, did we mention we got engaged?" Tim said.

My mother piffed her lips. "You're not engaged," she said with a derisive laugh.

"We are, actually," Tim said, holding up his hand to emphasize the ring he was wearing. I held my hand up, too, so she could see the matching set.

"No, I don't believe it," she said, irritated that we were persisting in the joke. After all, this guy was my friend, not my boyfriend.

My dad leaned over and said, "Would it help to know that Tim pulled me aside when they got here to ask if he could marry our daughter?"

Her eyes went wide as she turned to look at Tim. "You asked her and she said yes?"

Tim replied, "She asked me, too, and I said yes."

My mom sat back in shock, not sure what to do next. The unthinkable had happened.

*   *   *

Remember that bit about wanting to do my marriage *right*? As I thought about the actual getting sealed part, I felt uneasy. I had been to enough temple sealings that the wording of the ceremony had already cast its pall over me. I wasn't sure I wanted to commit to those words, those covenants. I had already found myself in the awkward position of being in the middle of my endowment and realizing that I was expected to make covenants I found distressing.

At that point in my life, I didn't consider marrying outside the temple an option, so I did the only thing I could think of. Tim and I went to do sealings at the nearest temple as often as we could. While we performed the proxy work, we listened closely to the wording. At the close of the session, we would pick the sealers' brains about what parts of it meant. The good news was that they each gave different interpretations. Their lack of consistency gave us permission to come up with our own version of what it would mean to us. After each session, we would flee to the celestial room and engage in intense whispered debates about what different words meant and what we thought of this or that part of the phrasing.

Through this process, we finally came to our understanding of what the sealing ceremony would mean for us, thus transforming the ritual into something directly between ourselves and God. The church would only be involved as the officiator.

*   *   *

The day I submitted my thesis, a week or so after my defense, my mother pounced.

"NOW! We need to plan your wedding! We only have three weeks!"

It was true. There wasn't much time. But, really, what did we need? We had already put in our request for sealing at the Portland Oregon Temple. That was it, right?

Wrong.

What about a dress, a cake, a reception center, a photographer, and. . . .

But no. We didn't want a big wedding. One of my closest friends had gotten married when Tim and I were just beginning our friendship. For eight months before the wedding day, she had planned and prodded the entire realm of existence into place so that she could have the event of a lifetime. And it was. I will never forget her wedding. She had planned everything down to the last bubble blown by the guests to usher the bride and groom to the limousine waiting to take them to their first night of marital bliss. It had been a truly amazing affair. And it was something I absolutely didn't want. I wasn't interested in "the most important day of my life" version of marriage, where everything after that is downhill. I wanted a wedding day that was about getting together and moving forward rather than spending a lot of money to fulfill a cultural expectation. Tim felt the same way. Even if my mother didn't.

We ended up having a couple of open houses at our parents' homes before the wedding. I wore a dress I'd bought at a secondhand store, a long cream-colored tunic with a tasseled hood; Tim wore a white tunic and black billowing pants with bells sewn on them. We were both barefoot and smiling. No long reception line, no photographs, no mints in little cups . . . just us.

We arrived at the temple each wearing white tunics and pants. At the reception desk, Tim said to the matron, "Hi. We're here to get married."

"Oh, I'm sorry," the woman replied. "That's only for members of the church."

Tim and I exchanged glances. "Um, we are. We're on your list," he said, pointing to it.

She asked our names, and yep, there we were, right on her list. But where was my big white dress and chunky diamond ring? Where was his tuxedo? And for heaven's sake, why wasn't I wearing a skirt, at least? I told her I had one in my bag, if there was somewhere I could put it on, and Tim had a button-down shirt and tie to change into. . . . Her eyes narrowed as she looked us over, her mouth puckering in disgust. She tsked with her tongue as she directed me toward the bathroom to put on my skirt. When we came again to the desk, she didn't even meet our eyes as she took us back into the temple.

Whew. Just thinking back on it makes me feel tired. But tired with a smile, because we did it our way.

After we came out of the temple, instead of lining up for endless photographs, we all went out to dinner and called it good. And it was.

*   *   *

Fast forward a decade.

We are still married. Very happily married, in fact. We've had plenty of challenges and difficulties over the years, but always we have put our friendship first. And guess what? We still like each other. We still crave time with each other. More and more as the years pass, actually. And our marriage doesn't look like anyone else's. It's ours.

I think we did it right.

Mormon Marriage Surprise

MARY ELLEN ROBERTSON

Six years of Young Women's lessons on temple marriage and making lists of the qualities I wanted in an eternal companion. Twenty years of Institute/young single adult ward lessons and firesides on dating, chastity, and temple marriage. Twenty-four years of attending church dances with varying degrees of enthusiasm because my parents met at a church dance and that method of meeting a spouse "worked."

I tried to follow the "ideal path" for a young Mormon woman's life: She lives righteously, chastely, modestly. She attends church and fulfills her callings. She hopes to be chosen by a returned-missionary soulmate who will spirit her off to the temple. Together, they will have children and live happily ever after.

The only problem? None of the relentless lessons on temple marriage prepared me for the path I took to matrimony or the realities I faced in marriage. Nothing about my process followed "the script."

Watching childhood friends, college roommates, and singles-ward compadres pair off and marry, it was hard not to feel defective or broken. I was doing everything I was supposed to do. So why wasn't I finding that special someone?

In my twenties, I'd had a couple of semiserious relationships wherein the topic of marriage came up, but none ultimately moved in that direction. In fact, I was often—*painfully* often—the last woman my boyfriends dated before they met, dated, and married "the one" for them. I felt like the last gas station at the edge of the desert. There were a few years when it was too excruciating to attend the parade of wedding receptions. Happy as I was for my friends as they embarked on their partnered phase of life, I felt my longing and envy would cloud their celebrations.

A few years later, there was a wave of divorces, custody disputes, battles over child support, identities in turmoil, vindictive exes, and single-again friends. One illuminating evening I accidentally showed up early to a birthday dinner and listened to two of my childhood friends complain about their husbands while we prepared for the party. The husbands didn't help around the house, they weren't as good with the children, they no longer initiated family home evening or family prayer or scripture study. My friends felt betrayed by the marked difference between dating behavior where the guys were spiritual giants and marriage behavior where the husbands hung back and let their wives initiate all the family's devotional activity. Not that they'd trade with me and go back to being single, the wives were quick to say. Putting up with laggard husbands was still preferable to being in the dating pool.

It was a revelation: even women who hit all the "ideal" benchmarks of temple marriage and starting families and staying home with the kids could feel unsatisfied or ripped off when the twitterpation of courtship waned and the realities of married life set in. Not that I was naïve enough to think married life was all smooth sailing, but I was surprised at my friends' vehemence, the disappointment they felt, the pain at being let down by their mate.

I was thirty-eight when I married. I'll call my husband *esposo*, Spanish for husband, and an endearment we used even before the wedding. It was esposo's second marriage, after his temple marriage of more than two decades ended. It was a package deal: he came with four then-teenage kids. We opted to marry civilly so that his children, all our family members, and our friends and loved ones could attend and celebrate with us. Since my brother had long since stopped going to church, my parents had envisioned their only church-active offspring getting married in the temple; a civil marriage was a disappointment.

I remember explaining our choice to my mom as we drove through downtown LA. Opting out of a temple sealing wasn't a worthiness issue, I said, even though some people assumed it was. Instead, I wanted one of our most significant life rituals open to the public—not done behind closed doors with members of our immediate families milling around the temple grounds until we emerged. I also said that I was uncomfortable with the church's irregularities in policy: Latter-day Saints in other countries could marry civilly without having to wait one year to have the marriage sealed in the temple. In countries that don't recognize private ceremonies as legally binding, church members marry civilly first and get sealed in the temple (hours or even days) later. This standard could be applied worldwide, but isn't. This was common knowledge among Internet-connected Mormons, but it was surprising news to many lifelong LDS folks. I felt resentful about a policy I found capricious.

What ultimately took the pressure off us was the LA Temple closed for several weeks during the summer for cleaning. We couldn't have been married there on the wedding date we'd chosen even if we'd wanted to.

The next contested point was who would perform the ceremony. My parents strongly advocated for my stake president, who was a family friend. If the wedding wouldn't be in the temple, at least we could have someone of church rank marry us. But that didn't fit with what we wanted, either.

I'd been to weddings officiated by LDS bishops and stake presidents; they often included references to the Proclamation on the Family or lectures about getting sealed in the temple as quickly as possible. I understand that these men are supposed to advocate for the cultural and doctrinal marital ideal. But I didn't care to be reminded on my wedding day that we were essentially doing it wrong—and that plenty of people disapproved of our choice.

I had attended graduate school with colleagues studying to be ministers; I had friends who had graduated from divinity school or were clergy in their own religious communities, and I told my parents about them: A lesbian minister and pastoral counselor. A long-haired vegetarian Unitarian youth pastor. A feminist professor involved with Roman Catholic Women Priests. A former tattoo artist turned Buddhist priest.

With each option I rattled off, my parents grew more wide-eyed. "Why can't you just choose someone who's LDS?" they asked. Though esposo and I were united in wanting an officiant we chose for ourselves, I was on my own in dealing with my parents, who pressed me to have a bishop or our stake president perform the ceremony. At one point, my soft-spoken, introvert dad was so upset that I worried he'd have a heart attack on the spot. It was a wrenchingly painful disagreement. But I was not giving in—I kept repeating that it was our decision as a couple and we would make our own choice.

I talked to a few friends about the officiant predicament. Someone mentioned that another friend, Mark, had obtained a one-day certification that allowed him to perform a wedding a few years earlier for a couple he knew. Maybe he could perform the ceremony? The state of California allows nonclergy to be deputized for a day to perform weddings. All it takes is some brief training about the requirements for the ceremony, submitting the paperwork in advance for approval, and paying a fee.

I'd met Mark through an informal LDS discussion group and knew him to be a thoughtful, smart, and hilariously funny guy. The more I thought about it, the more perfect he seemed to conduct our wedding.

Mark was surprised when I called to ask if he would consider marrying us; he needed to think about it. When he called back, he said he wanted to meet with both of us before making a decision. We went out for Indian food with Mark and his girlfriend, Marianne, and had a long conversation about marriage and commitment. At the end of dinner, Mark agreed to officiate at our wedding, and we started the process to get him deputized for a day.

I broke the news to Mom and Dad: it's not your ideal, but the officiant is Mormon, which is something you wanted; it's just not *who* you wanted. I explained that Mark and I had been friends for more than a decade, and we'd discovered that his parents and esposo's parents had been friends in high school and college. My parents were appeased by Mark's ties to both sides of the family, but still had reservations about this unconventional choice.

Mark's wedding ceremony was beautiful. He spoke about the paradox of cleaving—the word meaning both to divide and to join—and how marriage embodied this concept. He imagined esposo and I growing old together, sitting on a porch in rocking chairs and saying after many years together, "I love you. I thank God I married you. It has made all the difference." (For those of us close to Mark, his words were all the more poignant, as his longtime girlfriend was dying—we knew he wouldn't grow old with Marianne.) Mark's words were so lovely, thoughtful, and apt that my mom wept through the ceremony and afterward sang his praises. Any concerns about the officiant melted away faster than the ice in the reception punch in the record-breaking 113-degree heat at our outdoor wedding.

While our wedding was lyrical and lovely, I had a rough entry into marriage. I left my native Los Angeles to relocate to a South Texas border town where esposo had moved to work at the University of Texas after his divorce. Relocating to the Rio Grande Valley was almost like moving to another country—not Mexico, but barely Texas. I was culture-shocked for the first few months.

Moving also meant leaving a job I'd held for over a decade. I had been promoted and liked my work, but I looked forward to escaping office politics and a passive-aggressive office mate. The atmosphere at work was tense from a round of layoffs and the survivors were still tiptoeing around. I planned the entire wedding in secret because I couldn't afford to get laid off before I was ready to leave.

In the space of a few weeks, I went from being a single, independent, working woman to being a married, unemployed stepmother of four (who lived with their mom and visited us periodically), and chafing at being a dependent—not only on esposo's insurance benefits and income, but dependent for companionship in a new, strange place, and for everything else as well. I had the same last name and the same ornery cat; everything else in my life was different.

Given my many years in the dating pool and watching friends get married, one might assume I would be that much more prepared for my own eventual marriage. But that wasn't the case. It's like watching a soccer game versus playing soccer: they're fundamentally different experiences.

I was unprepared for how much being unemployed messed with my self-confidence and identity. I couldn't get hired at the mall at Christmastime—at a mall with some of the highest sales per square foot in the nation. I hadn't realized how much my self-worth was attached to having a job and doing it well.

During an epic fight early in our marriage, I tried to explain to esposo that while I'd been married in my mother's 1950s wedding dress, I did not aspire to the life of a 1950s housewife. I felt constrained by home and hearth. I had a hard time getting up in the morning and would somehow manage to be busy all day but without enough focus to have much to show for it when he got home, especially before I managed to get the house entirely unpacked. This job was left largely to me and felt utterly overwhelming, even though a friend flew in from Los Angeles to help me with it. I felt depressed and isolated rather than joyful about our new life together. I resented all the time he spent at work, leaving me alone in a new town where I had no friends and no money to go exploring.

I knew that the honeymoon, gloopily-in-love phase wouldn't last forever. But I wasn't prepared for the resounding thud of mundane, daily married life. The LDS approach to marriage involves little reality-based discussion beforehand. No one tells you how hard it is to merge your life with another's. Marriage is simply presented as sunny and seamless—the answer to one's problems, the reward for righteous living. You don't need to map out how you'll handle money and sex and childrearing and faith and whose career takes precedence and who will be the trailing spouse or stay-at-home parent. If you adhere to traditional gender roles and pray about decisions, knowing you'll receive unambiguous answers that will ensure you stay on the straight and narrow path, you don't have to sort those things out ahead of time. You simply live happily ever after—and prove this via relentless updates to the newly minted family blog.

No one tells you how much it can derail your well-being when the spouse you're supposed to be able to count on doesn't come through—or doesn't understand how to be there for you even when you explain how they can help when you're in distress. Or how different personalities or approaches to conflict can make the relationship more complicated. You'll fight about profoundly important, deal-breaker issues as well as the stupidest things imaginable. No one tells you that you may find the person you married utterly unfathomable from time to time, or that you may have to learn to manage anger toward a person who simply cannot see life as you do, though you've agreed to live it together. And because you can't learn any of that from church, you also can't learn about what these experiences can do, not only to your marriage, but to your sense of self, or how to manage when the rose-colored glasses break.

I asked my mom if she remembered her first big fight with my dad. She said as newlyweds, they fought about whether to keep the doors in their apartment open or closed. Mom grew up in a household with open doors. Dad went around closing all the apartment doors Mom had just opened until finally they had a blowup about it. I didn't grow up in a household of closed doors, so I think Mom prevailed.

In my own marriage, I would get irritated with esposo for not being more helpful around the house. As a newlywed, I was left to do virtually all of the cleaning, shopping, gardening, pet care, and upkeep around the house. We had fights about how dinner didn't just magically appear; my labor made it happen. Esposo didn't seem appreciative or offer to help with food prep or other household chores without prompting. He spent so much time watching *The Daily Show* that I not-jokingly referred to it as his "mistress."

It didn't help that a good chunk of money went toward child support. The support payment for all four kids was our single biggest monthly expense—even more than our mortgage. Of course I wanted esposo to support his children. But I felt like a bitch when I did the math and saw how little was left for us to live on. I was used to having my own income and being the sole arbiter of how it was spent. Having to be on a tight budget, setting aside money for the kids to come visit us in Texas, and fielding last-minute money requests from the ex-wife for a school field trip or sports tournament—this was unfamiliar territory for me.

Things eased a bit when a woman from church hired me to manage her reopening physical therapy clinic. A few months later, I applied for work at the University of Texas campus and was hired full-time in research administration. It was work I enjoyed and I felt more like myself than I had in months. I had purpose and a paycheck; I was in a position to ease some of the financial strain.

During a visit from his daughters, esposo mentioned that one of them had made a comment about our "two incomes," implying that we were comfortable while her mom struggled and couldn't afford the kind of frozen pizza they liked. I didn't take this well—it felt like she was being proprietary with *my* hard-earned income. I pointed out that the kids' mom had two incomes as well: the income she earned herself, and the child support she received every month. I didn't exactly feel charitable about her two incomes when one of them came from us.

Although we wanted to have children together, fertility issues derailed those hopes. So my experience with motherhood will be limited to stepmotherhood. I've found it challenging and rewarding, both in its own right and in terms of how it relates to my marriage to esposo. Lately, we've dealt with another change—resident children. Esposo's youngest two daughters moved to Ogden, Utah, a few years after we relocated there. Initially, they lived in our old house while we waited for the real estate market to pick up enough to sell it. After six months on the market, the old house sold and the girls moved into the new house with us.

I confessed to esposo one night that I felt a twinge of disappointment when I would turn onto our street and see the house lights on or the kids' car in the garage—meaning I wouldn't have the house to myself or be able to handle any after-hours work I'd planned to do. He surprised me by saying he felt the same way. While esposo loves his kids and is glad to have two of his daughters with us, it throws a wrench in his plans when they come over unexpectedly. He can't ignore them to work or have a quiet night with me if the kids show up with six loads of laundry and want to watch our cable TV. Occasionally, the date night he plans ends up turning into a quartet. Sometimes I go along with the revised plans and other times I opt out so esposo can hang out with his daughters and I can have some time to myself. But overall I'm glad that the proximity has helped us build stronger relationships as a blended family.

Marriages all hold surprises in some form or fashion. My path to matrimony was full of detours and surprises. The partner I thought I knew well after eight years together can still surprise me—sometimes pleasantly, sometimes not. For me, it's definitely been a long process of trying to figure out how to be myself and be part of a union, or how to be healthily interdependent with another person as opposed to being codependent or unhealthily enmeshed.

Even by-the-book LDS marriages hold surprises, as I discovered with my childhood friends discussing their marriages. Following the ideal Mormon path to temple marriage holds no guarantee of success. A college friend was shocked that her returned-missionary husband became physically abusive; she'd assumed that their love and the commitments made in the temple were a sort of insurance against things devolving that badly. Unfortunately, people can change for the worse; they can ignore warning signs; they can focus on the wedding rather than what their lives will be like postreception; and they can make spectacular mistakes in their choice of partner.

Some marriages are surprising in their endurance, some in their dissolution. I was flabbergasted when a particular couple I knew split up. From the outside, they seemed to have a great marriage, a balanced partnership, a deep respect for each other. Theirs was a relationship I observed, envied, and hoped to emulate. It turned out significant fractures lurked below the surface—infidelity, profound insecurities, jealousy, and resentment over one spouse's success—and significant work occurred to keep the happy façade in place before things finally, irrevocably fell apart. I was surprised at how ripped off I felt to discover that this relationship wasn't the idyllic marriage it appeared to be and had been profoundly painful and injurious to a friend I care about.

Recently, a Facebook friend sent me a list of random questions. One was "Do you think relationships are ever really worth it?" My answer: yes, but they take more work than anyone lets on. I'm not sure what the next eight years and more hold for me and esposo, but I'm hoping that the pleasant surprises will outnumber the other kind.

Postscript: About a year after I wrote this essay, esposo informed me during a couples' therapy session that he had given up hope for having any kind of a partnership with me four years earlier and therefore didn't see us moving forward together. Esposo had said nothing at the time because he didn't want to inflict the pain of a failed marriage on me—as if he inflicted no pain by checking out of the marriage four years before making his dissatisfaction and desire to officially end it known to me.

It wasn't just the end but the start of the relationship where the timing was off: we began dating ten months before his first divorce was finalized. I had refused to date men who weren't completely divorced and legally single, and I surprised myself by breaking my own rule—and lying to anyone who asked when our relationship started or how long he had been divorced. I justified my decision because his first wife had already asked for a divorce, and well, we were in love. The promise of a happily-ever-after was hard to resist. In hindsight, I'm chagrined by my behavior and hear a hollow ring in the way I tried to excuse something that just wasn't OK.

It wouldn't surprise me to learn that I have been similarly, preemptively replaced with a new woman prior to our divorce. As my soon-to-be ex is fond of saying, past behavior is the best predictor of future behavior. I have little doubt that someone new is buying into disparaging stories about me—commiserating over how I didn't understand him, making the same excuses about his marital status, consoling him after hearing about how I purportedly victimized him, and resolving that it will be different with her. Like I did.

Exploring the dissolution of Mormon marriage calls for its own collection of essays. Suffice it to say that things can change significantly, sometimes unexpectedly, and some partners are capable of more surprises than you can fathom. There won't be another eight or nine years of this marriage—and in many ways, that's a blessed relief.

Dreams Denied

KATRINA BARKER ANDERSON

As a typical Mormon girl, I had a dream of what my wedding would be like. I would marry a handsome, righteous returned missionary, of course. We would most likely meet at BYU. He would be premed, prelaw, or a business major. He'd come from a big Mormon family with lots of siblings and cousins all righteously living the gospel. We would be friends for a while, then date for several months before getting engaged. I would be no younger than twenty-one and no older than twenty-three; he would be one to three years older than I. We'd be married in late spring or early summer in the Bountiful Temple, our temple-worthy loved ones in attendance. We'd walk out of the temple hand in hand to our waiting family and friends; we'd smile and kiss as the photographer snapped that iconic Mormon wedding photo in front of the temple doors.

Sounds idyllic, right? I've seen many Mormon friends and acquaintances follow some variation of this basic script. But it turned out not to be mine.

I married a handsome, righteous returned missionary, of course. We met through an online dating website for Mormon singles. Jared was a PhD student in religious studies at the University of North Carolina at Chapel Hill. His parents divorced when he was a baby. His mother had been married three times. His father was dead. He did have some of the big Mormon extended family. In fact, one of my good friends had married his cousin the year before. Jared and I started talking in July, we met in person in September, saw each other a few more times in October, and were engaged in November. I was twenty-three. He was twenty-nine. He was divorced with three children. We were married in March at the University of Utah Museum of Art. We had our closest family and friends in attendance, including my non-Mormon family members and his three young children, none of whom would have been allowed in the temple. We walked down the aisle hand in hand. We took photos in the museum and at the beautiful courthouse downtown. It was a lovely, happy day. But a shadow loomed over it, of the dream that didn't come true.

You see, despite our happy union not quite fitting the ideal I had envisioned, I still absolutely expected to marry in the temple. I had spent my entire life being told that nothing else was as important. I had kept myself worthy and "pure." I had even chosen to receive my own endowment and go through the temple all on my own at age twenty-three.

When I met Jared, I had a degree in broadcast journalism, a career as a news producer, and a life. I wasn't just waiting around to get married. When we first started talking, I never thought in a million years that I would marry him. A divorcé with three kids?! I'd have to be crazy to do that. But I quickly saw how he was different from all the other guys I'd known and dated. He *got* me. He didn't put me on a pedestal. He saw me as a whole person, flaws and all, and loved me. I had never felt loved and known like that before. Nor had I ever dated anyone who let me into his heart and mind the way Jared did.

Despite attempts to keep things from progressing too quickly, from the first day we spoke, Jared and I never passed a day without talking. We would email, instant message, and talk on the phone every day. We are both excellent communicators, so the long distance thing worked for us. And through the luck of circumstances, we were able to see each other often in a couple of months' time. As soon as we got engaged, I made plans to move to North Carolina after the holidays. We settled on a March wedding date, and Jared began the process of applying for a sealing clearance.

A sealing clearance is permission granted to a man to be sealed to a woman in addition to his first wife. Thanks to the doctrine of plural marriage, Mormon men can be sealed "for time and all eternity" to countless women, while Mormon women can be sealed to only one husband. Although today polygamy is strictly forbidden within the mainstream LDS church, the doctrine still has practical ramifications for Latter-day Saints who want to remarry after divorce or the death of a spouse. When we got engaged, Jared was still sealed to his ex-wife because sealings are not cancelled until a divorced wife wants to remarry in the temple. In order to marry me in the temple, Jared had to get permission from the first presidency of the church to be sealed again.

The process of seeking a sealing clearance involves lots of paperwork, is emotionally draining, and often takes weeks or months to complete. But we felt little anxiety as we gathered information and filled out the forms, because we thought it was mostly a formality. Not for one second did we consider that the request might be denied. We believed that if our local leaders approved it, it was a done deal.

Several weeks after we left the paperwork in the hands of our stake president, who shared our expectation that our request would be honored, we were notified that it had been denied. The refusal letter was sent to our stake president, not to us, and was signed by all three members of the first presidency. No explanation was provided. There was merely a statement that we could reapply for a clearance in twelve months.

We were blindsided and absolutely devastated. To be told by the prophet that we couldn't marry in the temple, even though we were worthy, was incomprehensible. Did that mean God didn't want us to get married? I refused to believe such a thing. To me the only way it made sense was if it was a bureaucratic decision. My guess is that the applications are sorted based on criteria that aren't public knowledge, and that for fairly arbitrary reasons, some are rejected. In all the stories I've heard since then, that certainly seems to be the case.

In some ways, Jared took it harder than I. He felt so guilty that because of his past, I wouldn't have what I deserved—a temple wedding. We both shed many tears over the next few weeks. We had to rearrange our wedding plans. I had to call my old bishop, explain the situation, and ask him to marry us. More than once, Jared asked me if I was sure I wanted to marry him. He said he would understand if I didn't. He said he couldn't expect me to sacrifice so much for him. But I never questioned my decision to marry him. I wouldn't let some old men in Salt Lake City stop me from marrying the man I love.

So we got married. It was lovely. We even went to the temple on the morning of our wedding day to do an endowment session with our parents. Even if we couldn't get married there, we were still worthy to be there. We still wanted to start that day in a sacred place. We then were married at the Utah Museum of Art surrounded by Brian Kershisnik's beautiful paintings of ordinary people in daily life. Even at the time, I was grateful to share the day with all the people who could not have attended had the ceremony been solemnized in the temple. But in retrospect, I wish that we had taken more advantage of the situation. I wish we had written our own vows. I wish we had personalized it more. I wish we had included Jared's children more. I wish we had slowed down to really appreciate the ceremony instead of rushing through it because, even though we knew it wasn't our fault, we still felt some shame that it was happening outside the temple.

Being young, married, and Mormon but not sealed in the temple suspends you in a strange version of limbo. In our new ward in North Carolina, no one suspected that we were any different from all the other young grad school couples. We certainly looked like everyone else. But I felt like an outsider for the first time in my LDS life. I had been forced outside the box, living a script other than the one dictated to me all those years. With every lesson on or mention of eternal marriage, the wound on my soul was scraped raw again. Each time I saw a photo of a friend's wedding day with that iconic exiting-the-temple photo, I felt my heart break once more. It was incredibly difficult to wrap my brain around our reality, one so different from what I'd been taught to expect my whole life. The church was supposed to be a place of refuge from the hardships of life. It wasn't supposed to be the source of great pain.

Despite the pain around our wedding, we were blissfully happy together. Our relationship was, from the beginning, very easy. The circumstances were complicated and difficult at times, but what we shared with each other was beautiful. In our hearts, we did have an eternal marriage. We knew that our love and our relationship was no less valuable just because our marriage wasn't designated as eternal on the church's records. We knew that we had made a much more mature and thoughtful decision than the hordes of teen brides who line up outside of Utah's temples every spring to marry young men barely home from their missions. And yet. We still longed for the validation of knowing that God had sealed our union for eternity not just in our hearts but on those records too.

We even spoke to an apostle to try to gain some understanding as to why we had been denied the sealing clearance. I am sad to say that this apostle was neither helpful nor compassionate.

As the date neared when we could again apply for a sealing clearance, we met with our bishop and asked him to resubmit the paperwork. By this time I was newly pregnant. We asked the bishop to please include that in his letter. Our first anniversary came and went without word. Jared had planned a trip to visit his children in Utah at the end of March; rather last minute, I decided to go too. A week before we left, we got the letter saying that we could be sealed in the temple. We quickly let our families know and called the Bountiful Temple.

So it was that on March 29, 2008, five months pregnant, I put my wedding dress back on and was finally sealed for eternity to my husband. Being pregnant in the bride's room of the temple was not exactly how I had imagined the culmination of my Mormon experience. Although the cut of my dress camouflaged the pregnancy beautifully, it was plainly evident to the temple worker who helped me change. I have to admit I get a laugh out of it now. And you better believe I got a photo of us hand in hand as we came out of the temple!

We were finally sealed. We were finally truly married in the eyes of God and the church. I felt so relieved. I felt like I could finally be like everyone else again. But in reality, this experience changed me forever. It gave me an empathy I'd lacked before. I knew what it was like to be denied something I wanted desperately and truly felt I had earned, with absolutely no explanation as to why. I knew what it was to feel like an outsider. I knew what it was like to feel rejected by the prophet of God. And I knew what it was like to have the foundation of my testimony crack right down the middle.

The pain of this rejection still breaks my heart for the girl I was. And yet I can't help but feel some gratitude for the lessons I learned. Perhaps most important was that my decision to marry Jared was no one's but my own. I know too many LDS women who feel more than a little regret over the choices they made in their young adulthood. I have never once regretted my decision. I knew what I was doing. I married Jared with an open heart and with open eyes, knowing it would be hard but willing to make the leap of faith. Making that decision, even though it meant marrying him outside the temple, just forced me to dig deeper and be even more sure about my choice and my motives. I didn't marry him because God told me to, and I didn't refuse to marry him because the prophet put restrictions on where the wedding could take place. I married him because I wanted to. I married him because I love him. I married him because he and I fit.

It hasn't all been easy by any stretch of the imagination. My husband is a complex person who has had a very difficult life that has left scars. I am step-mother of three and mother of two very demanding young children. We have our struggles, as all couples do. Our worldviews have changed dramatically in the years we've been married. We've both changed a lot. There is still so much to discover about each other. There is so much life still to experience.

I'm just happy I get to do it with him.

PART III

Divorce and Other Endings

Figure 5. Leonard and Anita Tanner, June 1966, Osmond, Wyoming

Anita writes: "My husband and I look so very young and optimistic. It was a simpler time: I made all the decorations for the tables and the walls with tissue paper flowers and hand-written thank-yous for the guests. I made the punch and cookies. I sewed the dresses for the bridesmaids and maid of honor. I wore my older sister's wedding dress. When I look at the photo I feel such a sense of loss—the loss of my husband to cancer, the loss of time that passes so quickly, the loss of youthful maidenhood, the loss of youthful romance. However, I also feel a deep sense of abundance and gratitude for finding my soulmate and for his goodness and for our six children. I would choose him again. I would choose my six children. I would choose again whatever joy and pain that involved."

Reversal

ERIN HILL

My marriage was a tragedy.

Not because it was sad, though it was that, but because, in a strict literary sense, it was a rollicking story of my unavoidable downfall, a downfall facilitated by my ignorance and shortcomings that ended in my death—er, divorce.

Aristotle argued that the medium of tragedy should be drama, not narrative. However, since I don't have a spare amphitheater at my disposal and can't afford to hire actors to play out the ritual wedding-day cake-cutting or gloomy divorce-decree-signing, an essay must suffice.

Tragedy is a word we throw around freely, but a proper definition includes more than an unfortunate turn of events. Think Oedipus Rex, think King Lear, think Anakin Skywalker turning into Darth Vader—you get the archetype. The ancient Athenians held marathon drama festivals in the name of Dionysus. The Greek state knew that such productions conveyed something universal about the human experience, and that those watching the plays would be simultaneously entertained and educated—sort of like those ABC Afterschool Specials that aired in the 1970s.

The Greeks watched to see cause and effect unfold: if you do this, then here's what will happen. What happened for me is that after being sealed one clear August morning in the St. Louis Temple, and after ten years of doing all the expected marital checklist stuff—buying a house, filing joint taxes, having children—my spouse wanted the hell out of Dodge. I ended up with nearly all the furniture, the minivan, the expensive wedding china we had received plate by crinkly tissue-wrapped plate, and even our wedding rings, his gold, mine platinum—basically all the material souvenirs of us.

The "what I did" part of the cause and effect chain was a little more difficult to tease out. What was the cause for such an effect, I asked myself? When did our romantic comedy with its implied "happily ever after" morph into a dark tale of misery and shattered glass, that last detail being, in all honesty, totally my fault, since my first response to hearing that he no longer loved me was to punch the full-length mirror that hung on his closet's door, just so I could hear the satisfying crunch of shards crashing to the floor. Worth it, yes, but a pain to clean up.

Several years before I was punching doors, my sister and I sat on a shaded deck, eating nectarines and chatting about happiness. "Do you know anyone who really is happy in their marriage?" I asked casually, curious about the state of others' unions.

"Oh, you guys, of course," she responded. I suppose I might have thought so too, though such an assessment would have been superficial at best. My marriage, a little past its halfway point that summer, was already showing signs of strain. Of course, I looked the part of devoted wife and mother. I wore floral capri pants when I took our children to the park; I did all the laundry; I remembered to buy his favorite flavor of ice cream. I seemed a better wife than I probably was.

Aristotle's treatise on effective tragedy includes the caveat that the tragic hero should be neither entirely good nor entirely bad. Such a one-dimensional character wouldn't feel believable to the audience. The leading character of such a story should be a combination of strength and weakness. So it was with me.

Yet, the tragic hero was supposed to be someone of importance, someone with greater depth of feeling, greater intelligence, and so forth. I achieved that as well—at least in my own mind.

Here's me at twenty-two, my age when I met this man who would eventually divorce me: bubbly, hard-working, virtuous. Pictures from the time reveal that I even wore gingham dresses in public! In short, I was a fresh-faced Laurel with a couple of years of college under my red patent leather belt. Add to my youthful arrogance a certain instinctual selfishness and a conviction that I was a daughter of God entitled to a righteous priesthood holder who also brought me flowers and mopped the floor, and I fit the definition of a tragic heroine quite nicely.

And then I met a man—*that* man. We were coworkers at the college newspaper. I developed an infatuation the very moment I heard him play "Blackbird" by the Beatles. I began a dogged yet subtle pursuit of him in between headline writing and editing deadlines. After several weeks of friendly conversation whilst justifying column widths, he invited me to a party at his apartment. I arrived to a crush of people, throbbing music by Nirvana, and the shrill sounds of people trying to talk over one another. He took me into the kitchen, where we sat down next to his washer and dryer on a dingy linoleum floor. He had on Vans and I wore Doc Martens.

"So tell me about being a Mormon," he said quietly. "I have a friend from my hometown who goes to your church. He's a great guy. I've always wanted to know more."

I was surprised by the question, but flattered too. He was interested in me, and not in spite of my religion, but maybe because of it. So I told him, rather primly, considering we were at a college party, where we came from, why we were here, and where we were going, all while savoring the cosmic possibility that this golden contact could also be boyfriend material! He even started coming to church with me on occasion and put on a striped tie for the meetings he attended. I was glowing in the warmth of missionary service, or so I thought. I hadn't served a full-time mission, no, but felt pretty pleased with my outreach ministry.

So our falling in love got all wrapped up, at least in my head, in gospel ideals, chief among them the doctrine of eternal progression. "You make me want to be a better person," he confided shyly. I certainly saw his spiritual welfare as my stewardship. And from nearly the beginning, I wanted him to be something else. When we fell in love, he wasn't a member of the church. I wanted that to change. Someone with that kind of bespectacled charm and tenor voice needed the gospel. He took the discussions, read the Book of Mormon, and decided to be baptized. And while I wouldn't have admitted it then, our relationship was dependent on his joining the church.

After his baptism, he probably felt that he was in the club and everything would be fine. He was willing to attend meetings on a fairly regular basis, though not necessarily all three of them every Sunday. But when he joined the church, I wanted him to be active. When he started attending a ward pretty actively a few months later, I wanted him to propose. When we moved into a young marrieds ward after our wedding, I wanted him to be not only active, but involved. After he received a calling, I wanted him to be a better priesthood leader. After he was thusly called as elders quorum president, I wanted him to be a bold witness for the gospel. And so it continued, both day and night.

With each step closer to my LDS ideal of what a temple marriage should look like, I managed to conjure yet another to-do list entry. When he fulfilled his calling, I wanted him to attend ward parties. It wasn't enough that he put in an appearance; I wanted him to attend happily. If he was willing to attend Sunday sessions of general conference, I pushed for Saturday sessions too. And if he did watch on Saturday, I then wanted him to attend the priesthood session that night. When we had children, I wanted him to be a part of family home evening. When he did come to FHE, I wanted him to be a cheerleader for the lesson. And when he did pipe in with an occasional reminder to the kids to "sit up" or "keep listening," I wanted him to do so like he meant it.

After just six weeks of marriage, even before all our thank-you notes had been sent, we signed up for a celestial marriage class at the Institute. Most of the other fresh-faced students were young married couples like us. We were all there to learn how to make our marriages a heaven on earth. Interestingly, in class discussions, the level of surety held by a husband and wife that a particular concept in their relationship was "right" or "true" was inversely related to how long said couple had been married. Those with six months or less of matrimonial experience were the most confident that their approaches—"We never go to bed angry," "I always make a hot lunch for my hubby before I leave for work," and "I finally convinced my husband that watching football games on the Sabbath was a sin"—were correct.

Three weeks in, my husband said he wasn't going to attend the Tuesday night class anymore. "I don't feel like the other people there know any more than I do. I just want to figure things out for myself," he said.

So I soldiered on alone at the celestial marriage class. Did I stitch an M to wear on my chest? No, but I certainly felt the martyr. One appropriately rainy evening, I returned home from class, distraught that I had attended alone. I stayed in my car for the better part of an hour, my head on the steering wheel, eyes awash in tears, brain awash in fear. "What does it mean when my husband doesn't want a celestial marriage?" I kept asking myself. And I was certain that his playing hooky from the class meant exactly that, such was my all or nothing thinking.

I see now how all that wanting more was a poison. Buddhists call it attachment or craving. At the time, I felt justified in pushing him to ever greater gospel heights. After all, weren't we supposed to be celestial helpmeets? Sure, it felt ironic that I had to yell over scrambled eggs to get us to sacrament meeting on time, but didn't the ends justify the means? And while it wasn't very meek to nag him during church services to stop chewing on his nails and listen to the speakers, weren't we there to learn? It probably wasn't gentle persuasion when I basically guilted him into getting his patriarchal blessing, but he needed it, didn't he?

When a tragic character's actions produce an effect opposite of what he or she hopes for, we have, according to Aristotle, reversal of intention, or *peripeteia*. So my scowling Sabbath face (not unlike the vicious theatrical masks made by the ancient Greeks), instead of encouraging my spouse to love this day set aside for God, actually made him sick of church. And of me. I hastened the very outcome I was most trying to avoid.

And hastened it while giving 110 percent to my callings. During the years of our marriage, I served as Sunday school teacher, Primary chorister, Primary president, ward choir director, stake cultural arts specialist, and stake Young Women's secretary. I suppose I considered my church service mighty. He, however, suggested that I was putting my church service ahead of my family, an accusation I recoiled from at the time. I loved interacting with the members with whom I shared responsibilities. I genuinely enjoyed preparing and teaching lessons, organizing Pioneer Day candle-making booths, participating in cheesy musical programs, chaperoning mosquito-ridden girls' camp and poorly lit stake youth dances. I even managed to talk him into attending a dance once. Turns out, it isn't as much fun to do the Cotton-eyed Joe when one partner is on the verge of leaving the religion.

I wasn't consciously trying to put the church first; I had simply assumed that an equally yoked husband and wife would always make the church their top priority, and in so prioritizing, grow closer together while putting away folding chairs after an ice cream social. With every nag and nudge toward greater gospel allegiance, I was unpinning the bond between us. With appropriate dramatic irony, I didn't see that the threads tying us together had been cut until it was too late.

This is what clued me in to my culpability: after he left the church, but before he left me, he stopped wearing garments, the tangible symbol of the promises made in the temple. They sat in his dresser drawer for many months while he sorted out what he wanted to do with our shared life. And when he had decided that separation was necessary, I knew it, even without his explanation, because I came home to a heap of cotton/poly-blend garments, dozens and dozens, probably every pair he had ever purchased, in front of the bed.

"I'm going to throw these away," he said flatly, when I raised my eyebrows at the pile.

"Just leave them there. I'll do it," I said with a swallow.

And thus came my moment of recognition, or *anagnorisis*, a character's change from ignorance to knowledge, the instant when the tragic hero realizes her part in the drama that has been unfolding all along. Such recognition is necessary and leads to catastrophe, also known as the final scene of suffering. As I tended to the proper disposal of these garments, symbols of our promises to each other, scissors in hand, I cried real tears, not for his failures, but for mine. It was an Alma 5:18 moment: "Or otherwise, can ye imagine yourselves brought before the tribunal of God with your souls filled with guilt and remorse, having a remembrance of all your guilt, yea, a perfect remembrance of all your wickedness, yea, a remembrance that ye have set at defiance the commandments of God?"

I was experiencing, as described in Alma 11:43, a kind of call to judgment, "a bright recollection of all [my] guilt." I could see, finally, the way my hubris, or pride, and my *hamartia*, or tragic flaw, had brought about my suffering. I had put my callings first, before my relationship. I had exercised unrighteous dominion. I had been a real bitch. And I should have known better.

Just as Oedipus suffered for his arrogant ignorance and Hamlet for his waffling indecision, I too had a tragic flaw: my expectations. It came to me, tearfully, regretfully, that I had let my desire for a celestial family harden into expectation. And then this rush of insight: expectation is the enemy of happiness. At least it had been for me, him, and us. Expectation kills exploration. Expectation is a fossil, toxic, not life-giving. Expectations beget judgment, insecurity. Expectations beget control. Expectations are also hard to unpack.

I had spent too much time focusing on my goals and not enough time being truly charitable. I spent too much time in our twelve years together pursuing an ideal that just wasn't us. Because I wanted regular temple attendance, because I wanted happy-family-all-together-FHE, because I wanted the people related to me to actually pay attention during scripture study, not just prop their sleepy heads next to open Bibles, because I wanted constant progression and improvement for all of us more than I wanted actual love and harmony, I had foolishly written and starred in a tragedy.

The point of tragedy, even in the fifth century B.C., was to arouse both pity and fear in the minds and hearts of those watching. Those emotions led to *katharsis*, a kind of emotional cleansing that was meant to heal and empower the audience to improve their own behavior. The ancient Greeks might have walked back to their fishing boats and olive groves with this thought: "There, but for the grace of God, go I."

In my particular tragic production, staged from 1995 to 2008, I was both participant and audience. So although I was the one with both pride and flaw, I was also the one who learned the lesson. In my most believing moments, I've also hoped that perhaps—in the demise of my marriage, the trauma of divorce—there went I through the grace of God.

There is a wise saying, one I should cross-stitch into a pillow: "Only when the pain of the problem is worse than the pain of the solution will we change." I resemble that statement. And for me, the pain of the problem was excruciating. It took real suffering to teach me longsuffering. But once I learned it, my soul was changed.

Of course, regret can crush us. Too much regret undoes the good of katharsis. Nor is this recounting of my tragic downfall meant to imply that my former husband was a saint. It takes both a Lady Macbeth and a Macbeth to kill the king, right? But his part is his story to tell. In the end, I recognized, in addition to my hamartia and hubris, the eternal truth that I can change only myself. Wishing and wanting for others to change is folly and leads to unhappiness.

By the time I signed the divorce papers, I had digested this additional motif as well, that my Mormonism both hastened the demise of the marriage and helped me to survive the divorce. At church, I learned how to build paralyzing expectations, but in the teachings of Jesus, I learned how to take no thought for the morrow.

Like the ancient Athenians at the conclusion of the theatrical festival, I walked away from my tragedy uplifted and hopeful that I will be a better person for the experience. True, without the peculiar Mormon-ness of my marriage, I might never have suffered the pains of divorce. But without the pains of that divorce, I might never have learned how to truly live my religion.

Departures

BERNADETTE ECHOLS

Our strained and stoic goodbye hung awkwardly in the air by the back door before joining the billowing clouds of dust he churned up as he went rumbling, storming, careening down the dirt driveway.

Long, drawn-out days of sorting through belongings, of packing and throwing away. Of trying somehow to sensibly end a life together. Dealing with the baggage: the pain, the regret, the despair, the anger, and yes, the love—what remained, too injured to heal, too feeble to hold together what was plainly dead.

When the moment finally came, after months of awaiting its arrival, the departure was swift, empty, eerily silent, and still . . . not over.

I imagine the last goodbye between my cousin and her husband must have lingered in the air for hours, then days. Not in clouds of dust, but in each breath she inhaled thereafter.

His leaving, also long, drawn-out days of trying somehow to sensibly end a life together. The greatest preparation was his, completed in his living. He was allowed no baggage. And when he was gone, there were still boxes to pack, clothes to give away, things to sort, things to save.

His departure, a soft slipping-away—quiet, bittersweet. The "I love you" on their lips a promise that it was still . . . not over.

Striking, the difference between the death of a marriage and the death of a husband for two cousins, two girls who'd grown up together, not just cousins but friends. Sharp, the disparity between a young Mormon divorcée with four children at home and a young Mormon widow left with six. Immense, the contrast between pursed-lipped pity and open-armed sympathy. Endless, the gulf between a day of public mourning, open weeping, and acknowledged loss versus weeks of lonely struggle by one whose heartbreaking, suffering, and grief went unmentioned.

That first Sunday back at church, the empty space beside me on the pew informed the congregation of my loss. It was not unexpected. They knew. But no one said a word. No one offered even the smallest gesture of concern—there was no quiet smile or an arm around my shoulder. Above all, no one said, "How are you, sister?" or "I'm so sorry for your loss. Is there any way I can help?" or "Do you need to talk?"

Were they too ashamed of what had happened to me to speak of it, or did they imagine I was?

In Sunday school, the attendance role was passed routinely down the rows, checks placed by names. Stunned, I saw that someone had already erased his name above mine. The ward had already moved on. That simple act left me further disoriented for days.

A non-Mormon friend invited me to attend a six-week divorce recovery program with her at her Methodist church. I accepted her invitation; no such program was available in my own church. It was there, for the first time in my life, that I learned that "one is a whole number!"

My cousin's first Sunday back to church after the departure had been prefaced by priesthood visits and blessings, sympathy cards in the mail, flowers, houseplants, casseroles. Sisters came by to check on the family, run errands as needed, help with the children, sweep her floors.

In Sunday school, the attendance role was routinely passed. She placed a check by her name, and listened to the lesson that, once again, confirmed her unwavering belief that she was not a whole number, but half of an eternal equation.

I Do . . . to You and You and You

NANCY ELLSWORTH

I met John in the singles branch in the small town where I began my first real job after graduating from BYU. I was twenty-four years old and six feet tall, worried about ending up an old maid. John was a successful business owner a year older than I and the most interesting person I had ever met. He was a leader in our branch and by that I don't mean that he had a leadership call ing: his forceful, charismatic personality meant that everyone in the branch wanted to be around him. Having joined the church at age nineteen, he had a fervor about the church that other members found very appealing. He liked to arrange impromptu campfires in the mountains that invariably turned into testimony meetings. A debate champion, he made it his personal mission to know everything about church history and take on the anti-Mormons in town. He was good at it, too! Like everyone else, I was drawn to him, though his self-assurance sometimes struck me as arrogance, and though he was, of course, shorter than I—four whole inches.

We ended up serving together: he was Institute president and I was vice president. We became fast friends. Eventually I got over the height issue, he proposed, and we married.

Initially we were exemplary members of the church. We studied and philosophized and took our callings seriously. Then a couple of children came along very quickly and our spiritual lives unraveled. When we found ourselves spending more of each Sunday soothing our babies in the halls than in classrooms or the chapel listening to Sunday school lessons or sacrament meeting, it seemed easier to just skip church, at least for a while. I'm not sure if that's why things happened like they did—but it probably contributed.

We had been married seven years when John hired a new secretary, a beautiful blonde with a troubled marriage. I'll call her Natalie. John was convinced that many of her problems were due to the fact that although she was Mormon, she hadn't been to church in years. He devoted much of his work day to discussing her problems with her, offering advice, trying to help her feel the Spirit of the Lord and acquire a desire to return to church. Listening to him talk about her, I became interested in her life myself. I often dropped by the office and several times she and I met for lunch. I loved being around her. She was beautiful, and always so kind and concerned with how I was feeling. I could definitely understand why John would want to help her—I wanted to help her too. And I figured that because he would come home and tell me about their conversations, the whole thing really was a sincere, altruistic desire to help an LDS sister in need.

One night, as John and I talked in the living room after the kids were in bed, he said, "I really feel like Natalie is supposed to be a part of our family. In fact, I think we're supposed to find a way to live the law of polygamy."

My stomach did a flip. I let his statement sink in while I tried to figure out how to voice the confusion spreading throughout my body. "I know you like her a lot but is there . . . *something more* between you two?" I asked.

"Well, sort of," he admitted, adding, "there's definitely a sexual tension between us. I can't help but feel this is meant to be." His voice trailed off and he looked at the floor.

"But polygamy is against the law—and Natalie is already married!" I said incredulously.

He raised his face to meet my gaze. "Yes, but she's in a bad marriage and they haven't been sealed in the temple. . . ."

"So you're suggesting she leave her husband and be your second wife?" I asked. "I'm pretty sure you'd be excommunicated."

"Maybe," he said. "But I really feel that Natalie should be my wife. And if it's really God's will, there has to be a way to live the law of polygamy without violating any policies of the church."

Although personally uncomfortable with the idea, I was intellectually intrigued, especially given my history of thinking carefully about the big issues in the church. John and I talked about the doctrine of the plurality of wives and discussed the fact that our scriptures told us clearly that it was an eternal doctrine that brought blessings to those who lived it. Though it might surprise people a bit, I truly cared for Natalie and was genuinely excited by the prospect of a strong bond uniting the three of us in a family. It was also thrilling to be magnanimous enough to *let* my husband explore a relationship with another woman—especially since this wasn't just any relationship: it seemed to me something beautiful and sacred that God was orchestrating. John and I acknowledged that the church currently forbade polygamy but decided there had to be ways to obey both the doctrine and the ban on practicing it, ways to make the eternal principle a part of our lives. That was the catch: implementation. Though we never worked out the details of how things would unfold, our discussions always included the overarching theme that this was something God was inspiring us to research and learn about and consider. It made even the conversations we had about it seem almost . . . holy.

As a result, I didn't worry too much about what John and Natalie were doing. Why would I? I assumed that because John and I were openly discussing the situation and because Natalie and I were friends, nothing inappropriate was going on between them, and that he'd kept me up to speed on everything.

And then he left town on business, and while he was gone his partners put together a transaction with documentation that had to be signed in person. Natalie hopped on a plane to deliver the documents, and they had an evening together, and. . . . The upshot was that afterward, John expected Natalie to leave her husband and "marry" him, living as his second wife. It shocked John to discover that she wasn't interested in giving up her husband or the status of being legitimately and legally married. She quit her job and told him never to contact her again.

John came clean with me, confessing in startling detail the events of that night. I was crushed. We spent the next month working through the turmoil of the situation and the ideas of polygamy that we had discussed. It was heart-wrenching and hellish.

A month later, John interviewed a young divorcée I'll call Julie for the executive assistant position vacated by Natalie. Eventually the conversation shifted from a discussion of the job and Julie's qualifications to a discussion of religion and personal journeys and God's plans for John's life. A life-long member of the church from a prominent LDS family, Julie had been through the temple and knew what it meant when John confided that he truly felt that in order to fulfill his mission in life, he would have to live polygamy.

Julie instantly agreed. In that moment, John told me later, he felt like the heavens opened and angels sang. At that moment, he knew that Julie was the one who was supposed to be his wife.

He was so enthusiastic and happy when he told me about it that night after work. "It all makes sense now, Nancy," he said. "Natalie was just a distraction. Or maybe we made some bad choices so it didn't work out. But one way or another, God was preparing me to meet Julie! She's the woman I'm supposed to marry."

I was stunned, overwhelmed, and more hurt than I could express. "I don't want you working with her or any other woman!" I stated firmly, fighting the anger rising inside of me. "Not after what we've just been through!"

He gazed at me intently and said quietly, "I feel directed by God to do this and I will do it with or without you." I knew immediately that he meant what he said; I knew that I could get on board or leave. I wasn't prepared to leave, so

I did what I tend to do when starting something new: I jumped in with both feet.

Soon after, the three of us met in a park one night and I basically gave them permission to date. Even though it felt awkward and strange, I truly felt that God was somehow preparing us to be the pioneers of polygamy *in* the church. I honestly thought that perhaps God was preparing us because sometime soon polygamy would resume the position it was supposed to hold as an eternal commandment and doctrine of the church.

As the weeks went by, I tried to temper my jealousy but found it impossible. I was unprepared for this new territory. With Natalie I had been intrigued by the prospect of trying out a polygamous-type relationship; now I was actually living it, and it proved much harder than I expected. And Julie, although quite friendly to me at first, soon seemed much less concerned with how I might feel. I was also very distrustful of John's ability to keep his relationship with Julie . . . *appropriate*. I was so consumed by jealousy that I found it hard to think about anything else.

One day I decided to go to the temple to seek spiritual insight into our situation. I wanted a sure knowledge that the path we were on was approved by God, because it was becoming very hard very fast.

After completing an endowment session, I sat in the celestial room praying harder than I ever had. "Are we crazy, Father? Have we been deceived somehow? Please help me understand." The end table beside me caught my eye; on it was a set of scriptures. I had never noticed scriptures in the celestial room before. I picked them up and turned right to Doctrine and Covenants Section 132, the section about plural marriage. I began to read, and I felt the Lord was speaking directly to me:

> 1   Verily thus saith the Lord unto my servant [Nancy], that inasmuch as you have inquired of my hand to know and understand wherein I, the Lord, justified my servants Abraham, Isaac, and Jacob, as also Moses, David and Solomon, my servants, as touching the principle and doctrine of their having many wives and concubines.
> 2   Behold, and lo, I am the Lord thy God, and will answer thee as touching this matter.
> 3   Therefore, prepare thy heart to receive and obey the instructions which I am about to give unto you; for all those who have this law revealed unto them must obey the same.

Bam. I read that the Lord's house is a house of order, not confusion. I absorbed the details of how and when a man can marry a woman—or ten women. I learned that if a man and woman are sealed and either of them commits a sin or transgression, as long as it's not murder, they will still be exalted, provided they pay for their sins.

I had fully expected the Lord to confirm my feelings that what we were doing was wrong. Instead I felt the same comforting certainty I experienced each time I testified of the church on my mission. I felt the same sensation I always thought of as the Spirit of the Lord, with all its truth and goodness, that had guided me to that point in my life. Consequently I couldn't deny my sense that God approved of what we were doing. I wrote in my journal that day:

> I cannot describe the outpouring of the spirit that I feel. I feel the abundance of the universe and there is no room for feelings of scarcity and loss and negativity. . . . I understand better and clearer the doctrine of having many wives. I can see the blessings and joy that are associated with it. I can see the higher law and it doesn't have anything to do with giving *anything* up! By living the New and Everlasting Covenant of marriage to the *fullest*, everyone comes away with more. There is more love, more commitment, and more support. There is so much abundance it is phenomenal. . . . I know it, I understand it, and am prepared to live it. I *want* to live it . . . NOW.

For the next three years we lived a form of polygamy, though John insisted that he and Julie weren't having sex. Instead he was only engaged to Julie, who essentially became part of our family. At first she had her own house, but eventually she moved into our home and lived with us. John had come up with an interesting and creative way to marry her and still be a "good" practicing member of the church: he thought the two of us could get a civil divorce. We would still be sealed and then he and Julie would get married civilly and petition the church for a sealing cancellation to allow the two of them to get sealed since she was still sealed to her first husband. All I would have to do is give my permission. Then he would be sealed to both of us. He felt that a civil marriage was just a piece of paper that could be transferred back and forth as often as we wanted. He never followed through with that plan, though, because he didn't quite feel comfortable with it.

Those three years were the most miserable of my life. I can't explain how awful it felt to have my husband love another woman. I can't even describe the jealousy I experienced when he spent the night with her (just cuddling, of course) or bought her gifts like jewelry or flowers. She and I started out as good friends but as time went by, our mutual jealousy turned us into rivals. Even though we all went into the situation willingly, by its very nature it turned us into three very miserable people.

Several times during those years I told my husband that I was done with our little experiment. I told him that I wasn't capable of being in a relationship of three. I said, "You have to choose her or me. I just can't do this anymore."

"Do you expect me to just toss her out on the street?" he asked. "I don't break my commitments! I already chose you! I'm married to you!"

Things deteriorated when she lived with us. We would often argue over kitchen space or how things should be decorated. The worst was waking up in the middle of the night and hearing them having late-night conversations or cuddling on the couch. I told John that she needed her own place so we could stop stepping on each other's toes. Finally, after several conversations about her moving out, John said, "How about we finish the basement for her? That way she'll still be around but you two can have your separate space."

I opened my mouth to answer, to try and make him understand that having her anywhere in my house just wouldn't work—and realized there was no point. He would never give Julie up. Instead, I would have to give him up, and as soon as that thought occurred to me, I realized that I was completely ready and willing to do that: I was beyond *done* with the situation. So rather than say anything at all that night, I shrugged and went to bed.

I saved some money and began preparing for what would be a huge change in my life. One evening we went for a drive to get away from the kids for a bit. We discussed his business and other things happening in our lives. Something came up that involved the future and I knew it was time to tell him. Without any preamble, I said, "I've hired an attorney and I want a divorce."

"Well, it sounds like you've got this all figured out," he said.

"Yes," I said firmly. "I want you to marry Julie since you're already engaged to her. It'll be better this way. I just don't love you like she does."

John was sad but said he understood. I moved out three weeks later. Our divorce was amicable and I had every intention of continuing our "family" type relationship, just without being married to him. We even hugged in the parking lot of the attorney's office after we signed the divorce papers we had drafted and agreed on together.

Even though I had told him to marry Julie, I didn't expect it to happen right away. I thought they would wait a few weeks. I definitely thought that they would tell me when it would happen and that I would be a part of it. Our divorce was final on a Wednesday. Friday, a mere two days later, I stopped by the house to pick up the kids. John mentioned offhandedly that he and Julie had gotten married the day before.

I was livid—and hurt. I pulled him into the garage so the kids wouldn't hear and asked, incredulous, "How could you do this? How could you just go off and get married and not even tell me?"

"You're not my wife anymore," he said. "I don't have any obligation to involve you in all my decisions."

I was completely taken aback. It's true that I wasn't his legal wife, but according to the doctrines of the church, John and I were still sealed as husband and wife for all eternity. I had expected us to continue in a relationship where we were still "family" even though the civil marriage arrangement would be different—basically, something pretty close to what John had proposed all along.

I realized in that moment that I was being cut out of the family. Things only got worse. Julie was possessive of John and territorial of the space we had shared as a family. Even though I had found another place to live, I had been in no rush to find and pack up all my things at the old house. Julie wasted little time packing them and leaving them by the back door. She made it clear that the house was *her* space now.

What enraged me, though, and made friendship impossible, was when I found out she was pregnant—and much farther along than she possibly could have been if they had gotten pregnant on their wedding night. They maintained that they had *not* had sex before they got married, though all evidence clearly showed otherwise. Their baby was born twenty-nine weeks to the day after they got married, eleven weeks short of full term. To add insult to injury, it was also the date of our wedding anniversary! They took the baby home two days after he was born and insisted he was a preemie. I guess the lie worked: John and Julie are both still active Latter-day Saints and neither has ever faced any sort of church discipline.

That experience gave me a whole new perspective on marriage and relationships. Many people are surprised that it actually made me much more liberal. The entire time we were in a relationship of three, we had to keep it a secret—polygamy was both technically illegal and socially frowned upon then. But I decided that consenting adults should be allowed to do whatever they want in their relationships. I also realized that I'm not interested in something as binding as marriage—it's too hard to get out of if things aren't working.

As for polygamy . . . I always thought that if I had to live polygamy, God would give me the ability to deal with it. Turns out, he didn't. Some would argue that we were deceived and that God didn't really want us to live that law. Maybe, though I still think about the witness I felt I received. I spent a lot of time reading everything I could find on polygamy, including scriptural accounts and books detailing the first-hand experiences of those who had lived it. In all my reading, I found very few people who lived the law of polygamy and loved it. In every instance it seems there were a lot of messy, uncomfortable things. I can't imagine a loving God requiring his people to live this law. I can't imagine a God who would tell his apostles that this law had to be lived in order to attain the highest order of the celestial kingdom.

This was the beginning of my spiritual exodus. I don't really know how to categorize myself. I don't identify with Mormonism or any religion for that matter. I'm still trying to decide if I believe in God. I heard someone say once that they were an apathist—someone who just doesn't care. I think that's me now, and frankly, it feels good.

Signs

MICHELLE WEEKS

Although I'm a third-generation Mormon and was born in Provo, Utah, not until age twelve did I become active in the Mormon church. My family was living in South Carolina, where my father was stationed in the Air Force, when my mother decided we should start attending church. I loved it. The members in our small South Carolina ward really seemed to care about our family. When my father deployed to Vietnam, my mother moved us to Salt Lake City to be closer to her family. I thought Utah would be heaven on earth.

But I didn't fit in right away. To begin with, I was naturally reserved; second, I was an outsider, looking in on a culture others had participated in all their lives. It took me a while to understand and adapt to the Utah mold of who I was supposed to be. Crucial to this mold was training in how to choose a husband. I learned that I needed to marry a returned missionary in the temple—therefore I should date only young men who were active members of the church and had served or planned to serve a mission.

So that's who I dated, which meant I ended up sending a boyfriend on a mission. I was devastated. I'd seen him practically every day for close to a year and suddenly he was gone. He missed me, too. Although it was against the rules to write letters more than once a week, he wrote me daily, filling my room with stacks of letters. In one he told me that he missed me so much that he'd contemplated hurting himself so he could be sent home. The idea that his feelings for me might actually lead him to harm himself scared me. Eventually, his sugar-coated declarations of undying love became a burden. It felt like I no longer had a choice in whether we would marry when he got home, that I would have to marry him simply because he loved me so much. But as a student at the University of Utah, I met other guys in classes or at church, and when they asked me out, I said yes.

I was young, good-natured, and cute. I dated men who had already completed their missions. I dated men who hadn't gone on missions and didn't plan to, though I always reminded myself that things couldn't get serious with them. But I never found anyone who clicked just right or was quite who I was looking for. I knew what that was: I wanted the white picket fence and the handsome husband who would provide for me while I stayed home and baked cookies and made mouth-watering pot roasts. I would be the perfect wife.

I fell hard for a man I met when we both sang in the Institute concert choir. I'd thought things were going well when he suddenly stopped speaking to me. Heartbroken and desperately confused, I quit the choir and even withdrew from the university. How could I go to classes when he was still there? I couldn't bear to see him every day and have him treat me like a stranger when we were once so close.

I watched my friends marry while I continued hoping for the returned missionary of my dreams. We had all assumed that I would be among the first to find a husband, but I entered my late twenties still single. By Utah standards, I was an old maid. I was tired of dating, tired of looking for a husband; I just wanted to live my life. Some part of me still wanted the dream, but I didn't want to focus on looking for it anymore.

One day at a family dinner, an aunt who had married into the family mentioned that she had a single brother she thought I might like and asked if I would go out with him. I figured I might as well be polite. "Sure!" I said.

A few days later the phone rang. It took me a moment after I answered to realize Kirk was the brother my aunt had asked about. I told him I would be glad to go to dinner with him. After all, what would one date matter? The catch was that Kirk lived in rural Utah, hours from my home in Salt Lake City.

I was pleasantly surprised when Kirk picked me up a few days later. He was cute, with a boyish smile and blue eyes. We had a great time at dinner and Kirk assured me at the end of the evening he would keep in touch. Sure enough, he continued to call and drive to Salt Lake City to see me. As his phone calls grew more frequent, the pleasure I took in them grew as well. Kirk and I enjoyed each other's company and conversation. A returned missionary with a degree from BYU, Kirk was down to earth and hard-working. What was not to like about him?

Eventually Kirk wanted me to meet his family in Sterling, his hometown, a community of about 250 people, many of them cattle ranchers. Despite his clear directions on how to get there, I had a hard time finding the place because there were so few street signs, and I was surprised at just how many cattle there were. But his parents liked me and I liked them: that was what mattered, right?

Our romance blossomed. I suspected he would ask me to marry him. While I loved him—or thought I did—I couldn't help but worry about the differences in our backgrounds. But what was more important: the fact that this man and I might have different expectations for marriage, or that I was twenty-eight and single?

Late one night I helped Kirk finish up the day's farm chores. When he was done he walked to where I stood by the corrals. The moon was full and beautiful; a jumble of stars glittered in the dark, vast sky. Kirk could see I was chilly so we got into his pickup—it was smelly and old, but still some protection from a cold spring night on the high plains of central Utah. As we snuggled in the cab, Kirk looked at me and asked impulsively, "Marry me, OK?"

It wasn't exactly the romantic proposal I had dreamed of—nor did he have a ring. But I looked into Kirk's eyes and said, "OK!"

"There's one thing," he said after kissing me. "Can we keep this just between us, for now, at least? I want to tell my parents about this first."

My smile faded. Why should it be a secret that Kirk had asked me to spend the rest of my life with him? "I want to shout to the whole world that we're getting married," I said, hurt.

He squeezed my hand. "You'll get to—eventually," he said. "But I'll feel more comfortable if my parents know before anyone else."

I took a deep breath. "OK," I said, trying to be a proper cheerful fiancée. "I can wait until you tell them. Just don't take too long."

But time passed and Kirk didn't say a word to his parents. I found it so strange, and he never explained his actions to me. Six weeks passed before Kirk finally broke the news. I never learned why he was so hesitant to tell his parents about us. It should have been a sign—it *was* a sign—but I refused to see it.

As soon as Kirk gave me permission to tell my family and friends, I did. I'm not sure who was more excited with the news, them or me. I still didn't have a ring, however, and the wedding date was not yet set. I suppose that was another red flag I missed. But Kirk seemed like an answer to my prayers: after all, I was single and pushing thirty. I had to marry someone. Who else would I marry, if not Kirk?

We set a wedding date four months in the future. We didn't discuss any plans beyond the wedding itself. It was just assumed that we would marry in the Salt Lake temple. It was just assumed that we would live in Sterling. We didn't even discuss having children. There were so many things I should have brought up, but didn't.

We were married on a fall day in the Salt Lake Temple, and I moved to Sterling to begin my life as a Mormon country wife. It was quite an adjustment, to go from working full-time to staying home every day, caring for a new husband; to go from living in a city full of people I would never meet to living in a town of 250 where everyone knew exactly who I was.

Everyone at church was friendly, but I can't say I had friends. They were interested in what I could do for the church, not what I was thinking or feeling. They extended calling after calling, beginning with being a counselor in the Young Women's program. I had never before had a calling that entailed so much responsibility. I was expected to attend meetings and teach a gospel lesson to the young women during the week; on Sundays, I had presidency meetings after church.

Worst of all, there were many days when I hardly saw my new husband. Farming and ranching require a lot of time away from home. I was so lonely—I had never realized that days could seem so very, very long. Was this what the rest of my life would be like? I would try to tell Kirk how I felt; he would say that I needed to pray and read my scriptures—they would show me the way.

So I buried myself in my church callings and did everything I was supposed to. I was the best Young Women's leader I could be and the best wife. I cooked and cleaned the house. I cultivated a small but beautiful vegetable garden. When I could, I helped Kirk's mom. I could talk to my mother-in-law, even though I still wasn't sure she thought I was a good wife for Kirk. One day she told me that even though I was an older bride I wasn't too old to have a big family. But having lots of children wasn't in my plans.

And then, six months into our marriage, Kirk began talking about having a baby. "Have a baby?" I stammered. "I haven't even adjusted to living in this small town and being a wife. Now you want a baby?" I knew that having babies was part of the Mormon lifestyle, but I wasn't ready. Kirk knew that I had gone on birth control pills before the wedding but it wasn't something we had discussed in any detail. I didn't want to stop taking the pill. Kirk said we should pray about it. I wondered why this would require praying when I was the one who was expected to have the baby. When my birth control pills ran out six months later I didn't renew the prescription. I just decided that what would be, would be.

I had known that marriage required adjustments, but this was much more than I had anticipated. I had to do something to keep my sanity and decided the best thing would be to go to work, especially since Kirk and I struggled financially. I told Kirk that I had started looking for a job—it would be a good idea, I said, since I wouldn't be alone so much and it would also help with the bills. "I do not want my wife working!" Kirk bellowed. I was stunned. This was 1989. In most of the country, women's working outside the home was no longer controversial. But Kirk's disapproval didn't daunt me. I was an adult, entitled to make certain decisions for myself. My sanity was more important than fitting some stereotype. I just wished that Kirk could see this too. I found a job at the front desk of a hotel about an hour away. I enjoyed the work and the chance to meet new people. Just as I'd expected, it kept me busy and took the edge off my loneliness.

I continued to go to church and serve in my callings. I had hot meals ready for my husband. My yard was neat and clean, my house spotless. I prayed with my husband every night and every morning. Kirk was a good man, I admit.

He attended church, served in his callings, cheerfully helped neighbors in need in any way he could as soon as he was asked. An outside observer might think we were the perfect Mormon family, yet I felt something inside me dying. My husband was rarely home, and we shared very little. Even more than I had when I was dating, I wanted a husband who was a soulmate. Cooking and cleaning for a man who would pray with me but not talk with me: was this really all there was?

Years passed. Kirk and I still didn't have children. One Sunday the bishop asked us to meet him in his office, where he informed us that he thought that we might be having a hard time having children. Mormons tend to have big families and we weren't doing our part. I don't know why he felt this was any of his business, but there we were. He told us that he could submit an adoption application to LDS Social Services if we were interested. "Go pray about it," he instructed us. "Let me know."

Kirk and I prayed. We decided to pursue adoption; within a few months, we had a baby boy. He was a joy to us. He filled a void in my life and relieved my loneliness. I loved every minute of my new motherhood and took my son with me everywhere. I thought my delight in being a mother might heal some of the problems in my marriage. But something still seemed strained, amiss.

One day Kirk repeated a common Mormon aphorism: "No success can compensate for failure in the home." What did he think that meant? We both met many criteria for a certain kind of success: we attended church and served in our callings. We adopted a second child, another beautiful son. But I was dreadfully unhappy, in part because I knew there were ways in which our home was a failure. I wished that Kirk would pay more attention to me and our family and not spend so much time at church. Too many evenings he rushed home from a rough day on the farm to gulp down a meal so he could rush out to a church meeting. I looked at how often the church took us away from each other and our children. Although the church insists that "families come first," it sure felt like we were expected to put the church ahead of our families.

I suggested that Kirk and I go to marriage counseling. He refused. Maybe he didn't feel we needed it; maybe he thought that since we had the church, our marriage would be fine.

But we were both unhappy. Neither of us lived up to the other's expectations. Kirk would say I needed to pray and read my scriptures more. But the more I did, the more I began to question beliefs I'd had my whole life. I knew that if I admitted my doubts to Kirk, my marriage would be over.

I couldn't sleep. I couldn't eat. Naturally thin, I grew gaunt. After fifteen years of marriage, I finally told Kirk in no uncertain terms that we had to go to marriage counseling if our marriage was to survive. Our marriage was in trouble and had been for some time, I said, to the point where praying wasn't enough to heal it.

Kirk went with me to a grand total of two counseling sessions. After that I went alone. The counselor was professional, skilled, and honest. It did me enormous good to sort out and express fifteen years' worth of frustration and confusion. The counselor told me that her ultimate job was to save marriages, but that she had no techniques that would work for ours. All the techniques she knew were based on communication, and Kirk and I didn't communicate. She told me that no matter how hard it was, I had to be honest with Kirk and tell him what I had been feeling and what I needed him to hear.

I knew she was right, so I mustered my courage and sat Kirk down for a conversation about my questions and doubts concerning the church. I told him about sitting through a lesson on Joseph Smith in Young Women's. As the lesson progressed, the teacher said, "If you don't have a testimony of Joseph Smith, you don't have a testimony of the gospel."

With that one sentence, my doubts could no longer be repressed. Though I still believed in the importance of striving to know God's will and of living a moral life, I had to admit that I wasn't sure I had a testimony of Joseph Smith, and I didn't know what that meant for my relationship with God or anyone else. "I've been keeping this to myself," I told Kirk, "because I was afraid it would jeopardize our marriage. But I really want to try going to other churches."

Kirk was not happy with me. Our marriage already suffered from a lack of communication and intimacy, and just as I feared, this revelation from me made him withdraw even further. One day I came home to find an eight-page handwritten letter on the bed. Kirk detailed all the ways I had changed; he claimed my values weren't what they used to be. As I read the letter, Kirk walked into the room.

I looked at him, tears filling my eyes. I ripped the letter to shreds as Kirk looked on in shock. "I'm the same person I always was," I cried, struggling to speak through my tears. "I'm the same person you married. My values haven't changed. I'm just not sure what I believe about Joseph Smith. That doesn't mean I'm a different person."

Kirk stared right at me. He didn't say a single word. I looked straight back at him and said, "How dare you judge me so harshly? I'm the one person you're supposed to love more than anyone in the world." Still without saying a word, Kirk turned his back on me, walked out of the room, and left me in tears.

Kirk and I separated with the intent to divorce. It was bitterly hard. One reason I had stayed with him so long was the two children we adopted. The adoptions had been managed by LDS Social Services because the birth mothers wanted their babies to have two LDS parents in the same home. Who was I to deprive my sweet boys of this? I struggled and struggled, and finally sought advice from my therapist. No one plans on divorcing, she said; it's just not in anyone's life plan. She said that ultimately children know when their parents are fighting and that a miserable home isn't a good environment for kids. It's better for a child, she said, to have two happy parents who live apart than two miserable parents who live together.

I found a new place for me and my sons in Salt Lake City. Sterling was just too small for my soon-to-be ex-husband and me; I couldn't bear to stay there with everyone knowing our marriage had failed, and I needed a fresh start. I had always regretted dropping out of college. I went back to school and am happy to say that I graduated with my bachelor's degree five years after my divorce. It was a monumental challenge, being a single mother, working full-time, and going to college, but I did it! I made my own life work in ways I could never make my marriage work.

Of course people wondered if I would date again after my marriage fell apart, but I decided the most sensible thing was to make the best life I could for me and my two boys. I still think it was wise to spend most of my time away from my job or classes with my children—they are happy young men with bright futures who provide me with a lot of love and good company.

I also needed time to heal before I could even imagine being in a relationship again. My failed marriage left me jaded; I found it hard to trust men after the way Kirk hurt me. I never want to experience again the pain I felt going through a separation and divorce. I promised myself that if I do find someone and marry again, it will be because I'm crazy in love and not because I feel I have to marry to fit a certain lifestyle. And I'll make sure to communicate about everything beforehand.

Eventually I decided I don't want to stay single for the rest of my life, and I started to think about what I want in a partner and to pay more attention to the single men I meet. I also signed up for an online dating service. Dating at my age is difficult at best. The dating pool has shrunk, and, not surprisingly, the men who are available often have the same sort of trust issues I do. The fact that I live in Utah but am no longer a believing, practicing Mormon also makes it hard to find a man who accepts me for who I am.

But in the last few years, I've fallen in love with life like I've never done before, so it's important to me to have friends to enjoy life with. I find that I miss the company of men, so I'm going to try dating again after about a year's sabbatical. I've also joined social groups where I can interact with single men and women. I find that my friendships are stronger because I've finally learned to be authentic. I was always hiding behind a mask and trying to live up to Mormon expectations when I was married. Now I like who I am, and I want others to know the real me.

My Next Scene

BRITTNY GOODSELL

No one wakes up and thinks, "My life will fall apart at 11:58 A.M. when I'm in the middle of an email." But mine did. It was August 2011. My husband, Troy, was reading in the next room. I was emailing pictures of a recent get-together with friends from Troy's graduate program at Arizona State University.

Someone knocked on the door.

Troy answered.

There stood Brian, the husband of a woman in Troy's program. I entered the room and Brian held out a book he had borrowed from me. "Didn't you love it?" I asked.

"Yeah, it was good."

Silence. Followed by me noticing his overly sweaty forehead, a shaken look in his eye. "You OK?" I asked. "You look sick."

"Nah, I'm fine. Just wondered if Troy could help me with something I have in my car for you." They walked outside at midday in the blistering Arizona summer heat.

Ten minutes passed. I looked out the window, trying to see where they went and wondering what Brian and his wife, Laynie, were giving us. A TV? Used bookshelf? An old mini fridge?

Finally, Troy walked up the stairs. Empty-handed. Alone.

I've had a few bad days in life. I can vividly remember the top three. And though I didn't know it at the time, that day was number one.

"We need to talk," Troy announced. He started by confessing that he and Brian's wife, Laynie, had kissed. Unable to imagine the entirety of it, I initially thought kissing, emotional intimacy, and the desire for more were the extent of the betrayal.

The minutes didn't slow down the way I imagined when a person experiences a staggering reality shift. And the minutes didn't become a sharp memory I can replay if I'm triggered by the right song or smell. Instead, my brain broke. It fell onto my white-tiled floor like pieces of glass. I heard the symbolic shatter and looked down.

I remember the floor because I kept looking at my smashed brain next to my maroon rug and coffee table, the one we used as a footrest during our nights of watching *The Office*. During our nights of games with friends. Halloween parties, family visits, hours-long conversations about politics and religion. During the shared nights of our lives.

I felt a humiliating nakedness, a violation. My worst fear was realized and I had no safe hold, no foundation, nothing to break my fall.

Ironically, somewhere outside the suffocating horror of my husband's affair, I realized my email was unfinished. Odd to think of something so insignificant after something so major. The email was never sent, though. The day demanded a pleading phone call to a close friend, a call to Brian about how he uncovered the affair, a broken discussion with Troy about sleeping elsewhere, an inner debate about calling my sisters.

As far as I know, the affair ended that day in August, but confessions and details continued in the following weeks and months. Not until mid-October did Troy admit that the affair had spanned more than a year and involved much more physical and emotional intimacy than he first described.

The following weeks were a blur of crying, of headaches, of sleeping on couches, of yelling "Why" inside myself, of yelling "Why" at Troy—all during our final year of graduate school.

"Why" was a question I had to have answered. On paper, the scene wasn't logical: why would a man have an affair with a beautiful, young, intelligent woman enrolled in an ambitious graduate program when he was already married to a beautiful, young, intelligent woman enrolled in an ambitious graduate program? I resolved to find the logic, which required a brutally honest look at myself.

I never used to have a problem with sex. Let me clarify: I never used to have a problem with the *idea* of sex since faithful Mormons—Troy and myself included—choose not to have sex before marriage.

Still, my sexual outlook appeared healthy. My Mormon girlfriends and I watched the steamy, extended sex scene from *The Notebook* over and over, indulging in arousal even though we didn't act on it. In college, when I was both single and curious, I wanted to write a book about sexual fantasies Mormon couples could act out, like, "Meet in a bar, pretend you don't know each other and then go home together—while drinking only Dr Pepper, of course." The thrill of getting picked up at a bar was a part of sex I would never experience but still wanted to explore, with a Mormon twist.

I strove to be a good girl—I tried to keep my clothes on while dating. I was plagued by guilt if I gave in to the heavy petting so frequently warned against in church lessons. I didn't masturbate. I dreamed of marrying someone who had "waited" for me. I wanted to be his first. To me, that was sexy.

I was a close-call virgin when Troy and I married in the temple in June 2006. We had dated for almost two years and daily felt, but still resisted, the urgency of sex. As Troy often said while we made out in his parents' basement, "Looks like we'll never have problems with our sex life." Our make-outs were that hot, just on the edge of remaining technically worthy to marry in the temple while also on the edge of losing all control—an extremely fine line. I could orgasm with my clothes on. What could possibly go wrong when we finally got to do it?

A shitload. After your husband cheats on you, it's normal to think, "This is all my fault," while simultaneously thinking, "What a bastard; it's all his fault." The tug of war erodes your confidence until you're eventually left with "This is all my fault." If you have a good counselor—which I did—that phrase changes to "Troy's affair is not my fault. He *chose* to have an affair. But what parts of the stage were set before this first act opened?"

An affair makes you look at the part you played, intentional or not. My part was being in a marriage that didn't include sex. It didn't start out that way of course, but that's what the new normal became. How I went from "I'm so horny I could do you sideways" in 2006 to "Don't touch me" in 2011 was the evolution from one person to another. I became a nonsexual person.

The day I started the pill, my sex drive left abruptly, slamming the door behind it. I blamed it on wedding stress—jitters and planning. Chalk it up to first-night nervousness, too. Whatever caused the decrease couldn't be permanent—at least, that's what I told myself. But instead of improving, my sex drive kept decreasing. I went to sex toy parties, bought lingerie and products, was even open to watching porn with my husband if asked. Nothing helped. Rather than solve the problem, I hid it from my logical self. Being a sexual failure in your marriage is humiliating. It's the new "going to school naked and everyone points" dream, the adult version of having a shameful secret you're desperate to hide. I confided in a few people—a sister, a girlfriend. I always cried, always said I felt like a failure. In the deepest parts of my soul, I knew I was damaged and couldn't be fixed. I felt utterly helpless. And even still, with that bleak outlook, I was in denial about how deep the problem was and how much it threatened my marriage.

Second, I was deathly afraid of pregnancy. I had watched an older sister go through two pregnancies fraught with life-threatening complications, and I felt sure our shared DNA meant my experiences would be similar. More importantly, I feared motherhood would destroy my identity and leave me an empty woman. Even when Troy and I shared heavy make-out sessions with clothes technically still covering various body parts, I became obsessive-compulsive about making sure his cum didn't come near me. That semen was not to penetrate my vaginal orifice. But it got to where even trying to orgasm with clothes on—known as dry humping or zipper sparking in Mormon circles—ended with me thinking, "What if his semen seeps through my jeans, swims up my vagina and makes a baby?! Ack!!"

Third, sex hurt. If I wasn't physically turned on but I still wanted Troy to orgasm and have a fulfilling sexual experience, I would tell him to continue. My hands grabbed pillows to distract myself from the feeling of something too big entering something clinically too small. My face contorted in pain, not pleasure, and my eyes watered in the dark bedroom of my marriage. I was irritated and frustrated that Troy wanted something "normal," but giving something "normal" stretched me until I broke—physically and emotionally. If we didn't have lubrication we didn't have sex because sex felt like rubbing my vaginal walls with sandpaper. After, Troy would say he felt bad that I didn't orgasm or wasn't into it, and that he couldn't enjoy sex if I didn't. He encouraged me to see someone for what I was experiencing. I just thought, "I'm so far off the grid of sexual dysfunction, there's no way I can be fixed."

I experienced a profound shame that I guarded defensively. After the affair, I quit my hormonal birth control and tried an extremely low hormonal-dose IUD in hopes of repairing my sex life. It took three separate attempts, multiple doctor's appointments, four numbing shots in my cervix, pills commonly used during abortion procedures for cervical dilation, and multiple-sized dilators, before the sexual health specialist successfully inserted an IUD into my damn small and damn tight cervix—forty-five minutes of hell complete with the worst cramps of my life. All for Troy, I told myself, so it was worth it.

Of course, I didn't know the sources of my sexual inadequacies. A brilliant counselor uncovered these truths over many months. She helped me see that while it's not the church's fault that I experienced low sex drive, fears of pregnancy, and painful sex, my past beliefs about sex, motherhood, identity, and marriage all stemmed from my Mormon upbringing and worldview. I didn't know any different, so of course my cultural and religious background influenced how I dealt with my biological and emotional sexual issues.

I didn't talk about sex with my Mormon friends. Not really. In rare moments, we superficially discussed some aspects of sex, such as how often we had it and whether we liked it. But the topic produced discomfort about being really honest with ourselves or each other. Our conversations were always impersonal and vague. No one ever talked about masturbation or vibrators, about fetishes, about the devastating damage of low sex drives, about ways to orgasm. My Mormon friends and I mostly talked about how wicked porn was and why we still performed sex with our husbands even when we didn't want to because it was the right thing to do. Was this the best wisdom Mormons had to offer on sex? My premarriage perspective of what successful sex involved wasn't founded on reality, clear information, or experimentation—just a curiosity about sex, a belief that I'd understand it when I could do it. And my married perspective of sex was so far from normal that my shame blocked all forms of sexual progress or healing.

Troy seemed threatened, like he wasn't good enough, if I ever pulled out my vibrator. And I felt like we should both always orgasm if we each had sex, as if quality of sex should always trump quantity of sex. I was never naked just to be naked. There were no blow jobs. Cunnilingus was rare because I felt self-conscious about Troy spending time in an area I didn't understand. We didn't explore any sexual avenues beyond the few we already knew. I didn't believe in spontaneous sex. It got to a point where I scheduled sex so that I would remember to do it and prepare my body and mind in a false effort to get turned on. But Troy hated scheduling sex. So we went back to having sex when he was brave enough to ask for it and not feel rejected, and I sometimes agreed because I never initiated and felt guilty. And it sucked. I actually got to a point where I felt disgust and resentment for him when he wanted sex, and that's when sex stopped.

In my honest moments, I know I stayed with Troy after the affair because I felt guilty for failing him and our marriage. I owed it to us to stay, to see if our marriage stood a chance, and I owed an honest effort, which I made. The most vulnerable parts of me were exposed. I went to marriage counseling once a week. I went to individual counseling once a week. I saw doctors. I visited a physical therapist once a week whom I paid $125 per session so she could put her finger up my vagina and retrain my muscles for an hour. I bought $90 dilators to daily stretch myself in the bathtub. I bawled when my IUD wouldn't go in the first two times. And then I shuffled to my car, bent over, wracked by painful cramps after my IUD was finally inserted, and cried on the way home for how hard I felt I was working. I offered to give Troy a few blow jobs, to try sex-related activities. He always declined. Our intimate life didn't improve.

I couldn't work any harder. I have never felt so emotionally naked in my life. I have never felt so betrayed and yet so forgiving. I kept thinking of how this woman came onto my husband, this woman who, I assumed, didn't experience my sexual inadequacies. This woman who probably didn't have to endure the emotional, physical, and mental pain I did once the affair was discovered. I imagined her life after the affair: emotionally hard, sure, but nothing near the depths of failure because of my sexual issues.

I gave my all.

Shortly after 6 P.M. on a Tuesday in May 2012, I made Troy take a picture of me with mop in hand after I finished cleaning our apartment for a final checkout.

We returned our keys to our apartment manager, never to step foot in Arizona again. The sun was setting, right at the point where families gather for barbeques and get-togethers at the start of a summer evening. Our life was in a U-Haul; we were bound for the East Coast and my new job. I couldn't wait to escape the city where the worst chapter of my life had unfolded. We could finally heal.

We drove to a Circle K, filled the U-Haul and the car with gas, then pulled into two parking spots to plan our first leg of the trip. I hopped into the U-Haul cab where Troy sat. "OK, so how do we want to drive to the Grand Canyon?" I asked, opening up an atlas.

I looked at him. I waited. His eyes were emotional, shaken. I knew that look. "I'm not going with you," Troy said. "I got a job somewhere else."

A familiar wave of anxiety awakened in my chest. I felt sick to my stomach. I had lost. I began to cry as I moved closer to him. "What?"

"I got a job in Alaska. I start next week."

"What?" The sunset shone through the window behind me, casting shadows and sunshine on Troy's face, the man I had loved for eight years. I sat in that U-Haul wounded for the last time. I knew it was over. And I was angry—I learned later he knew he wanted to leave me in March and quietly started to plan a new life for himself so he could take off after we graduated in May. That new life didn't include me. And I didn't find out until he couldn't hide it from me an instant longer—in that final moment, when our life was packed in a U-Haul and we were on our way to the Grand Canyon. In an act of breathtaking cowardice and selfishness, he literally waited until the last possible second to tell me he was leaving me.

It was like finding out about the affair all over again: another betrayal, another secret he'd kept from me, another way he'd rejected me, chosen something else over me, admitted it only because circumstances forced him. I felt an emptiness swallow my heart so completely it seemed my heart would be lost for years to come.

I imagined what people thought of me blubbering in a U-Haul truck parked in the front stall of a gas station, fighting for what was left of my marriage. People kept walking in and out of the Circle K with their Mountain Dews and bags of chips as the sun set on the world and on my marriage. How could life be so normal when mine was ending, especially after all my hard work?

That was the second worst day of my life. My sisters bought me a plane ticket and flew me home to Utah the next morning. My dad picked me up from the airport but I don't remember the ride. I don't remember walking into my parents' home or what I did the first few days. I just wanted to sleep my reality away. I cancelled my job. I didn't talk to my sisters when they came to see me. I just lay inert in an emotional coma.

I lost the second half of my marriage that day in the U-Haul. I lost the first half when Troy told me about the affair. In hindsight, mourning my losses seemed easier the second time around because I had mourned the first time and survived.

But perhaps I really lost my marriage when it first began, when I didn't realize the intricacies, the complexities of sex in a relationship. And once I realized my inadequacies, it was too late—even though I eventually did the work, I never got to see the results of my sexual journey.

So, there I was. Divorced, thirty years old, a post-LDS woman with vague notions about sex and not much experience. I was shoved onto an open stage without a script. I felt the world would watch me fail.

Until November 2012. That's when I experienced a sexual awakening. I decided that life was fragile, that risk was necessary, that courageous change would bring healing. So, I fumbled my way through the unknown. Exploring a sexual world at thirty after being a virgin at marriage is a trip. There are vibrators, there is porn, there are one-night stands, there is sex with old friends for the sake of experimentation or to express affection, there is good relationship sex, there are emails to my former counselor about how I just orgasmed three times in a row and am so proud. There is excitement wondering how long I will wait to have sex with the man I'm publicly flirting with, the exchanges so hot I check my clothes to make sure they still adorn my body. There are gynecologists who educate me about sexually transmitted infections and safety measures required for sexual activity outside of marriage—crucial information I was never taught in my conservative Utah high school health classes. There are new ways to flirt, there is sexting (OMFG!), there are sex manuals, there are ways to get dirty in sex, just as my counselor encouraged me to explore—and that I'm happy to say succeeded. There are conversations with non-Mormon friends about sex, about masturbation, about fetishes, about relationships. My purse holds condoms. And there's no need for lube because I get turned on enough now on my own—first time ever.

Perhaps I've hit another extreme. But this sexual awakening is my next scene, a new way to recover from an unhelpful Mormon past where sex was hidden, where sexual inadequacies were shameful and nondiscussable. And now my sexual awakening explodes in a forum where I feel accepted, normal, and uninhibited, among people who engage in sex outside of marriage. I feel sexy, more competent. I'm a new lady.

Sex—and my unwillingness to admit my failure—destroyed my marriage within religion. Now, I'm embracing sex outside of marriage and religion. Finally, for the first time ever, I can say that I genuinely embrace the joy of sex and all it offers.

Acquiescence

KATE PORTER

A DNA Mormon—that's me. With relatives in Utah and ancestors who crossed the plains in the nineteenth-century Mormon migration, I couldn't help but view my connection to the world through the lens of kinship, in ways that made my religion feel more biological than cultural. With few Mormons in my social groups, I was keenly aware of my "otherness," of how my religion set me apart from friends and schoolmates. My childhood diaries were filled with sugar-coated words about the church, the ward members, and the overall "rightness" of the precepts I was taught. I think I bore my testimony in those pages more than any missionary recently returned from a really cool country.

I attended almost every church activity available, volunteered for any and all assignments, attended four years of early-morning seminary, served a mission, and earned my BA at BYU. But somehow, church activity gradually moved from the center of my world. As a single woman, I felt myself becoming invisible. I felt increasingly unwelcome as wards simply didn't know what do with an adult single woman in an organization geared for families and couples. One ward actually put single women on its list of inactive members, believing that the same approach to fellowshipping inactive Latter-day Saints would work for single women, regardless of their activity status.

Even still, I continued to value, almost cling to, a close circle of Mormon friends. Our get-togethers were centered on long conversations about church history and current events. Eventually, interaction with this group became my only link with the church.

One day, at one of these gatherings, I met Vicki, a somber woman with a wild, oddly dyed haircut. She dominated the discussion with her piercing questions and strong opinions. The story of Vicki coming out to her family as gay and their near-immediate shunning was well known in our group. Such courage and self-acceptance drew my attention at a time when I was just beginning to explore my own situation. I was terrified and often preferred to avoid such difficult questions.

Instead, I reached out to Vicki, and before I knew it, we were dating. I took comfort in the fact that Vicki's background was so similar to mine and that she understood the nuances of dealing with sexuality as a Mormon, the concept of accountability, and being in a community where conformity often masqueraded as obedience. She also appreciated the challenges, the hurt, and courage it took to deal with gay sexuality in an environment where marriage, family, and eternal relationships were central to our upbringing. Best of all, she took everything (pardon the pun) straight on and celebrated her individuality in ways I found admirable.

We bonded quickly. I couldn't imagine life without Vicki. We made promises of fidelity and respect. We planned for the future and set goals, like any good Mormon couple. We both had parents who married in the temple and honored, through thick and thin, the vows they made to each other. I easily assumed Vicki and I would take on the same depth of commitment and fidelity in our relationship.

My life took on a vibrancy I never thought possible. Everything—simple errands, evening meals, parties, weekend trips—seemed so much richer, deeper, and more vivid when shared with someone. Thinking in terms of "we" rather than "me" seemed to offer both joy and completion. I felt I had finally been let in on life's big secret.

I confess we were a bit smug about our relationship in the early days. We rarely argued, and we imagined that the respect between us was the envy of our friends. We felt a bit above the fray of typical couples' drama and often spoke of the need for honesty, being true to one another, and keeping the lines of communication open. Despite not having much experience in relationships, we were sure we had cracked the code on keeping a long-standing relationship, well, long standing.

Still, the relationship wasn't fully realized. Family members and most Mormon friends had to be kept apart from my relationship with Vicki. As open as Vicki imagined herself, there were still people and situations from whom she hid her sexuality and personal life. Such limitations hindered the relationship in ways I didn't understand until much later.

Within a year, Vicki accepted a job several states away. As she worked to reestablish a relationship with her family (who coincidentally lived a few miles from her new place of employment), our relationship flourished too. After a few years of long-distance dating, I opted out of my job, accepted a position in the same city as Vicki, and we began housekeeping together. It was a daunting but heady time. I was leaving behind my whole life, on the promise and anticipation of a new life with the woman I loved. I sold my house, left a delightful neighborhood and a slew of dear friends. I was scared silly.

My new job wasn't the best fit for me. Navigating the new city was frustrating and confusing. Aside from Vicki, I knew no one, and progress on making new friends was slow. But if anything, those defects in my new life only served to make my relationship with Vicki more real. So much was unfamiliar. But the woman at the center of it all was familiar and tangibly, wonderfully solid. I was with someone I loved who loved me back. Life awaited us on our terms.

Though not really. Vicki had endured over two years of absolute silence and abandonment by her family; any thought of replicating such a situation sent her into a fit of shaking and tears. Our life was dictated by her need to keep peace with her family, keep the elephant in the room well fed and quiet, and for me to support that effort. Which I did without reserve, believing such a sacrifice on my part was necessary and appreciated. By that first year in our new house, holidays were spent apart. Vicki celebrated them, as well as many other occasions, with her family, while I fended for myself, often hanging out in the basement with the TV for company. I was the roommate, essentially. I rationalized it away, but now I see that such actions eroded the legitimacy of our relationship, that it was becoming less real.

It was an unhappy thought for me, that I displaced my entire existence to become a "roommate," but I tamped it down with reminders that I was doing the Right Thing; that family is crucial, that keeping the peace for Vicki and her family was a worthy sacrifice. I wanted to show my support for Vicki by agreeing to be "less than" in public for her.

Plans Vicki and I made together were often usurped when a summons from her family arrived. Vicki's acquiescence to them was nearly absolute. Sad as it is to admit even now, I see that Vicki chose the approval of her family over the integrity of our relationship. How dumb was I not to see this as a blazing red flag, flashing atop the highest hill? Of course, at the time, the concept of seeing and recognizing red flags in a relationship I believed would be enduring was simply impossible.

One especially cold winter evening, about three years after we moved in together, Vicki thundered downstairs to my little sanctuary in the basement and announced, without any preamble, "We have to talk." I wanted to laugh at the classic lead-in to so many break-up conversations, but when I saw that she was serious, I shut down. I found myself unable to do anything but listen in growing horror and desperation to her litany of prepared comments, all carefully bulleted on a legal pad.

"This isn't working. I was just upstairs and realized that it won't work, no matter what we do," she said.

"There's nothing we can do? Nothing? It's over? Just like that?" I asked.

"You know we both haven't been happy. I can't see how anything can make it better," Vicki said, staring at her notes.

My brain stalled. I couldn't call up any semblance of a coherent response. Not that it mattered, since Vicki wasn't waiting for one. She continued, "We haven't formally registered as domestic partners, so you should have paid attention to that. And when you went on that business trip last year and I didn't go with you, you should have paid attention to that. You never took to this area and that bothers me. The pressure of keeping you and my family happy is too much. And you are far too much in the closet."

I kept thinking that what was happening surely wasn't. Vicki couldn't be serious. What was with this list of items she kept rattling off? Why couldn't I make my brain form a coherent response? Why was she only now telling me of concerns that she'd harbored for months, perhaps even before we bought a house, maybe before I moved out to her new city? Why was it all coupled with such an urgent, decisive exclamation point at the end of her sentences? Why such an adamant refusal to work things out?

My voice unsteady but not yet inflected by tears, I said, "I need to think about this. Can we talk again later? Can I have some time to absorb this?"

"No. I've decided." And off she went. Watching her ascend the stairs, I found myself hoping she'd look back at me. And when she didn't, I felt a coldness deep inside my heart. It was the not looking back, more than anything else, that convinced me it was indeed over.

Vicki was unshakable in her determination to end things, despite my earnest pleas for joint counseling, for us to revisit the idea of moving to another city together, anything I could think of to help her see my point of view. Ending a relationship that we had invested so much in, with the belief that it would be for always, was to me the worst possible option.

Friends suggested that perhaps Vicki was having an affair. It would explain her eagerness to end the relationship and her refusal to see if it could be repaired. I huffed in indignation and defended us both. Of course Vicki would never be unfaithful—not to me, not to anyone! Look how loyal she was to her family!

I tried to start my new life. I began housesitting for a friend in a time zone far away, struggling to figure out my life without Vicki. It was there, alone, that I discovered, proof positive, that she had indeed cheated on me. The news staggered me. Her new relationship began months before ours ended; plans were already afoot for her to establish a new life with this new woman. All the while, I was oblivious. When did she cross the line and not look back? And to conceal it so astonishingly well? And then never tell me, never acknowledge it?

The shock was as total as it could be: I spent months and months in my new town, unemployed and not knowing a soul, agonizing again and again over how I could have missed the core of Vicki's character that made it OK to make such an awful decision. The discovery that the Vicki I knew wasn't at all who she actually was chilled my heart. Thinking of it, my breathing would grow ragged and I'd once again tumble into tears. I'd gaze around my new surroundings, realizing that I'd been discarded and abandoned, forced to pull together a new life without the person who meant the very most to me. I never imagined that heartbreak could be so painful.

During what I called my "crash and burn" nights, my brain wouldn't turn off and my body would be racked by sobs and cries I didn't know I was capable of creating. Time seemed a thick awful goo that I had to wade through, with memories and pain haunting every moment, the blight of betrayal and abandonment irritating every nerve and fiber in my body. Even now I continue to have occasional crash and burn nights, when the shock and pain flood back to remind me that my life is now marked, irrevocably, by Vicki's cruel choice to betray key promises of our relationship. I'm angry that her choice will forever mark my life in such a bluntly negative way.

For a time, I doubted I would ever recover. I understand how people can fall out of love. Ironically, Vicki and I had talked about this matter many times; both of us agreed that it would be far better to be upfront with a partner, as difficult as that might be, rather than cheat and violate the fidelity of a relationship. Her cheating trumpeted to me that our relationship, complete with all of the sacrifices made (I did mention that I moved across the country, disrupted my career, and sold my house, didn't I?), meant little to her. How much less painful it would have been for me had she ended things with me before embarking on her new relationship. What a gigantic difference that would have made.

Equally difficult was managing the emotions of still missing and loving this person. While I lost all respect and admiration for Vicki, I still pined for her almost constantly, a feeling always accompanied by the gnawing knowledge that she preferred to love someone else. That my deepest, rawest fear was realized: I was loved but found to be lacking, insufficient.

Through those dark times, I reached out to friends who knew of my relationship with Vicki. All were supportive, open, and warm in their willingness to help, to listen, and to let me be candid with my feelings and hurt. A fairly private person, I would have found such behaviors anathema at another time. But there I was, sharing the most intimate, most devastating pain of my life. And they responded with such love and care that it takes my breath away even now to think about. One friend, after telling me of a story of infidelity she experienced, described life afterward as one with an overarching darkness to it, but through the darkness, when something wonderful happens, its brightness appears more glorious. She likened it to Van Gogh's painting of "The Starry Night." At the time, I rejected her view, but I now see how right she was. And I suspect that many who've had such an experience feel similarly.

I still can't help but devote countless hours to sorting through memories and trying to make meaning from it all. I'll seize on a strand and wonder if that was the thread that actually started the Big Unravel and how I contributed to the fraying. I wonder how my hasty assumptions contributed to the ultimate awful ending. Had I been arrogant to assume that because we had such amazingly similar backgrounds, our approach to honoring promises and being true would be the same? Simply because we knew the same hymns and had missionary scriptures highlighted with red pencil? How was it that in trying to honor such a key piece of the religion we were raised in, the concept of eternal families, our relationship was undermined and made less real? Or, maybe, did Vicki and I both fail to see the relationship as truly genuine simply because we had to hide so many aspects of it to so many people, most of all to her family?

I was also stunned by the stark realization that I had become invisible—strikingly familiar to how I felt in my last few years of church activity—in the most important relationship of my life. I allowed who I was to be subsumed by outside factors and acquiescence to something I down deep disagreed with. I was submissive, far too agreeable, and in so being, hid my true self from the person I loved and expected to live my life with. Were my actions as dishonest as hers? I cringe remembering how often I lost my voice in the years Vicki and I were together. Quite often, when I tried to speak, particularly in a social setting, my voice would come out raw and weak; I'd have to clear my voice and start over. Often, I'd feel like I was shouting, even though the timbre of my voice was frail, nothing like the voice I sported when working in radio broadcasting years prior. I even experienced a bit of a stuttering problem that has never returned. How telling is that?

I still struggle with what I've learned through this chapter of my life. The integrity of our relationship was sacrificed long before Vicki cheated and ended it. Time and time again, she chose the approval of her family over the honesty of our relationship—with my implicit approval. My acquiescence to her wishes and plans further undermined the situation. Any relationship worth having is worth working for and making a priority. Pondering why I didn't see that leaves me feeling shame, regret, and that nagging "well, duh" sensation.

I wish I could say I'm over it. I'm not. However, I've gained some valuable insights and learned more about myself. I'm more open and willing to be vulnerable, though paradoxically, my instant trust in people is nearly gone. I'm guarded, cautious, and very aware of the decision on when to open up. I'm still surprised by the intensity of kinship that arises with friends old and new who've had similar experiences of heartbreak and betrayal. It binds us in a collective that makes us a bit more scarred, but also more sensitive to things of the heart.

I still work and hope for a positive end to this story. Some days I think I'm near the final chapter; other days I see that I've so much to learn before I can understand what is still so very un-understandable to me.

Here are the rules I abide by right now: Trust yourself and learn to value what makes you who you are. Honor and truly love all your relationships. Be honest with others by letting them know the real you. Strive for truly equitable relationships. Pay attention.

Oh, and never spend holidays alone in a basement.

The Crash

AMY WILLIAMS

It was the night before our wedding. We sat in a black Fiat hatchback at a red light on the Avenida Paulista in Sao Paulo, one of the most famous thoroughfares in all Brazil. My future brother-in-law Marcelo was at the wheel, my fiancé, Rey, in the passenger seat, while my father and I watched from the back seat as the frenetic metropolis bustled around us. Suddenly I felt a powerful jolt and heard the sound of crunching metal and shattering glass. I braced myself for the worst and looked at my dad, who had covered his head with his arms to block the flying glass. The driver of a Mack truck had fallen asleep at the wheel and awoke to find his truck mere feet from our bumper. He rear-ended us going twenty five miles an hour in a truck carrying three thousand gallons of water. Our car was propelled into the back of a sedan in front of us and buckled between the vehicles. For a moment it seemed we would be crushed inside this tiny tin can Fiat dared call a car.

Finally the crunching stopped. We all remained still for a moment, stunned both at what had happened and that we were alive. "Dad!" I shouted, once I realized I could. "Are you OK?"

"Amy?" Rey said, fumbling with his seatbelt. "Are you guys OK?"

"I'm OK—I think," my dad said.

"We're OK, Rey—are you?"

"I'm fine," he said, climbing painfully out of the crumpled door. There was a great deal of shouting and gesturing as Rey and Marcelo confronted the truck driver. After what felt like hours, my father and I took a taxi back to my apartment, while the brothers stayed to talk to the police and argue with the driver.

Back at the apartment, I was overwhelmed by dread. For months, I had prayed for a sign from God about my upcoming wedding. I couldn't help but wonder if the crash was it. Ever since I'd gotten engaged I'd felt confused, unsure that I was making the right choice. I'd prayed and prayed and prayed and never felt at peace. No one knew I'd changed my mind a thousand times—except God. So I finally asked him to give me a sign, a clear, unambiguous sign I couldn't miss or misunderstand. Was this God's way of telling me not to get married? Had he stretched his arm down from the heavens and pushed that truck into us to get my attention? Was God so against this marriage that he had basically just smacked me upside the head as if to say, "Don't do it, you numskull!"

I feared he had, but I told myself it wasn't so. *I was being ridiculous, it was just a coincidence, I mean, God doesn't do signs, I shouldn't have asked for one, that's not how it works.* Yet I couldn't shake the feeling that it was in fact the sign I'd prayed for. I woke the next morning in a state of panic. I wanted out of the wedding. But my parents, at great expense, had flown to Brazil for the wedding, and they'd helped pay for my dress. One of my brothers had also flown in for two days, just for the wedding, as a surprise to me. The cake was made, the flowers paid for, and everyone expected a wedding. I *couldn't* back out. And what about Rey? I couldn't break his heart. So, when my mom saw me crying and asked what was wrong, I said I was just stressed. I should have told her the truth; I wish I had told her the truth. My life would be totally different if I had. But I didn't. I told myself it was just cold feet and everything would be fine, and then I went to the temple and bound myself for time and all eternity to a man I barely knew.

So, why did I get married? When it seemed that God, the universe, or at least my subconscious, was screaming at me not to? This is something I've asked myself often.

I was twenty-four, practically an old maid by LDS standards, and I believed whole-heartedly that it was my job in life to figure out what God wanted me to do, then do it. I accepted, lock, stock, and barrel, the idea that my ultimate role in life was to be a wife to one of God's righteous priesthood holders and have lots of children with him. So when a righteous priesthood holder wanted to marry me, I figured that must be what God wanted too. In fact, Rey told me that God had revealed this to him in the celestial room at the temple—that I was the one he should marry. So I believed it—God wants this. I never asked myself if I wanted to get married. It was just, *Does God want me to marry? Is this who God wants me to be with?* I never asked, *Is this the person I want to spend my life with?*

Was I in love with Rey? I thought I was. After all, he was Brazilian. I had spent eighteen months as a missionary in Brazil. And I fell absolutely, madly in love with the place. Some of the Brazilian missionaries I'd worked with on my mission called me a "gringuinha brasileira," the little Brazilian gringo, an affectionate title I wore with pride. Once home from my mission, I was obsessed. I couldn't stop thinking about Brazil: the people I'd met there; the friends I'd made;

the language I'd learned; the food I'd eaten; the music I'd heard; the beautiful, complex, exotic, thoroughly intoxicating culture that had captivated me. I felt I'd found my true home and it was Brazil. I wanted nothing more than to go back.

After the beautiful, charming Brazilian men I'd met, American men seemed stiff and pretentious and—especially the ones at BYU—annoyingly pious and self-righteous. So when an exotic and handsome priesthood-holding Brazilian wrote to me declaring his undying love, I was hooked. His letter cemented my plans to return to Brazil. It was a sign that Brazil was my destiny. I ignored warnings from friends concerned that Rey might be using me to get to America. The thought crossed my mind, but I brushed it off. It couldn't be a problem because I didn't want to come back to the States. I intended to live in Brazil and had told Rey so.

When I arrived in Brazil we had been corresponding for eight months. Two months later, we were engaged. We saw each other daily and spent as much time together as we could. But we still didn't know each other well. Much later, I realized that we had each presented ourselves how we had wanted to be perceived.

I didn't do this on purpose; it was just something I had learned to do as a Mormon without even realizing that I did it. It was like dressing up for church: you wear your Sunday best, including a smile. As you file into the meetinghouse, people only see the well pressed slacks, the freshly laundered modest skirts, the neatly combed hair, the sunny smiles—and they assume all is well. No one knows that five minutes earlier your mom was screaming her head off about how you didn't clean your room, or raging at your older brother for coming home drunk the night before. No one knows that dad skips church not because he's out of town on business like your mom claims, but because he became an atheist and refuses to attend a church he finds morally reprehensible. You don't discuss your problems. You smile and say you're fine when your teacher asks you how you are even though you've been contemplating suicide. That's how it's supposed to be. Of course I had learned to present my best self to the world and of course it was mostly a façade and of course I didn't even have to maintain it consciously.

What I didn't know was that my husband also had a façade, one he'd constructed quite deliberately.

Our marriage was hard. We never had time to ourselves to get to know each other and adjust to married life. We ended up living with his parents for the first several months after we got married. After we left Brazil so he could attend college in the United States, we lived with my parents in Idaho. I got pregnant right away; before our first anniversary we had a daughter. I didn't adjust well to motherhood and this put a strain on us too, especially after I started a graduate program studying English. It's not that we didn't get along or that we fought a lot;

it's that we were truly poor in both time and money, and we didn't really connect. We discussed mundane daily routines—school, work, church, kids—but never our feelings. When I would try to tell him about my emotions or ideas, I never felt that he listened to me or that my opinions or feelings mattered to him. He wasn't mean or disrespectful, yet somehow I never felt appreciated. I think he felt the same way.

From the outside, Rey seemed like the ideal husband. He loved to cook and often prepared delicious, elaborate meals from scratch. He did a lot of cleaning and housework, usually without being asked. He helped take care of the kids, changing diapers and all the rest. He worked hard in school while also working full-time. He could do my hair and makeup better than I could. He loved to shop and picked out great outfits for me. But when it came to emotional support, affection, and intimacy, he couldn't deliver.

I couldn't put my finger on what was missing, nor was I very conscious of the fact that we lacked a real emotional connection. I just knew that I was lonely and unhappy, though I couldn't articulate why. That vague, unsettled feeling I'd had during our engagement persisted. Something just felt *off*. Deep down I felt I'd made a mistake, but it was too late. There was no going back: we had a baby and we'd been married in the temple. It didn't matter if I'd chosen the right person—Rey was the one I'd sealed myself to for eternity so I had to suck it up and make it work.

I thought we were making it work. We both finished school, he got a promotion, and I taught English part-time at a junior college while raising our daughter. He was transferred to Dallas, far from anyone we knew, but we had a ready-made community at church. We bought our first home and had our second child.

And then, about a year after we'd moved and seven years into our marriage, Rey changed. At first I thought he was stressed out because of work. He worked long hours, was under a lot of pressure, and felt unappreciated by his bosses. Depressed, he stopped eating and started seeing a therapist. He found excuses for us to spend time apart, sent me and the kids to visit my parents, started working nights. He wanted to request a transfer so we could move to Utah, closer to my family. Even though I liked Dallas and our new house, I agreed, thinking it would be better for his career.

But as soon as we arrived in Utah, he found excuses to return to Dallas. Two months after we moved, he essentially deserted me and the children, saying the move had been a huge mistake. He took a leave of absence from work and lived in our empty house (without even a bed to sleep on) in Dallas while searching for a new job. He decided that the children and I could make do in our small apartment near Salt Lake City for a few more months. We could move back to Dallas when he found work.

Clearly something was seriously wrong. I tried talking to him about us, but all I could ever get out of him was how bad things had been at work. I was angry at him for convincing me to move to Utah and then leaving us there—he'd even missed our son's first birthday. His actions struck me as selfish and irrational, yet he seemed baffled by my anger.

A little over a month into this new arrangement, Rey came to see us for a weekend. My parents were also visiting and agreed to watch the kids while we went out. As we sat in a sushi bar, I finally asked, "What's going on?"

"I'm not happy," he said.

"I know. Is it work? Are you homesick?" He hadn't been back to Brazil in five years.

He looked down at his hands, then up at me. "Sometimes I think we should have never gotten married."

I stared at him, shocked. I had always felt that way, but had no idea he did too.

"I think we made a mistake, you know?" he said, as if he hoped I would agree. "Everything happened so fast, the kids, school, living with family—we never even had time for ourselves, to get to know each other."

I was relieved to hear him express things I had felt all along. It was the first time I really felt we were connecting. Still, it hurt to hear him say marrying me was a mistake. "It's a little late now," I said.

"I don't know what to do. I love you, but I'm not *in love* with you," he said.

I couldn't respond to this because despite my best efforts to hold them back, tears began to flow.

"I think we should separate but live close to one another and raise the kids together, as great friends," he said. This shocked me more than anything else he said that night. Despite all my misgivings, I had believed he loved me, that he wanted us to be together, and that we would somehow make things work. In my mind, divorce wasn't an option.

"How long have you felt this way? Why didn't you say something?" I asked.

"I'm sorry. I should've told you sooner. I'm so sorry. I didn't want to hurt you."

I just cried.

He left the next day. I felt sick and suddenly very desperate. I didn't know what to do, but anything seemed better than staying where I was, so I continued to make plans to move back to Dallas. It fit the façade I'd learned to construct.

Then, two days later, Rey sent me an email that read, "I think I might be gay." While it was shocking to see those words on the screen, at the same time, something clicked in my head; it suddenly all made sense. Of course he was gay. That's why it had never felt right, never during all eight years of our marriage. That's why I wasn't happy. That's why he wasn't happy. That's why something was missing and we'd failed to connect. That's why he never looked at other women. That's why we felt mismatched. Because we *were*! Of course he's gay; why didn't I see it? Why didn't I heed the warnings? Why hadn't I listened to my inner voice?

But even after I knew he was gay, I thought we might be able to make things work. Believe it or not, I moved back to Dallas. I went to be with my gay husband who wasn't sure he wanted us to be together. I thought maybe we could stay together for the kids. I thought maybe, even though I knew being gay wasn't a choice or something he could change, I thought maybe he could choose me and our family and that maybe, just *maybe*, that could be enough, for both of us.

Or maybe I was just so terrified of being a single mom that I thought anything would be better.

But then I found a letter.

I knew in my gut there was someone else. Right after he came out I'd asked him point blank if there was, but he swore there wasn't; he'd been faithful and would never put me at risk like that. But I did what I hadn't done in the aftermath of that car crash: I trusted my gut. I searched his clothes, his bags, his personal things. And that's when I found it. "Dear Thomas," it began. I remember reading and rereading those two words, trying to make the letters transform into the shapes that form my name. It had to be to me. The letter had to be to me. But it wasn't. And the things he'd written were things he'd never said to me. Words like *soulmate* and *destiny* were used abundantly. He was clearly madly in love with this man. This man whose name refused to look like mine. This man whose body looked nothing like mine. This *man*. Reading that letter, I felt physical pain in my heart and thought I would be sick.

When I confronted Rey that night, he tried to deny it at first, but eventually he admitted he'd been having an affair for nearly six months. It suddenly made sense: he'd tried to run away to Utah but then couldn't do it. It wasn't Dallas he hadn't been able to leave behind, it was his lover.

Two weeks later I left him and moved in with my parents. Rey didn't love me and maybe never had. It's a hard realization to make: that the person you'd promised your life to had used you to cover up a lie he'd been telling himself and everyone else his whole life. I felt used. And worthless. And totally disgusting—the least desirable woman on the planet. I'd never had great self-esteem. I'd never thought men found me attractive, and the one man whom I had believed did find me attractive and love me, and whom, right until I'd read that letter, I had trusted completely, turned out to have never been attracted to me. In fact, he had rejected not only me, but my very sex.

Eventually I filed for divorce, but it was a long process—a year and a half. Financial difficulties, including bankruptcy, prevented us from divorcing right away. Our house—the one we'd moved back to—went into foreclosure. Not surprisingly, the financial fallout of the divorce has been far-reaching.

Nearly five years have passed since the divorce was final. There is still some pain and anger, but it's lessened considerably. I sometimes get angry that he took so many years from me. That he used me to perpetuate a lie and to obtain the things he believed, as a devout LDS man, he was entitled to—an eternal marriage, a wife, children. And that he did so without bothering to let me in on his secret. I don't know if I would have married him had I known he was gay—as a devout Mormon, I very well might have—but he withheld that choice from me.

My self-confidence has never fully recovered. It's hard not to blame yourself when your husband tells you he'd rather be with a man. While intellectually I know it has nothing to do with me, emotionally I felt that I was so awful (ugly, fat, bitchy, whiny, whatever) that I drove him to men. It's ridiculous, really, but I would be lying if I said I've never felt that way.

Sometimes I tell people the real reason I got divorced but more often than not I keep it to myself. Some people don't understand how I couldn't have known. Some people think there's something comical about a woman discovering her husband is gay. Others think it would be a relief, as if being cheated on with a man is somehow better than being cheated on with a woman. But I remember feeling the complete opposite. If he'd had an affair with a woman, I think we could have stayed together because I could compete with another woman, but how could I compete with a man? I don't have the right equipment. I simply couldn't give him what he wanted or needed. I felt I had been cheated out of the right to fight for my marriage.

People also wonder about the sex. How could a gay man sleep with a woman at all? I can't really answer that except to say, a need for sexual release can overpower many other desires. And how could I not tell a difference between a gay man in bed and a straight one? It was simple. I was a very inexperienced virgin when we married. Rey was the only person I'd ever even kissed. That means I got my first kiss at the age of twenty-four. This seems unfathomable to most, but I was very shy and naive and had been deathly afraid of committing any type of sexual sin. I kept my distance from boys, which was easy to do at BYU, where there was a cult of uber chastity. Many of my friends and I wanted to save our first kiss for our future spouse—we called this the "Virgin Lips Club." I was a proud member.

I didn't particularly enjoy sex at first. Switching off the part of my brain that had always believed sex to be dirty and sinful and forbidden was difficult. It's not that I never enjoyed it, but I still had a lot of inhibitions and hang-ups that made it hard for me to fully embrace the experience. In the first few years of marriage, I found myself turning my husband down, frequently. There were times when I felt bad about this, like I was rejecting him, but we never discussed it. It wasn't him, I just didn't want to have sex, but I'm sure he felt rejected. Because he always initiated things and seemed to want it fairly often, I never had any reason to think he wasn't interested. At some point, though, the roles reversed. I don't remember exactly when this occurred. But I do remember, maybe three or four years in, there were times when he turned me down. I remember feeling surprised: isn't the guy supposed to always want it?

Eventually it began to take him a really long time to climax. At the time, I thought that meant he had great stamina and had learned over time how to have more control. Now I know it was because he wasn't really turned on by me. He once told me that he had really believed that getting married would make his homosexual feelings go away. He said that in the beginning of our marriage he thought that it had worked, but that within the first couple of years he realized he'd made a mistake. He said he'd totally lost interest in me by then and the old feelings, of wanting men, had returned.

The thing many people fail to realize about a mixed orientation marriage is that it's not just unfulfilling for the gay person; it's equally unfulfilling for the straight person. Rey was encouraged to marry a woman and told that it would help him overcome his same-sex attraction. At the time, that was the church's standard operating procedure: marriage was offered as a cure, or at least a successful treatment, for the ailment of homosexuality. Perhaps this was in large part because the men giving this advice were heterosexual and couldn't imagine how a man would want to lie with another man, especially once he had tasted the pleasures of being with a woman. Perhaps, because straight men do find women so desirable, the assumption was that it would be impossible for a man not to be smitten by the allures of feminine beauty. And I think it was beyond the leaders' mental scope to even imagine that a straight woman wouldn't be satisfied with a gay husband—after all, a man is a man; a penis is a penis.

What those straight Mormon men and many others failed to realize is that homosexuality, while it has *everything* to do with sex, also has *nothing* to do with sex. This is what I didn't get until long after we had separated. It's about intimacy and creating an emotional bond that is expressed through sex, yes. But that cannot be and is not nurtured through sex alone—yet, paradoxically, it cannot exist as the unique bond that it is, without sex.

So, can a gay person and a straight person in a romantic relationship connect sexually and intimately in the same way that people with compatible orientations can? Maybe, but I think it's very rare and that very few can sustain it for long. Can you love someone you aren't sexually attracted to as intensely as you can love someone to whom you are sexually attracted? People who encourage gays to marry straights think you can. They say other things matter more: friendship, mutual respect, shared values—those things supposedly outweigh the sexual problem. But here's the thing: while sex may not be the most important component of a marriage, in Mormon marriages, at least, it is a defining component and something that sets the relationship apart from every other relationship those two people have. And if you have sex without any real sexual attraction on one side, there's an imbalance. How can that lead to a healthy sex life?

Some women knowingly choose to marry gay men, believing what they hear about how other things matter more than sex. But I think they underestimate how much the sex matters too. And how much it can hurt that your partner doesn't want you. I'm not talking about respect or admiration or fondness or dozens of wonderful things he may feel for you. I'm saying, does he *want* you? Does he lust after you? Does he look at you with lascivious eyes, think about the curves of your body, imagine his tongue on your nipples, his hands caressing your hips as he thrusts in and out?

No matter how much the straight wife may love and want her gay husband, nothing can make up for not being wanted in that same way by the one she loves most. That is fundamental to a fulfilling sexual relationship and, by extension, a fulfilling marriage. Every woman deserves to be cherished by her husband, not only for the friendship, love, and support she provides but for her body, her femininity, her sex.

Encouraging gay people to marry straight people, which unfortunately some cultures still do, is entirely about the gay person, about their obligation to change. They must stop being who they are and become something else to placate a society or a God who will reject them if they don't. It's tragic and cruel.

But it's also tragic and cruel to treat their spouses as acceptable collateral damage. The straight spouse's needs never enter the discussion. What is the cost of this farce to the straight spouse and to any children born into such a marriage? This question should also be asked.

For me, the cost was too high. Divorce is like a death, a devastating and permanent loss. But ours was a death that should never have been. I didn't have to suffer. My ex didn't have to suffer nor hide who he was. Yet, the Mormon culture we were raised in encouraged this suffering. It set us up for failure. And still we pay the price; our children pay the price every day. I sometimes wish I could give my kids the kind of stability and security an unbroken family can provide. I mourn that loss for them and for myself. But I don't regret ending a marriage that was ill-conceived and built on lies; it was doomed from the start. And while just a coincidence, it seems poetic that our wedding was preceded by a violent car crash—like some kind of cosmic foreshadowing of how our marriage would crash and burn.

As it happens, I did move back to Dallas, and Rey and I continued to live together, sharing our small house as roommates until the bank took it back. He slept on the couch; I slept in our old bed. Then I moved into a rental and let him sleep on the couch until he could afford to move out. Throughout all the tumult we managed to remain friendly, though I wouldn't call him a friend—there's not enough intimacy or trust for that. We're more like relatives. We have our children and are tied to one another by the shared blood that runs through their veins, but we aren't close. I wouldn't choose to hang out with him. I wouldn't call him just to say hi or send him a Christmas card, yet there he is. We still occasionally do things as a family—me, Rey, and our kids. It's funny: in a lot of ways our relationship hasn't changed much. We talk about work, our kids, and our mundane daily routines. We don't fight. I don't share my feelings with him and he doesn't share his with me. But we don't have to bother with the pretense of sex a couple of times a month. And somehow that makes all the difference. I'm free. He's free. It works.

The Last Valentine's Day

VIV B.

Scene: A Mormon Chapel, 8:57 on a Sunday Morning

Enter: foyer left. A man in his mid-thirties. He wears a dark suit, white shirt, and one of the 657 ties in his closet. (The count is down this month; he's given some older ones to the missionaries. He'll replace them before long, with Versace or Oscar de la Renta.) He sees that the only bench commodious enough for his entire family is near the front. He glances behind him, then marches proudly up the aisle. Following him are six stair-step daughters clothed in matching dresses, one small son, and a petite woman holding a swaddled baby girl. They file into the row just as the bishop steps to the microphone to begin the meeting. They sing the hymns loudly, without referring to a hymnal. The parents nod in recognition when the speaker mentions Prophet David O. McKay's motto: "Whate'er thou art, act well thy part." After the meeting, they are deluged with invitations to dinner. They offer acceptable answers to the question of "What do you do?" Later, the husband will be called as high priest group leader and the wife will be the Cub Scout den mother.

We were born actors, all of us, and our Mormon audience applauded in all the right places.

A Conference Talk

"Pride is a very misunderstood sin, and many are sinning in ignorance," said President Ezra Taft Benson, my husband's hero, in a 1989 sermon. "In the scriptures there is no such thing as righteous pride—it is always considered a sin. Therefore, no matter how the world uses the term, we must understand how God uses the term so we can understand the language of holy writ and profit thereby." After that talk, I stopped using the word *proud*. Instead, I was "pleased" with my children when they earned perfect grades in school. I was pleased with my large family. I was pleased that my husband was a righteous priesthood holder. He had been abused as a child by an alcoholic father, and the gospel had helped him overcome his own tendency for violence. I was pleased with him for the changes he'd made in his life. He had hit me only a few times early in our marriage, and when he later found himself out of control with one of our teenage daughters, he vowed never to discipline any of them again. That responsibility fell to me, the stay-at-home mom. It was a heavy one.

Two Temple Vignettes

We attended the temple as often as possible in the early days of our marriage. George enjoyed serving as the witness couple. It wasn't hard to be chosen for this honor. You showed up early, sat in the front of the chapel, and held hands. An officiator would approach to ask you to represent the company by kneeling at the altar several times during the temple ceremony. Once we did this when I was newly pregnant. I staggered as I rose after kneeling, lightheaded. I was escorted from the room to a place where I could lie down. An elderly woman stepped in to finish the session with George. On the ride home, he pontificated on the symbolic nature of this incident. If I did not start living up to my covenants, he admonished, I would be taken from him and someone else would take my place.

Another day, I kept catching the eye of a young woman watching me. After the session, she approached and asked how many children I had. I said I had eight children. She said she knew I had many children, because I radiated the spirit of a "Mother in Zion." I went home and looked at myself in a mirror. Most of my wrinkles were laugh lines, so they didn't look too bad. But my chin was definitely saggier. I held my arms out to my sides and jiggled them. No "Relief Society arms" just yet. Despite nursing eight children, my breasts were OK—round and soft. Legs in good shape: no varicose veins after eight pregnancies, despite a hereditary propensity! I was pleased with that. Problem area: my stomach, which George teasingly called my "Botticelli belly." Yes, I had a "Mother in Zion" stomach.

The Day My Domesticity Died

Having grown up in a liberal Massachusetts household, I was performing a kind of rebellion by playing Molly Mormon. I ground wheat, made my own bread, and had as many children as my body could produce. Little by little I was cured of my fanaticism by the challenges of real life. The homemade bread went by the wayside during a Hawaii summer when I was almost ten months pregnant with no air conditioning. Cloth diapers were jettisoned when I had three babies in nappies and two were nursing. Someone gave me a gift of Pampers; I never looked back.

One day I brought a vegetable quiche of my own recipe to a Relief Society luncheon. I was proud of how the dish turned out. It looked lovely, and I received many compliments from the ladies, so I decided to repeat the experiment for my family that evening.

I knew that this dish, with feta cheese and no meat, wouldn't be a raving success in my home. George, a real man, would occasionally eat a meatless dinner I served, but afterward, feeling that he hadn't really eaten, invariably ordered a meat-lover's pizza. But I figured I had a sure-fire way to encourage everyone to enjoy this gustatory experiment: I made chocolate chip cookies. And if everyone ate their thin slice of veggie quiche, they could gorge themselves on cookies for dessert.

After I explained the relationship between quiche and cookies, the dinner table erupted into pandemonium. Daughter #1 held her nose, shoved the entire plateful into her mouth and swallowed. She then received her cookies, which she slowly savored, waving them in front of her distraught siblings. Daughter #2 made fruitless attempts to swallow small crumbs from the side of the quiche, gagging loudly when they touched her tongue, until her eyes bulged from their sockets. Daughter #3 threw herself under the table, sobbing dramatically and uncontrollably. Daughter #4 sullenly mashed her portion with a fork, over and over, until it was unrecognizable. Perhaps she hoped it would disappear, but the properties of matter would not be evaded. With the four oldest children behaving that way, it was no wonder that the younger ones also wept and wailed, terrified of trying something, anything, new.

George was no help. Rather than telling the children to sit up, behave, and eat their dinner (support my own father would have provided my mother), he commanded me to just give the kids the cookies. Weeping, I insisted that if I did, no one would ever take me seriously again. When George commandeered the plate of cookies and began handing them out, I slunk to my room, feeling broken.

The next day we had frozen pizza for dinner.

The Gardener

When we lived in California, very close to the border with Mexico, our accommodations included a gardener who poked around the grounds a few times a week. In part because he spoke little English, my interactions with him were limited to the occasional "hola" when I walked by. Nevertheless, he was the source of some agitation for George, who was certain that I was romancing the man in his absence.

One day I caught my husband grilling our three-year-old. "Did Marcos come in the house when I was gone?" George demanded.

"No, Daddy. . . ."

"Are you sure?"

"Uhm, mmmhmm," the child stammered, doubting herself in the face of her father's disbelief.

"He came in, didn't he? DIDN'T HE?"

"Uh, yes."

Furious, I confronted George. "Can't you see she's telling you what she thinks you want to hear? You're bullying her. Leave her alone!"

This incident was all the proof George needed that I was cuckolding him with the groundskeeper.

Purse-Snatching

We started our marriage with a paradigm of equality, but as Mormons—especially Mormon men—will tell you, "Someone has to be in charge." President Howard W. Hunter taught, "A man who holds the priesthood accepts his wife as a partner in the leadership of the home and family with full knowledge of and full participation in all decisions relating thereto. Of necessity there must be in the church and in the home a presiding officer. By divine appointment, the responsibility to preside in the home rests upon the priesthood holder."

Even when I had been absolutely committed to my priesthood-holding partner and our marriage, George doubted my loyalty to him. Eventually, years of mistreatment made it harder for me to feel or express the love George thought he should command. He became increasingly distrustful and controlling. For instance, he removed my name from our bank account, allowing me a small sum with which to do the weekly grocery shopping. Sometimes he wouldn't give me any money at all, electing to accompany me to the store, forcing me to defend each purchase.

I learned that it wasn't a good idea to threaten to leave home when we were having an argument. George would confiscate my purse, my driver's license, my car keys, and my phone, then deny me access to a computer. Though not technically a prisoner in my own home, I often felt like one. On a few occasions I did walk out the door and start down the street with only the clothes on my back, but he would get in the car and follow, very slowly, twenty feet behind me. He'd trail me until my feet got tired, and I admitted to myself that I had nowhere else to go.

I started a savings account in my own name, where I could deposit money I earned from part-time jobs. George referred to this as money I was "embezzling" from the family.

Sweet Nothings

At midnight, after the Holy Ghost had gone to bed, George would begin to whisper in my ear. It always started the same way. "You're a slut and a whore," he'd murmur. "When you stand before the judgment bar of Christ, he will cast you into outer darkness." He would continue this litany for hours on end. "You covenanted to belong to me before angels and these witnesses. You can never leave." And I wouldn't.

But why wouldn't I? Why did I feel that night after night, month after month, year after year, I had to submit to this ghastly ritual? Why didn't I just get up and leave the room when he started berating me in those chilling whispers? Sometimes I'd wake and his mouth would be to my ear, the tones he was uttering so hushed I couldn't catch more than a cuss word here and there. I'd lie still, my eyes closed, listening, but pretending I was asleep.

A Family Conversation

HUSBAND: (*out of the blue, to fourteen-year-old son*): Your mother is a pseudo-intellectual.

SON: What's a pseudo-intellectual?

MOTHER: Someone who thinks they are intelligent, but they're really not.

SON: Why is she a pseudo-intellectual?

HUSBAND: Because she and her friends like to blog about theodicies [mispronouncing it "thee-oh-DICE-eez" instead of "thee-OD-uh-sees"] and other strange things.

SON: What are theodicies?

MOTHER: A theodicy is a theory of why God allows pain and suffering in the world.

SON: Why don't they stop blogging about it and just go do something about the pain and suffering in the world?

HUSBAND: *laughs so hard that tears run down his face and he gasps for breath.*

A Family Secret

You know what a family secret is, right? It's one of those things everyone in the family knows, but no one ever talks about. We had a family secret: George was hitting me again. Sometimes, it was a whack on the back of the head, the way a redneck might cuff a dog. Other times he would pummel me methodically about the head and shoulders—but only when I deserved it. Once or twice he gave me a black eye. I would never miss church over something like that, so I covered it with heavy makeup, and wore sunglasses in the chapel.

THINGS I DID THAT PROVED TO MY HUSBAND I WAS CHEATING ON HIM

- Bought new sheets and a bedspread for the bed without prior approval ("very suspicious")
- Visited a girlfriend in Santa Fe for a weekend
- Spent too much time doing genealogy
- Stayed out late at ladies' book club meetings

- Talked to men on the Internet
- Wrote blog posts about controversial subjects
- Studied Mormon fundamentalism
- Forgot important things (like picking up my children from school)
- Experienced several bouts of not-able-to-get-out-of-bed-for-weeks exhaustion

George reported actions such as these to church leaders. He felt it was his duty to inform on me each time I wrote, said, or did something he disagreed with. As time went on, stake presidents and general authorities were also asked to mediate over issues such as whether I should attend LDS symposia or have access to a cell phone.

Come, Let Us Reason Together

One day I happened upon an online article discussing why people cut themselves. I had never before wondered why I engaged in this practice. I paused to consider my motives. Once during an argument, I had scratched bloody, angry welts into my arms. It stopped George cold; he stared at me in horror. Thus I discovered that I could control how much violence I endured in a fight if I inflicted it on myself. I kept it up: when a fight became too scary, I attacked myself before George could hurt me either physically or verbally. And even when I was alone, I took to nicking myself with a knife or razor. I was hurting so much, and I wanted to make my outside match my inside. I liked the localized pain and the sight of my own blood—it distracted me from the fact that I was a filthy slut, a hideous whore, a lying bitch no one could love.

Hot Tubbing

To George, my scratching myself was proof that I was mentally ill. The same goes for the time following a chilling scolding by George when I ran a scalding bath and huddled in it, fully dressed. I was so cold. I couldn't think of any other way to get myself warm, but I felt too vulnerable to take off any of my clothes.

I admit: these are not the behaviors of someone with a thoroughly healthy psyche. But they might be the behaviors of someone struggling to survive an intolerable situation.

Behind My Back

I pulled into a small park to take the call coming in on my cell phone. It was a former missionary I'd served with in Quebec and just reconnected with through Facebook.

"Viv, our chat this morning was really disturbing," he began. "I, uh, had to call you and clarify some things."

"Our chat this morning?" I repeated, a small knot of dread growing in my stomach. "I wasn't on the computer; I was out shopping!"

"We talked on Facebook. You told me you loved me and wanted to know what my feelings were. . . . That wasn't you?"

Shame and anger flushed my face. My pulse raced and pounded in my ears. George had somehow found my computer passwords. He had hacked my Facebook account, and, with one of our daughters as accomplice, pretended to be me. I drove home erratically, so nauseated by the betrayal that I truly thought I would be sick.

I didn't know much about how computers worked, but I did know how to change all of my passwords. I did that first, on my own computer on the desk in my bedroom. Then I figured out how to look at my history and any programs that had been added. The first thing I saw was a keystroke logger, which gave George access to everything I typed. Then I noticed that a program I'd never heard of had been purchased and installed. I googled to see what it was. Horrified, I read something like this:

> Self-help Subliminals is a special computer program that enables you to display your own subliminal messages and use them to change your life. You use the program to display your own positive affirmations subliminally. You are in total control of the messages, which are displayed in word or picture form.
>
> Subliminal messages appear for such a short period of time that only your subconscious mind registers what it sees. This means that you are more susceptible to the subliminal ideas since your conscious mind cannot form arguments against the suggestions.

I leaped up and yanked the plug from the wall as if I had just seen porn. What manner of messages had been placed in my mind without my knowing? Flinging myself on the bed, I grabbed the sheets with my hands and pulled, trying to rip them to shreds, like a woman in labor.

I don't know if I ever got all that horrible stuff off my computer. George apologized, and said he'd removed it all, but how could I be sure? I never quite trusted it after that.

The Triathlon

I was forty-seven when I decided to enter my first triathlon. I'd been athletic in the past, but children and Mormon Jell-O culture had taken their toll. I needed an inspiring goal, and the Uintah County DinoTri—a half-mile swim, thirteen-mile bike, and five-kilometer run—was it. I was already a strong swimmer, so I only needed a few months of practice to improve my speed. I figured the bike segment would be easy. But getting in shape for the run took dedication.

During registration the night before the race, I almost chickened out and withdrew. One of the oldest participants, I was the only one who needed a size "large" T-shirt. Hard bodies and muscled thighs strode by me and my Walmart bicycle. If people noticed me at all, it was with an eye roll and a shrug of condescension. But courage and determination prevailed, and somehow I made it to the starting line the next morning.

When I finished the swimming segment, I was thrilled to see that I was ahead of about half the pack. I wriggled out of my wetsuit and mounted my bike. Two miles straight up and out of the canyon I pedaled, at a crawl. "On your left!" I heard, again and again, as everyone passed me. When I dismounted at the end of thirteen miles, my wobbly legs would hardly hold me up. I ran the three miles on what felt like a pair of toothpicks. There were only a few people behind me, and some were limping.

Finally the stadium came into view. I wanted to put on a burst of speed, like everyone else was doing, but my body wouldn't cooperate. Still, I felt a surge of exhilaration as I crossed the finish line. I had done it! I had trained for and completed a feat of strength and endurance. I hadn't given up. I had endured to the very end.

George arrived shortly before the end of the race, and came right over to inform me that two people had passed me on the way into the stadium. He didn't offer a single word of congratulation or praise or concern. Not expecting any, I merely nodded, grabbed a water bottle, and went to congratulate someone I knew. George became angry: I was taking too long. He was sweating in the hot sun. I saw him turn to leave, shouting at me to ride my bike home.

Seven more miles. Seven more miles, when I was already on the verge of collapse. But somehow I mustered the vigor needed for that additional achievement, even as my legs trembled with exhaustion and my face contorted with weeping. Somehow I did it. I did it for the same reason I did so many things in my marriage: because really, I had no choice. Where would I go but home, and how else would I get there? The sun, too hot for George even to stand in, beat down on me as I rode; the wind dried salty tear tracks down my face.

Something You Have Probably Already Figured Out

I can't help feeling a little guilty that I'm presenting a skewed portrait of my marriage. George wasn't all bad. I married him and bore his children because I loved him, and despite all the ways he hurt me, I continued to love him in ways that mattered very much to me. If there hadn't been something to redeem the marriage, I would have left ages ago. For twenty-nine years there was enough good in the marriage that I could justify putting up with someone who beat me, abused me, told me I was worthless.

And then, one day, there wasn't.

The Last Valentine's Day

Taking his cue from an article in a church magazine titled "Fidelity in Marriage: It's More Than You Think," George became distraught over any friendship I cultivated with anyone but him. One evening, he was driven to blows by his frustration over an online conversation I'd had with a man. One of our daughters came in the bedroom, worried by the noises she was hearing. She saw me curled into survival position, George hitting me repeatedly with a clenched fist on the back and side of my head. "Dad, stop it!" she pleaded. He stormed from the room. For hours, he recited his litany of grievances to the grown children gathered downstairs, while I lay upstairs, silent and still, staring at my downy blue striped coverlet. In the small hours of the morning, he crept into bed and we clung to each other in the marital embrace.

I awoke on Tuesday, February fourteenth. George had left for work, my youngest had gotten herself to school, and I was alone in the house. My eyes were puffy and gritty, so I closed them and lay back against the pillow. Random events from the night before spun through my mind, one in particular growing in significance. I recalled George hollering up the stairs: "I divorce you, I divorce you, I divorce you!" A year we'd spent in Saudi Arabia ensured our understanding of this thrice-repeated ritual statement. It was all a husband in that country had to say in order to legally divorce his wife. Our marriage was finished. I would always love George, but the spiritual ties that bound us had been severed. I called a friend and arranged a place to live on the other side of the continent. With a credit card, I booked a cross-country flight. I packed two suitcases. I called my visiting teacher to give me a ride to the airport. This Valentine's Day, I would honor no man, but I would give a gift of love to myself.

Two hours before my ride was to arrive, George came home unexpectedly. He had a bouquet of flowers. He had a pearl necklace and earrings. He had a sheepish expression on his face—until he saw the packed suitcases by my closet. Enraged, he grabbed my purse. I knew that if I didn't have my driver's license or credit card, I couldn't board the plane. So I caught hold of the bag and held on for dear life. Pulling me by the strap, George flung me left and right, into door frames and walls. He dragged me outside, where he wrested the handbag from me and attempted to throw it on the roof, out of my reach. "Give it back to me!" I screamed. "Help me! Help me!" Several neighbors came outside. "Help me!" I cried again. George let the purse drop. I seized it and ran inside the house, frantically locking the door behind me.

The police, the bishop, and my eldest daughter were called. I assume my daughter was the one with the key who let them all in the house. George, our bishop, and several police officers crowded into my bedroom. I could hardly look at all those men standing in my personal space, assessing me and my life. In order to make a report, the police wanted my driver's license. Hysterical, I refused to give it up.

I didn't care if there was any legal record of George's hitting me. I didn't care what these men thought of my marriage. I cared only that I had finally decided to escape and that this episode with the police might prevent it. I clung single-mindedly to the thought that my visiting teacher would arrive soon.

Everyone seemed to realize that George and I needed to be separated for a while; my daughter offered a bedroom in her home and the bishop suggested that the ward could put me up, or even spring for a hotel room. But I lugged my suitcases downstairs one by one, clutching my purse to my chest all the while. When I heard a car horn honk in the street, I carried out the only possessions from my old life that I would be permitted to call my own in my new life.

In the side yard, I saw my son-in-law, holding my two baby grandchildren in his arms. I went to hug them and say goodbye, but suddenly my daughter was in front of me, snarling like a mama bear. "Don't you dare go to them," she hissed. "I don't want them to remember this."

Questions I Wish Someone Would Ask George

If I was such a filthy slut and a worthless, wicked whore, why isn't he glad to be rid of me? Why would he want me back? Is it to prove he's the better person? Does he want the power that comes with possessing me? Or does he need some-one to blame and to forgive for all that is not right in his life and in his family? Perhaps he can't bear that I did what he said was impossible and wrong: I left him and found happiness on my own terms.

Two Nightmares

The night before I sat down to begin this essay, I had two horrifying dreams. In one, I grasped a bird by its bloody tail feathers and bludgeoned it to death. I didn't want to—I recoiled in horror and shame even as it happened—but I somehow couldn't stop.

The second dream was this: I was going to a fair and for some reason I had carried several heavy things in with me. I didn't want to drag them around, but it would have been inconvenient to return them to the car. I searched for a safe place to store bags, books, papers, and clothing for a while. I found some shelves and lockers where I could leave my belongings, but as I tried to situate them, they kept disappearing. I looked around, growing more and more agitated. Finally, from the corner of my eye, I saw George, snatching my pink purse from the pile. He didn't bother to look at me, just grinned to himself with satisfaction and pride.

Rocks and Flowers

I'd left home before—once for several weeks—but this separation was permanent. My children were ages twenty-seven, twenty-six, twenty-four, twenty-two, twenty, nineteen, seventeen, and thirteen; most of them had already left home for marriage, missions, and college. But they all felt like small ones abandoned by their mother. They were lost little Mormon children with a selfish parent who had ruined their eternal family. Daughter #1 spoke to me once on the phone and then determined that I was best left to "hit rock bottom" so that I could repent. But "rock bottom" is what I hit when I kept returning to a husband who beat me and claimed it was my fault. My eldest did her best to convince the others to have no contact with me. Most of them agreed, but some would occasionally respond to my overtures. Infrequently, my youngest would text back, or reply to a Facebook message. Finally she said, "We just have to realize that we have lost you."

George says he won't give me up. He's made a hundred changes, and friends and family say he's a new man. But sometimes, at 3 A.M., he'll start sending me texts. They're short and ungrammatical, filled with religious verbiage, and go on for an hour or more. Occasionally I wake up and read them, and they sound like the whispers I used to hear late at night.

Some messages aren't so bad. About a year after I left, as winter ended, he texted to say, "The bulbs are beginning to come up." I could picture the daffodils I had planted all around the trees in my front yard. I always loved spring in South Carolina, because it starts so early—often in February. Here in Washington, it's still so cold. But there are hardy plants that thrive here, and pots on my patio that will be greening up soon.

Sole

ANITA TANNER

But love has pitched his mansion in
The place of excrement;
For nothing can be sole or whole
That has not been rent.
—William Butler Yeats, "Crazy Jane Talks to the Bishop"

I gave my hand to you before I knew that space remained between us. We whispered altared promises and gazed at the mysterious puzzle of each other's eyes until we found the image of ourselves returning that stare. Puzzles before we knew how time and space like sieves releasing dailiness down a long corridor of mirrors, could separate the two of us who hand-in-hand embarked.

Not long until the children came, the last two of six while you were bishop. They were my focus since you were off to work, at church, or gone with those who needed care. We lived to please the faceless goddess of necessity who ruled our lives. We lost each other's eyes. How could we see clearly who the other was—or who we had been, reflected in them? The very church who sealed us to God divided us, alone together. I'd stop to gaze out windows of our home, missing you. I carried that knot of loneliness like a seventh child inside our years of child rearing.

In ways those years were fullness—so much to do, our duty clear: the church and family. But too soon the crown of marriage became meniscus, the rim of goblet, where fullness turned to spillage. We couldn't track, much less manage, the overflow: schools, graduations, missions, marriages, grandchildren, and through it all, unaccountably, we'd grown older and away from one another. Both wounders and wounded could only mean renewed resolve for many mornings to begin again. . . . We had space and time.

But scarcely thirty-five years together, one evening you weakened, your heart in stress—the beginning of the end. Too late was every diagnosis. Cancer all but filled your liver. Little could be done but buy you time, a few mere months. Every thought, medication, blessing, prayer—to one end, but in April you breathed your last.

The funeral morning I slouched from bed and dragged myself to the bathroom mirror: "Today's the day I bury my husband and the father of my children." Other details about those hours remain a cloister of smoky images that still singe my eyes.

With life reduced to inanimate, it's not *who what where when* or *how* but *why* that became my early widow's mantra amid rebirthing my identity, remaking a self to face an altered world: b.h., a.h., *before him, after him*. To claim a piece of happiness I must: Sole my feet to the ground every morning where his absence is so present. Remember joy and beauty in the rush of our meeting, courting, marrying, raising children. Live simply, one day at a time, sometimes one hour, maybe a few minutes. Face the way it is. Try to fall in love with the world again. Refuse to allow his memory to vanish. Turn toward my own good ending. Find sovereignty in involuntary solitude. Be deepened by heartbreak. Remake our marriage. Minimize regret.

PART IV

Second Chances

Figure 6. Lynne Burnett, left, and Janet Welling, September 2014, Provo, Utah. Courtesy of Aynn Ford Photography.

Lynne writes: "I didn't know that twenty years after I fell in love with Janet, we would share a moment at Provo's first Pride Festival showing our delight in being married."

Best Friends

LYNNE BURNETT

I married my best friend. I heard straight people say that for years but could never buy it. How could the subtle beauty of my relationships with women, the mutual understanding and respect, be replicated in a relationship with a man? If my experience and perception weren't like other women's, I needed to figure out where the disconnect began. You know how sometimes you'll try to check how "normal" you are by casually dropping a few seemingly innocent questions? In conversations with women, when someone would bring up sex (thank goodness for friends who bring up sex!), I would shyly ask, "Don't you find women's bodies more beautiful? I mean naked bodies? Right?" Invariably, the answer was yes, women generally find other women's bodies more beautiful than men's. Whew!—I'm normal.

It never occurred to me to carry things a step further and ask, "Don't you think it would be more fun to sleep with a woman than a man?" I know now that if I had asked that one, the answer from straight women would have been a resounding NO. Straight women might find other women's bodies more beautiful than a man's, but only gay women want other women in their beds.

At first I did marry a man. He was and still is a good friend. We had a lot in common, and I knew he would be kind. We had kids, we held church callings, we bought a home. He taught special education in the same school district for thirty years until finally retiring at age fifty-five. Me? I spent the first twelve years of our marriage as a homemaker, then held a string of jobs after that. Either way, at home or in the workplace, I was restless.

Working as a nurse's aide in a nursing home, I met Janet, one of the Mormon hippie mom types you find every now and then, clad in a denim jumper and Birkenstocks. We clicked instantly. At first I thought my attraction to her was due to our like-mindedness. But then one day, I watched her walk away from me down the hall—and realized that the feelings I was having were the "wrong" kind.

I immediately began therapy with LDS Family Services—where else does a Mormon mom go for help? The well-intentioned therapist admonished me that if I ever told Janet about my feelings for her, I would likely lose the best friend I could ever have—not to mention my husband, my children, my extended family, AND my church membership!

For a while, those horrible consequences made my choice seem easy. I stuffed my feelings deep inside, and Janet and I forged an amazing friendship. We both installed phones with really long cords in our kitchens so we could do all the things moms have to do and still stay on the phone together. When our kids were small, we'd bundle them into our respective cars and take them on outings together. The kids were happy to do something different, and we were happy to do something together.

When our kids got big enough to do without us for a few hours, we started taking time for ourselves, by ourselves. OK, I'll call it what it really was: we were dating. Not that we could have admitted it at the time. We were both painfully aware of the strong attraction between us that we didn't dare discuss. We knew we loved each other. But was it *love* love? We couldn't even *go* there. We were Mormon! What would we do with that?

I'll tell you what we did. For nine years, we nurtured a wonderful friendship, with and without our kids along. We even went on a few "double dates" with our respective husbands—awkward, but we were trying to make things work. We shared everything it felt safe to share.

Then, one May, we drove to Mesquite, Nevada, for a weekend escape. The few times we'd traveled together prior to that trip, I had made our hotel reservations and of course requested a room with two beds. But when we opened the door of the room the first night of that trip, a solitary king-sized bed loomed before us. I turned to Janet, horrified that she might think I had done this on purpose. I stuttered out an apology—it was a mistake, and of course I would go back to reception and get us another room. She laughed, a bit uncomfortably, and said, "We're big girls and this is a big bed. We'll be OK. You don't need to change the room."

That night, we each clung to the edge of our side of that big bed, as much space as possible between us, terrified that an errant limb might accidentally brush the other person and ignite some kind of flame. But despite that tense night, we passed the weekend just fine, talking nonstop and laughing ourselves silly.

We were fine, that is, until the drive back to our families in Utah. Each time we returned from a trip together, Janet would grow very quiet and more than a little sad. As we drove north on I-15, she began to cry. "I don't know how much longer we can go on like this," she said.

My heart rose to my throat. I swallowed hard. "Like how?" I asked.

"Like this!" she said. "Pretending we're just friends, when we both know we're more than that."

She gripped the steering wheel and stared straight ahead, waiting for me to respond. For one moment, I was excited, thinking, "Here it is! We're finally going to be honest!" But reality and the magnitude of change this would mean for both of us was too heavy. "We can't talk about this," I said. "I do know what you mean, but we can't talk about it. We can't ever say it, out loud. We'd lose too much."

I was nauseated with fear and tension, but deep in my belly, all throughout my heart, there was also a feeling of elation and relief: I finally knew, really *knew*, that Janet felt the same about me as I did about her.

At least, that's how I remember the drive home. Janet doesn't remember crying at all. She remembers admitting that she wanted to touch me during the entire weekend and felt very distracted by that desire. She remembers giving in and touching the inside of my arm, saying, "That's just what I've wanted to do all weekend." But either way, there was no resolution.

I returned to a husband frantic with anger and worry. My doctor had been trying to reach me all weekend, and my husband insisted that I hadn't even told him where I was going. Given that we had four kids at home and I was seldom irresponsible, I found and still find that almost impossible to believe. . . . But if it's true, it's an indication of all the craziness and confusion I felt: forgetting to share crucial information, too focused on my time alone with Janet.

Doctors rarely call you on the weekend unless something big is going on. So I called my doctor, and he read me the pathology report of a biopsy he had done the previous week. Even though I'm a nurse, it was very difficult to understand. He had to tell me twice that I had uterine cancer.

Finding out that you have a life-threatening disease is often a serious "come to Jesus" moment for people. It certainly was for me. Forty-five years old, I examined everything in my life. I decided that whatever time remained to me, I wouldn't spend it being dishonest—not with myself, not with the rest of the world.

Throughout my illness and recovery, Janet was my most dedicated visitor, staying after everyone else went home. I treasured the ordinary but thoughtful gifts she brought daily during my recovery: broccoli (my favorite comfort food), a Winnie the Pooh bookmark, reading material. But most of all, she brought love. Her intangible gestures forged an even stronger connection. I felt increasingly estranged from my temple marriage and the LDS church. I knew that no matter what the consequences might be to my "eternal salvation," I would divorce, leave the church of my birth, and somehow come out of the closet.

It was an incredible time in my life. I allowed all those feelings of attraction, deep love, and budding lesbian lust to explode. I kept a journal. I wrote torrid love letters to Janet that I never delivered. Because my confrontation with myself about what I felt for Janet was so serious, I couldn't help but bring her into some of it. We began having more honest conversations. We acknowledged our feelings. It was terrifying. We discussed potential consequences, though neither of us could comprehend them.

Over the course of the next year, I separated from my husband and left the LDS church. Those losses were real and I mourned them even as I rejoiced in my new opportunities. To my relief and surprise, my children did not disown me. The same went for my extended family and most of my friends. They loved me as they always had.

I began going to wonderful support group activities with Parents, Families, and Friends of Lesbians and Gays. Janet wouldn't go with me. My friendship with her was one of the few deeply affected by my coming out of the closet. She distanced herself from me and immersed herself in her family, home, and church.

Our meetings during the next nine years were infrequent and painful. I left Utah to complete my schooling. Occasionally one of us would phone and we would try to connect, but it was obvious we were choosing totally different paths.

Until her path veered off in another direction. Her marriage was unhappy, her children grown and out of the house. Her steadfast commitment to the LDS church changed in 2008 when it supported Proposition 8, repealing gay marriage in California. She could no longer associate herself with a church that could be so bigoted and unkind. She also separated from her husband of twenty-four years.

Shortly thereafter, I moved back to Utah. I had just ended a relationship so painful it made me doubt my ability to choose well. I knew I wanted to see Janet again but was wary of the consequences. We'd had little contact during the "dark years." She didn't really know me as a lesbian. And she had barely come out—what if she changed her mind and wanted to be Mormon again? What if the chemistry that both sustained and terrified us had somehow disappeared?

Seeing her was overwhelming. She hugged me. We didn't want to let go. One of the first things she did was touch the inside of my arm. She was my same Janet. Within minutes, we both knew: the best parts of our relationship had survived. We hadn't run out of things to say to each other. At times there would be an odd moment and one of us would say, "Lynne, it's me, Janet." Or "Janet, it's me, Lynne." And we would remember.

We were married in Victoria, British Columbia, nearly two years after our reunion. The marriage was performed by a sweet female wedding commissioner and witnessed by our hotel clerk and his lesbian roller derby friend. After our return to the United States, we had a beautiful reception, attended by many friends and family who lovingly (or at least tolerantly) stand by our sides. We feel like the luckiest girls in the world.

This is my marriage: life with a partner who thinks I'm the best thing since sliced cheese. I feel the same about her. I share my thoughts and hopes and failures and fears, knowing that she wants to know me completely. I bite my tongue now and then because I've tried to learn what hurts and don't want to cause her pain. We want the best for each other. I appreciate her and let her know this often. We bring each other joy. Sometimes we giggle into the night as if we're having a 24/7 slumber party. On the best days it's a dream come true: I'm finally married to my best friend. On the not so good days, we've cried and tried to make smoother the path we're on together. Given what we've been through to get here, we know we have a good thing that will last. We both say, "Finally."

Becoming a Couple

JARI CARLTON CANNON

John was the youngest of twelve in an affluent LDS family; we met when I was a junior in high school. The proud owner of a shiny, new, black Honda CRX, he let me drive it 100 mph going south on I-15, just for the rush. He introduced me to great music, including "There Is a Light that Never Goes Out" by the Smiths, "Tom Sawyer" by Rush, and "Comfortably Numb" by Pink Floyd. He was voted best dressed boy the year we met, and, after our friendship turned into something more, wrote me the sweetest love notes ever. He was different from other boys, more mature. He always had time for me. Together we discovered and explored Jackson Hole, Wyoming; Silverton, Colorado; as well as Lamb's Canyon, Park City, the more exciting parts of Salt Lake City, and countless other places in northern Utah.

Things could not have been better. I celebrated with him when, midway into my senior year in high school, he received his call to serve in the Korea Pusan mission. He would be gone for two years but we would write weekly. We decided I would date others while he was gone but my heart would belong to him. And that's essentially what happened.

When John came home, we picked up where we'd left off. But it was different this time around. He'd changed, and I probably had, too. Little things seemed off—he told me his mission president hadn't liked him and that he'd caught one of his companions going through his things. I chalked it up to cultural differences and personality clashes, but the suspicion gnawed at me that there might be more to the story.

Even though I couldn't put my finger on whatever it was that didn't seem quite right, this was, after all, John, my friend and confidant with whom I'd shared so much. So in 1993, despite some reservations, we were married in the Salt Lake Temple and settled into newlywed life. John got himself a fancy briefcase and began working on his real estate license, and I continued my undergraduate studies and held a part-time job as well. It was a very typical beginning to a Mormon marriage, and the future seemed as bright as the latches on that briefcase.

But after only a few short weeks he began to distance himself emotionally and physically from me. Given our long history, his behavior was as inexplicable as it was painful. Something was wrong. I came to believe he must be hiding something. When he'd leave on a Saturday to hold an open house or take a couple house-hunting, I began to search, though I didn't know what for. I went through every drawer in our small home, opened every closet, checked under the mattress and searched through the boxes left packed up in the basement. It made me feel dirty, like I was the one doing something wrong. I had been told that trust was the foundation to a good marriage, but something was dreadfully amiss, and it didn't feel right to trust John this time.

But I found nothing. I had dated a fair share of guys in high school but had been emotionally "serious" with only a handful of them. Add to that the fact that I was married at twenty-one and the Mormon prohibitions against premarital sex and cohabitation: I was pretty naïve. But I had instincts and I heeded them. I couldn't explain away the fact that within a few months of our temple marriage, John was telling me I didn't look sexy in my garments; nor could I resolve his obvious sexual dissatisfaction and frustration, especially since he refused to discuss it—aside from criticizing me.

His locked briefcase was the only place he could be hiding his secrets, and I became obsessed. After weeks of checking almost every time he brought it in the house, I finally found his briefcase unlocked. While John mowed the lawn one unseasonably warm April afternoon, I quickly and quietly placed the briefcase on the floor and opened it, my heart pounding and my hands shaking. Maybe I would find nothing scandalous, in which case I could put my fears to rest and work on my marriage. But maybe, just maybe, the answer to whatever was happening in my marriage was contained in that usually locked briefcase. I opened it. Mystery solved. The briefcase was literally bursting with dozens and dozens of pornographic magazines and videotapes.

My heart broke. I knew next to nothing of such things. My mind immediately raced back to a time during middle school when my friends and I had found a pornographic magazine in a nearby parking lot. We innocently opened the magazine to see what it was, agreed it was disgusting, threw it in a nearby dumpster, and never talked about it again. Even so, I could still recall clearly the pictures I had seen that day, and I knew my husband had similar pictures in his head all the time. Was this the reason he had distanced himself from me?

I scanned the magazines with curiosity and revulsion. There was no question in my mind that these images were the root of our problems. I'd always had pretty good self-esteem, but I knew right off I couldn't compete with these women. I now knew what he found arousing, and it wasn't me.

I pulled myself together, wiped the tears from my eyes and cheeks, and stood up tall, breathing deeply. I hoped to confront John with what little remained of my dignity. Then, I went to the front door and calmly asked him to come inside for a minute. He turned off the mower and, after what seemed like an excruciatingly long time, came into the room where I sat, his open briefcase before me.

I don't remember saying anything to him. I didn't need to. Our eyes met for a blisteringly painful moment, and then he hung his head. "I'm so embarrassed," he said. "I'll throw everything in the garbage and I won't get more. I promise."

And that was that. While he picked up the contents of his briefcase and took them to the trash outside, I sat on the floor and sobbed. *Maybe he can let this go and we'll be OK*, I thought, but I didn't believe it.

I didn't see how habits that had clearly become ingrained over time could be eradicated with his few words of reassurance, and I was painfully aware of the fact that he could get more whenever he wanted. Over the next few weeks, I asked him countless questions: *How long had he been involved with pornography? Where did he get it? When did he look at all that stuff?* But he refused to discuss it.

We had been married only a few months and I didn't want to admit, to myself or anyone else, that I had made such a monumental error in judgment, so I tried every way I could think of to fix our relationship. But it was hopeless. For all my trying, I couldn't trust him, and he seemed uninterested in regaining my trust. About a year later, we got into an argument, he threatened divorce for the umpteenth time since the discovery of the pornography, and I finally gave in. I called my parents to announce the news (something I had to do to make it final), and my eternal marriage ground to a halt after sixteen miserable months.

I felt humiliated and alone. In 1994, porn addiction wasn't something that came up in Relief Society. I didn't know anyone else who had this problem, and I couldn't point to anyone my age who was divorced. When friends asked me why John and I divorced, I told them I would prefer not to rehash things; that we had grown apart. I didn't know if I responded in that way to protect his reputation or to protect mine, but sometime later, after countless sessions with a psychologist who specialized in addiction, I realized my protecting him was only hurting me.

After that, whenever someone close to me asked, I told them the real reason. I remember one friend being shocked—she had assumed we divorced because he was gay! I opened up first to my parents, then to my siblings, and then to my grandparents, afraid all along that someone would jump to the conclusion that there was something wrong with me. After all, I had always understood that "it takes two to tango." Even with the support and understanding of family and close friends, I had never felt more alone, especially since it seemed to me that the other young wives I met were all so happily married. Of course I know now that many of those young wives suffered similarly then and that many more suffer today as the epidemic of sexual impropriety and infidelity escalates. I understand their heartbreak and damaged self-esteem.

Thankfully I had never given up on my dream to attend law school, and in 1995, I began my studies at the University of Utah College of Law. I started dating again, but kept myself emotionally distant. I was in no hurry to settle down. Even so, I felt obligated to tell the guys I dated about my past. They had a right to know I had been married, but should I divulge that fact right off the bat or wait until we'd had a few dates? Both scenarios seemed wrong. In the end, I usually disclosed my status as a divorcee after a couple of dates—before things got serious, so he could walk away if he chose. However, the fact I had been married and divorced mattered little to the guys I dated. This surprised me, especially since my psychologist had warned me it would "raise a red flag." I knew I would be concerned dating a divorced man and would have a lot of questions if things were reversed. But none of them asked questions or judged me. I couldn't help wondering if all these nice Mormon boys were understanding because they, too, had their own experiences with pornography but thankfully did not become addicted. I didn't know the answer to that question, but the optimist in me pushed that notion aside.

Halfway through my second year of law school, a guy I'd dated a few times in high school pestered my best friend to line us up. He hadn't been unattractive or a jerk in high school, but he had seemed self-absorbed and arrogant. She kept bugging me, but I couldn't see a reason to give him another chance.

Eventually I relented. It had been ten years since I'd seen Chris. I didn't know what to expect when I opened my door that night—maybe balding, maybe overweight—but he was neither. We went to dinner and a movie; the conversation was relaxed. He'd served a mission to what was then Czechoslovakia and currently worked as a brokerage trader. That was more than I had expected of him. What didn't surprise me was that even though he was a year older than I, he had only completed a couple of years of college. Initially judgmental, I learned that the reason for this was that he had taken time to travel. I envied that. While I had been stuck in a loveless and demeaning marriage, he had hiked through the Himalayas to the base camp of Mt. Everest, taught English to Korean kids, and played basketball in Israel.

Whatever the reason, we hit it off. Like the other guys, he was unconcerned about my divorce and we continued to date.

Chris was everything John was not. While John had been quiet, introverted, and calculated, Chris was talkative, extroverted, and direct. If he thought something, he said it out loud, no matter the repercussions. It was refreshing. I had been lied to for I didn't know how many years and I needed to hear the truth.

He made me homemade bread, wrote and performed songs for me on his guitar, put up with my road rage, and defended the matter-of-fact nudity in movies such as *Schindler's List*. Given my past experiences, I felt that nudity in films was always inappropriate, but the fact that he would openly disagree told me I could trust him. Here was someone who told me what he really thought, not what he thought I wanted to hear. Things intensified quickly. By month seven we were engaged and by month nine we were married.

Yet despite my love for him, or perhaps because of it, the walls I had built around my heart during and after my divorce did not come down on our wedding day. Instead, they held steady, every brick, for the next two years. I married Chris because I trusted him, but even in marriage I still kept a certain distance, just in case.

In 1998, we moved to the D.C. area so Chris could attend law school and I could begin my career as an attorney. We heard about the Marine Corps Marathon and agreed it would be a fantastic way to see the city—the race began at Arlington Cemetery, then followed a complicated route past such landmarks as the Lincoln Memorial, the Washington Monument, the Capitol, the Supreme Court, and the Pentagon before it ended at the Iwo Jima Memorial. The amazing route wasn't the only attraction; Chris wanted to add the Marine Corps Marathon to the list of marathons he had already run, while I wanted to check "ran a marathon" off my bucket list. But we had very different ideas of what it would take. Chris had never trained for a marathon and had done well in several, finishing one race just fifteen minutes shy of the time needed to qualify for the Boston Marathon. He reasoned that the constant exercise from training would only cause an injury and was therefore not only unnecessary but also ill-advised. (He was only partly serious; the real reason was that he hated training.) I believed that training was crucial and looked forward to the exercise.

For all my good intentions, however, our training regimen was dismal. In the four weeks leading up to the race, we jogged only three miles two or three times a week. Our longest run was five miles. My weekly total probably never exceeded ten miles. I was wholly unprepared to run 26.2 miles and I knew it. But I decided I had to do it anyway.

My first marriage, with all its secrets, had primed me to pretend I could do things when I knew I couldn't, to say I was fine when I knew I wasn't, and to decline help even when I knew I needed it badly. Overcoming that kind of self-deception takes time and positive experiences. Chris believed absolutely that I could finish the entire race despite my lack of preparation. In the days leading up to the race, I realized his seeming obliviousness to my very real fears and doubts wasn't because he didn't care about me but because he believed in me and wanted me to believe in myself.

That realization caused the walls to begin to crumble. It dawned on me that asking him for help wasn't a sign of weakness but rather something two people who love one another do. I didn't know anything about running a marathon. Chris, despite his aversion to preparation, at least knew the basics: how to attach the timing chip to my shoe, what to eat, what to take with me, where to find a bathroom, and especially what I should do if I just couldn't complete the race. Where would we meet? How would I get back to the starting line?

So I asked him to attach my timing chip to my shoe. Then I popped an Advil because he told me my body would start to hurt. I took to heart his promise that he wouldn't leave my side even though I knew that would mean a bad marathon time published next to his name.

The first few miles were easy. Adrenaline kicked in and the time and distance flew by. The many fellow runners made it almost impossible to slow down. Endless cheering crowds lined each side of the street, boosting my spirits. Before I knew it I was at the halfway mark. But miles 13 through 18 were another story. As the crowds and runners now stretched thin, I "hit the wall" and seriously doubted myself. Keeping his promise, Chris stuck by me, literally running circles around me. He encouraged me to get to the next mile, and then the next. When I urged him to run ahead because I didn't want to ruin his time, he dismissed my pleas and said he would much rather see me finish than improve his own record. I think in the end, with all that circling, he ran a marathon and a half. But he kept his word and, hand in hand, we crossed the finish line together. It was at that moment that we became a real couple, equal parts strong and equal parts vulnerable.

It's strange that this relatively unimportant event would prompt such profound change in my life. But this one race did exactly that—and not just for me. Chris later told me that it was the most meaningful single event in our marriage prior to the birth of our first child.

I'm not sure why we were willing to enter into such a serious covenant as marriage when we both knew the scars from my first one hadn't completely healed, but we did. The subsequent years brought us four kids, multiple career changes, and everything that raising a family entails. Our kids now range in age from twelve to four. They aren't yet old enough to know my story, but I've often wondered what I'll tell them: not necessarily to wait until a certain age to marry, nor to date for a certain amount of time before marrying, nor not to marry at all, nor to marry no matter what. I think the answer is to trust themselves. Had I not trusted my instincts in my marriage to John, I might not have discovered the contents of his briefcase and might still be suffering, wondering what I was doing wrong. And had I not trusted Chris on that October day in 1999, not only would I not have finished the race, I may not have discovered, as I ultimately did, what it feels like to trust someone enough to love him.

Its Own Reward

C. L. HANSON

"It's too late to say no now," I thought. "The decision's already been made; the dresses and cakes and decorations have all been bought. . . ."

I stood before the justice of the peace, surprised by my own hesitation as I listened to the vow I was supposed to agree to. I had sort of followed my nose all the way to my wedding; in more than two years of planning, I somehow hadn't asked myself whether I was ready to make this commitment for life. It was too late to do otherwise, though, so I said, "I do."

I was raised Mormon, so it's not surprising that I grew up believing that my worth was based on my ability to attract and land a desirable man. Sure, it's not just Mormonism—girls also get these sorts of negative messages about their own value and importance from the culture at large. But Mormon culture shouts them with a megaphone. Women are explicitly excluded from the church's leadership hierarchy, so they generally derive their status in the Mormon community through their husbands and children. Being the wife of a bishop, for example, is a high status role, and having many children who serve LDS missions and marry in the temple is prestigious too.

In our chapel, there was a plaque on the wall with the names of all of the Eagle Scouts our ward had produced. As I recall, it was donated by the bishop's wife, who had four sons. In the court of honor in which a boy is awarded the rank of Eagle, his mother would be decorated with a pin as well. The moms would wear their pins proudly and joke amongst themselves that they were the ones who had really done the work to earn the award—and it was funny because it was true. My brothers' names ended up on the plaque, but we girls didn't have such plaques or ceremonies honoring our achievements. Instead, we could aspire to get in on the honor by someday producing sons.

Starting from age twelve, I got church lessons about marriage and motherhood, and I was encouraged to look at my male peers in terms of their romantic potential much earlier than that. Memories of being matched up with little boys from my ward extend back as far as my memory goes.

I recently read a memoir by a Mormon woman that reminded me of my own experience. The memoir consisted entirely of a huge sequence of guys she met and her flirty conversations with them. It's the same story I was writing in my own journal as a teen. It's a story that says, "I think the most interesting thing about me is the guy who might be interested in me."

There's a comedy type in TV and movies that I hated: the unattractive woman who's madly in love with the story's male protagonist. Everyone gets to laugh at her pathetic attempts to throw herself at a guy way out of her league. I absolutely didn't want to be that character. Yet I was incredibly and sincerely nerdy and socially challenged. Too shy to make friends, I would wander around in my own fantasy world, talking to myself, making the other kids think I was nuts, or at least very weird. To make matters worse, I was a late bloomer and lacked the assets to make boys spontaneously notice me. I found myself in real danger of being that character.

I could have escaped this fate by deciding that I didn't need a boyfriend. But I was attracted to boys. My culture put them at the center of attention, and I couldn't help but want one for myself. Despite not growing breasts until I was nearly sixteen, I had spontaneously discovered masturbation well before the age of twelve; I had a very healthy libido. So my formative romantic experiences were characterized by unrequited sexual desire as well as unrequited love. I was determined to beat the odds and attract myself a boyfriend or two.

Available Mormon girls, unfortunately, vastly outnumbered available Mormon guys in the suburbs of Minneapolis where I grew up. In high school, I found that I could beat the odds by choosing math and science nerds instead of Mormon guys. Not only did I share their interests, but it was a community where the gender ratio was heavily tipped in my favor for adventures in love and lust.

Then my parents sent me to BYU.

BYU was not the best place for me. As a senior in high school, I'd stopped believing Mormonism's truth claims and rejected a lot of things I'd learned from the church. In particular, I embraced feminism and rejected the church's sexism. Yet some of the sexist messages were too deeply ingrained for me to recognize and reject entirely.

Even though I lacked the independence and self-confidence to organize myself a non-BYU alternative, I pitied those girls who were just there to earn their MRS! I fancied myself a feminist and a math whiz—and I even found myself a boyfriend who lived in his own trailer in a trailer park on the far end of Provo. I managed to sneak in some partying with other closet nonbelievers, but I was focused on my studies and highly motivated to get out of there ASAP. I graduated in only three years and lined up a fellowship for myself in mathematics at a good graduate school on the East Coast.

I was finally free of the church's control and my parents.' Financially at least. Mentally, perhaps partway. The summer between BYU and grad school, I told myself, "Now I'll be surrounded by really desirable guys instead of those silly LDS returned missionaries. Now I'll be able to find myself a husband."

And it was almost easier done than said! The month I arrived at graduate school, I went to a bar with my new fellow grad students to celebrate my twenty-first birthday. That night I hooked up with Tor, the tall, blond Bostonian who became my first husband.

Within a few months, we were engaged. The following fall, we moved in together and started planning our wedding. Sure, we could have just lived together as boyfriend-and-girlfriend, but I was already in my early twenties and didn't see any particular reason to wait—despite the fact that this was the mid-1990s and most of my secular peers were in absolutely no rush to get married.

At the time, I still harbored a bit of competitive spirit with my younger sister Cathy, who entered BYU herself the year I started graduate school. Cathy and I were two years apart in age, but my mom had named us "Carrie and Cathy" in accordance with her childhood fantasy of having twin girls. Mom even used to make us matching dresses to wear to church. This wouldn't have been a problem were it not for the fact that Cathy and I were struggling to define our own identities while trapped between two brothers who held the keys to my parents' dreams and status. John was the golden boy whose brilliance outshone the sun (as far as my mother and our ward were concerned), and adorable little Ben went by his middle name because my Mom had wanted him to have a name with a leading first initial—"R. Benjamin"—in anticipation of his one day becoming an LDS general authority.

In the manner of close siblings, Cathy and I were friends—yet locked in mortal combat over the few crumbs of parental attention left for the girls. (As for the slim pickings that remained for Laurie, the youngest—I shudder to even think about it.) Of the two of us, I considered myself not only "the smart one" but also "the pretty one"—but such subjective estimations count for nothing. The proof of the pudding is in the eating, and in Mormon-girl terms, that's the husband she lands. Consequently, my thoughts about my wedding didn't center on the idea that this man is the person I truly want to spend my life and raise a family with. My thoughts were more like, "Yay!! I won!!!"

I was also seduced by the beautiful images in the tower of bridal magazines I'd bought myself. This was ironic because my mom had taught me not to fantasize about a big wedding ceremony. A Mormon temple wedding didn't involve a long walk down the aisle to stand before the congregation to say "I do." You don't even say "I do," she explained; you say "Yes." So the big church wedding was never a fantasy of mine, but that didn't stop me from dreaming about how gorgeous I'd be in my dress at the receptions, nor did it keep me from imagining all of that beautiful china, crystal, and silverware we'd get!

My parents could certainly have afforded to throw a big reception with a dinner and everything, but it wasn't even entertained as a possibility. In my experience to that time, the ceremony itself was a quiet affair, and then you traveled to each spouse's home town to throw an open house in the LDS meetinghouse, invite the whole ward and anyone else you know, and serve little cups of mints. The very idea of serving all the guests a sit-down dinner (with drinks!) seemed like a crazy extravagance—not to mention an unnecessary limitation on the pool of people who might give you presents. (On the flip side, while some people are generous beyond the call of duty, many figure out that if they're not invited to a real reception, then they're not socially obligated to offer a real gift.)

Being an atheist, I rejected the idea that a marriage ceremony creates a marriage through an incantation pronounced by an authority—magically transforming sex from a heinous sin to a sacrament. In my mind, the legal ceremony was simply one of the steps in the evolution of the relationship. So I decided on having a small civil ceremony that no one should travel to attend (I didn't even invite my future mother-in-law, which hurt and disappointed her), and then having three receptions: one in Minnesota, one in Boston for Tor's family, and one for our friends in New Jersey where we lived. The one for our fellow grad students was a wedding-themed postdinner drinking party, but the other two were just open houses. In Minnesota, once the guests had left, my out-of-town Mormon relatives were treated to big buckets of KFC, ordered as an afterthought—why would they need more than that? So, despite rejecting Mormonism, I perversely managed to get married Mormon-style.

In so many fairy tales, the only thing after the wedding is "and they lived happily ever after"—that's the end, that's what you get once you're married. But I discovered too late that the wedding not only didn't guarantee a happy ending, it wasn't even the end of the story—and frankly, I didn't want it to be. Before the wedding, I'd hardly thought about whether I really wanted to be with Tor for the rest of my life because, hey, who doesn't want "happily ever after"? If the best way to get it is marriage, what Mormon girl would hesitate over the commitment of taking a husband when she's got one lined up? Unfortunately—*stupidly!*—I had to cross that line and get to the other side of the commitment to see that I wasn't ready to be there. Tor was a great boyfriend, but I didn't want to have kids nor grow old with him. I didn't want it at that point in my life, nor did I want to be locked into that future. I had just completed one exciting and successful round of "get a husband," and I wanted to play some more!

Tor and I returned from our wedding tour just as the new semester started— and with it came the next batch of graduate students—some of them more advanced students arriving from other countries. And then I fell in love, but hard.

Of course that's not how I interpreted it at the time. It seemed just another silly infatuation—one made all the more inconvenient by the fact that I was now married and, hence, shouldn't be out looking for new romance. But instead of fading away, the infatuation grew progressively stronger.

Emmanuel was as socially awkward as anyone in the math department, but so cute with his outrageous French accent! He was an exotic French-variety math nerd. Since he was one of the star students, his shyness made him seem distant and aloof—but I could make him laugh. Every day I would look forward to the coffee hour when I would have the opportunity to exchange a few words with him. All my daydreams were devoted to remembering our exchanges and imagining the witty things I could say to him next.

I had to remind myself that I was *married*. I was a new type of animal: *a married woman*. Even if I wasn't entirely sure that's what I wanted to be, I knew for sure that I didn't want to be a failure at marriage—doomed to wind up like Liz Taylor, with a string of so many failed marriages that people lose count.

I made a friend who, like me, was trying to stick out her marriage. Monica was a Jewish girl who'd gotten a grand stadium-scoreboard proposal and a big rock from an up-and-coming stock broker. As with me, Monica's "Yay!!! I won!!" reaction had distracted her from asking herself whether she really wanted to be married to that guy. Her conclusion was essentially that marriage is for appearances, and affairs make it bearable.

Monica's advice seemed reasonable, so I propositioned my new love. Twice. And he refused, twice. We didn't talk about it, and I assumed that his refusal was because he didn't find me attractive. From that point on, I mostly left him alone for the rest of our mutual graduate studies. I still feared becoming that comic character throwing herself at the uninterested man. I found some other affairs to put my sorrows to bed.

The pointless affairs were the part of my story that makes me go, "*What the hell was I thinking?!?!*" But I'd like to take that question out of the realm of the rhetorical and ask myself sincerely, "What was I thinking?" Not to excuse or justify my choices, but to understand them.

If it had been about wanting more sex or more sexual variety, then I'm sure I could have had a joyful open relationship with Tor. But that wasn't it. It was that almost all my fellow female grad students were unmarried and out having all these fascinating relationship intrigues—crazy breakups and flings and love triangles—that sounded so exciting! Even the student who introduced me to Monica had a boyfriend she was cheating on at one point.

Also, given the unrequited love I was suffering from, I'd concluded that true love is tragedy. Love isn't about happiness: it's about the delirium of reveling in passionate sadness—drinking and singing along with sad songs and feeling more alive as emotion fills your whole heart. Because I was so miserable myself, hurting someone else somehow didn't seem like a big deal—especially since I also wanted some distraction from the stress of math research.

Another factor was that I had rejected the idea that marriage had the magical ability to make sex good or bad. I'd learned for myself that it wasn't true. So it seemed logical to reject the corollary that "adultery is bad because it's sex outside of marriage." The message "adultery is depraved sexy sex that went rogue and escaped the marriage corral" was so glaring that it overshadowed the real reason not to cheat on your spouse, namely that it's a betrayal of a promise to someone you care about. When you've learned your moral framework as a series of "don't do X because it's a commandment," rejecting that framework means figuring out a new moral framework on your own. Sometimes that requires a bit of trial and error.

Around the same time, my sister Cathy was at BYU, busy winning her own round of "get a husband." And what's worse, her new husband, Erik, was as tall as Tor!

That was when it finally sank in how destructive it is to treat this critical life-decision—whom to marry—as a competition or a status symbol that signals your worth as a person. I didn't want to "win" against Cathy. I wanted to be nothing but sincerely and genuinely happy for her that she found such a great guy. And Erik is a great guy. They've been happily married for fifteen years and have three adorable kids.

My approach was all wrong. Sticking with a marriage just for the sake of sticking with it—and making it unspeakably worse in order to make it bearable—was about the wrongest possible solution. It was time for me to stop wrecking my own life and Tor's. I moved into my own apartment and began divorce proceedings. (Unsurprisingly, Monica did the same.)

The following spring, Tor, Emmanuel, and I all finished our PhDs and went our separate ways. My lingering secret fantasy romance with Emmanuel had led me to teach myself to speak French fluently, and—figuring that he wasn't interested in me—I set off for an adventure in France on my own. But I couldn't forget him. That December, I reconnected with him through mutual friends while he was in Paris visiting family for Christmas.

Then, when we finally talked seriously, I found that he was, in fact, quite interested in me—he simply hadn't wanted to get involved in a tawdry affair with a married woman. In retrospect, I'm glad he refused. Had he accepted my offer, there's a good chance that we would have had a quick fling that burned through the love I felt for him, and then he would have been forever tainted in my mind by the shame I feel about that part of my life. He would have been wound up in the web of deceit and lies and misery that I would rather leave behind. As it is, the fact that he had too much self-respect to become someone's plaything made him that much more desirable.

Soon after our reunion in Paris, I moved back to New Jersey where Emmanuel had a postdoctoral position. There, we lived together as an engaged couple for two years before marriage—the same length of time I'd lived with Tor before marriage. But although the length of time was the same, the two intervals couldn't be more different. Those few extra years made a huge difference in my maturity level. In my late twenties I understood myself better, and I understood better what I wanted from life. And the experience of going through a wedding and divorce taught me not to take that decision lightly again.

Again I got married in a small civil ceremony, though this time it was mostly because it was simpler for various reasons to get married legally in the United States before moving to France, where we held the reception—which included a dinner and drinks and dancing all night. There were no open houses or cups of mints. I'd attended a number of friends' weddings in the meantime, and I'd learned that the party is not just an unimportant, obligatory sideline! The trick is to invite the people who really want to celebrate the joyous union, rather than trying to invite every single person you know. Because all the guests had to travel to the reception (we had just moved to Bordeaux where Emmanuel had gotten a job as a professor), we rented a château so that all the guests could stay as late as they liked. And since Emmanuel's mother's hobby is gourmet cooking, we had a fantastic buffet without breaking the bank.

Today we've been married for twelve happy years and have two wonderful children.

I realize that the "me" character in this tale probably comes off as very selfish and foolish. I won't try to temper or disguise it—in my early twenties, I really was immature, and, yes, selfish. The two things I'll say in my defense are, first, that I sincerely believed the terrible messages I'd been taught about women and marriage, so of course I acted on them. Second, I'm willing to admit my failings and mistakes, which gives me the opportunity to learn from and correct them.

It bothers me when people claim that no-fault divorce harms "the family." Without it, I wouldn't have my happy family. Looking at statistics—and even at my own circle of friends—I've learned that these sorts of "starter marriages" are actually quite common.

Treating short "starter marriages" as standard fare may be disrespectful of the seriousness of the commitment of marriage. But it's also disrespectful to encourage young people to jump into marriage at the first reasonable opportunity—enticing them with status and distracting them with party preparations and dreams of bridal glamor, and forbidding them any sexual outlet unless they are legally bound to the one and only person they're allowed to have intercourse with—rather than encouraging them to take this decision seriously, and to wait if they're not sure they're ready.

Because I've gotten past the LDS training that made me define my worth in terms of the men I attracted, I believe more strongly than I ever did as a Mormon that a marriage relationship can be a comfort and a joy. People don't need to be tricked and then locked into it—marriage is its own reward!

Sacrifice and Sacrament

A Mormon Marriage

MARGARET M. TOSCANO

I'm a sixth-generation Mormon woman who was excommunicated on November 30, 2000, for my feminist writings advocating priesthood ordination for women and the worship of our Heavenly Mother based on her full godhood and membership in the godhead with the Father. I've long argued that the current structure and doctrine of the LDS church hinder the equal partnership between men and women it claims to embrace. According to church doctrine, my excommunication ended my eternal sealing to my husband, Paul, a convert to Mormonism. Because we were married in the Salt Lake Temple in September 1978, our four daughters born to us between 1979 and 1984 were "born under the covenant" of our marriage, and thus are part of our eternal family. Of course, when Paul was excommunicated in 1993 for his criticism of the Mormon priesthood hierarchy, we were told that our sealings to each other and our children were severed and that we had no hope of celestial glory, unless we repented and yielded to priesthood counsel.

While my faith in God and my belief in Mormon theology has waxed, waned, and metamorphosed over the years, the idea of eternal relationships still appeals to me. If there is an afterlife where we retain some kind of individual identity, and I have some hope that there is, then I want to be connected to those I have loved so much here and now. I don't believe that LDS leaders have the power to break bonds that are sealed by God's love—or by our love for each other. When Jesus tells Peter in Matthew 16:19 that he has the keys to bind and loose on earth, it's only what has already been bound and loosed in heaven, as I read the text. The ultimate power resides in the divine alone, which is what is meant in Mormon scripture by something being ratified by the Holy Spirit of Promise. And perhaps our own desires are crucial here too. Do we all ultimately get what we want, for good or ill? I think we do. I believe that the sealing bond between

Paul and me still holds, even if only by the power of our own feelings and desires. But this doesn't make things easy; marriage is always a crucible.

After thirty-five years of marriage to Paul, I can honestly say I've never been bored, but I'm often extremely annoyed, and have even been tempted occasionally to kick him while wearing high heels. How can any relationship last for eternity? One of Joseph Smith's revelations states, "the same sociality which exists among us here will exist among us there, only it will be coupled with eternal glory, which glory we do not now enjoy" (D&C 130:2). Perhaps eternal glory makes all things possible and eternally alive. I hope so.

Paul isn't my first husband, though our marriage was my first temple marriage. In my mid-twenties, I was married for two years to Guy, a British convert I met at BYU. I was romantically and passionately in love with him, but it was always a troubled relationship. Guy was a womanizer. He'd been married and excommunicated for adultery, which is why we couldn't marry in the temple. I knew what I was getting into when I married Guy, not just because of his problems in his previous marriage: his eye, and more, had wandered while we dated. I thought my steadfast love would heal his wounded soul, or whatever underlying issues caused his infidelity. In the end, he left me; my forgiving heart didn't make him want to stay. When he finally left, I was very relieved to see him go.

Guy liked the Mormon doctrine of polygamy, at least his interpretation of it: that a man needs many women to fulfill his needs. And Guy thought he was good at fulfilling women's needs, at least their sexual needs. But respect, honesty, and trust were difficult for him, I think because his own family history hadn't embedded these qualities in him. Like many Mormon women before and after me, I dreaded the prospect of living the doctrine of plural marriage, but also felt on some level that I should be willing to accept it, if I was just spiritual enough. This of course is odd, given that the modern church has always distanced itself from both the practice and the doctrine. And yet any believer who knows the church's history and reads Joseph Smith's words in Doctrine and Covenants Section 132 struggles with the question of whether polygamy is a celestial law required for exaltation. Neither Guy nor I had fundamentalist leanings, at least intellectually and politically, but he liked the idea of being part of an elitist, esoteric group. And I longed for spiritual purity at that time of my life, which meant that I thought I should be willing to give some ultimate sacrifice. It was only later that I saw how unequal sacrifice ruins any marriage.

Before I met Guy, I was a good girl who followed the rules. (OK, so my reading and movie-watching were never orthodox, but my behavior was exemplary.) But being married outside the temple to a man who wasn't a worthy priesthood holder, I found that a woman's status in the church is only as good as her husband's. Though I had already gone through the temple when I married Guy and was worthy of a temple recommend, one bishop refused to renew my recommend because I was officially married to a "nonmember." I was tainted on some level. My relationship with Guy made me question LDS notions of "righteousness." I had already thought deeply about the issue because I was intellectually curious and wondered about the underlying nature of morality and goodness. But after the lessons of my marriage to Guy, I *felt* it on an experiential level.

As a smart woman at BYU, I came up sharply against gender inequality in the church. No matter what anyone said about women being valued, my time at BYU showed me how male priesthood leaders controlled resources and discourses, how men were more important than women in every arena, how men's voices and opinions always dominated, and how invisible women really were. I began to notice this pattern in the Mormon marriages around me too. I was often the only woman involved in lively graduate student discussions of philosophy, theology, and Mormon history. The married men's wives stayed home while their husbands were off engaged in educational and intellectual pursuits. The men said their wives weren't interested in these discussions, but I began to wonder how there could be mutual respect when Mormon marriages so often divided along traditional roles of women occupying the domestic sphere while men inhabited the public realm.

I also suffered from depression over issues involving my own worth. It isn't that I thought I was worse than anyone else; it wasn't a matter of self-esteem. It was a deeper existential issue about my failure ever to be good enough at anything. I didn't realize at the time how much this was tied to being a Mormon woman, how I had been trained by a set of unrealistic LDS cultural values to feel inadequate. It took me many years to realize that I had internalized, deeply, women's inferior status in Mormon culture. How can a woman live up to the highest ideals of righteousness and the intelligence that is the glory of God if her worldview tells her in so many ways that she's handicapped from the beginning? Mormon women get a mixed message. On the one hand, they're told they're daughters of God and should be the best they can be, but that best isn't *really* the best compared to the model for men. All of the ways Mormon culture devalued me as a woman and an intellectual played into my existential anxieties about my worthiness before God and my ability to live up to my own ideals. But I didn't see this connection for a long time. I just felt keenly the many ways I fell short, and never seemed to improve enough, no matter how heroic my effort.

This led me on a spiritual quest that at first seemed to leave me in despair. But when I thought all was lost on one or two occasions, I felt myself encompassed by an overpowering love from an unseen power that pervaded the core of my being. I sensed this was God's love, the love of Christ who valued me just because I was myself. It didn't matter what I had done or not done; I was infinitely precious.

Such experiences freed me in ways that changed how I approached my second marriage. I no longer had the fear of plural marriage hanging over me. My experience with a loving God made me confident that heaven couldn't be a punishment for women. If there was anything true about plural marriage, it had to be something more than the patriarchal polygyny that has permeated a number of cultures, including Mormonism. My heart was open to mystery. And Paul was no womanizer. I chose my second husband on the basis of friendship, mutual respect, common values and interests, and a mutual passion for Christ's gospel and social justice. Now, don't get me wrong; I was very drawn to Paul physically too. His charming demeanor and charisma have always enlivened his whole person. I couldn't help but be in love with him and enchanted with his sense of humor, creative intellect, eloquent and forceful use of language, and ironic balance of self-deprecation and self-assertion. Paul has never lacked confidence the way I did. But he's a man. Even though he likes to talk about feelings and hates televised sports, he's still a man, and of an age and a training that he bought into Mormon notions of male priesthood, with the duty to preside, provide, and protect. This has created tension between us. I'm fine with nurturing, the duty supposedly ordained for me as a woman, but I resist being presided over, provided for, and protected.

Paul and I have been blessed by the fact that our paths in the church have been parallel; we moved out of the mainstream together; we became more liberal and radical together; these things have helped us stay together. But there have been two major struggles in our marriage: negotiating sex and each of us maintaining our sense of self. Sex is a vitally important component of marriage or partnership, but too complicated and personal to discuss here. Let's just say our relationship has been a struggle between people of two very different sexual temperaments and temperatures.

Instead, I'll focus on the problem of self and other. An issue in any relationship, it's central in Mormon marriages because Mormon theology asserts eternal personhood and eternal gender as part of eternal marriage. Developmental psychology, in all its different manifestations and approaches, tells us that we each develop a sense of self by interacting with others and the Other—our parents, siblings, friends, sex and marriage partners, god figures, value systems, etc.—all of which create a series of conundrums for every person. We need the Other, but we're always in danger of either overpowering or being subsumed by it. Simone de Beauvoir explores these complexities in her foundational feminist text *The Second Sex*. Women function as the Other against which men define what it is to be male; in this way, women are simply a placeholder, a mirror, showing men their own reflection.

Rather than seeking to understand women, men often simply project their own feelings onto women, whereas women's secondary status makes it necessary for them to be more culturally bilingual. They're trained to know both the dominant male discourse as well as the language of women.

Paul was thirty-three years old when we married. Like Mormon men in general, he had been under terrible pressure since he was twenty-five to find a wife. His single status had even been the focus of public ridicule more than once. But he couldn't bring himself to get married just because of social pressure. A maverick at heart, Paul lacks the personality to do something just because it's expected. Part of him feared marriage because his parents had such a bad one (his father was abusive), and part of him leaned toward monasticism. He would have made a good medieval monk, someone who prefers the life of the mind and spirit over the life of the body. He hates hedonism in all its forms; he can't fathom how people can seek their own pleasure while an infrastructure is falling apart.

But still Paul did want to marry on some level because being a full citizen in the LDS community includes marriage; Paul cared enough about his place in the community and his ability to influence it through priesthood leadership, which requires marriage, to keep himself open to the possibility. He tells me he proposed because I was the first woman with whom he felt he could have a long-term, honest relationship. We had known each other for seven years at that time; we were very good friends, liked each other very much, and enjoyed each other's company. We met through Guy, my first husband. In fact, Paul was a witness at my first marriage. Though I am a romantic at heart, after the pain and failure of my first marriage, I was very open to a marriage based on friendship rather than passion.

What I didn't expect was the difficulty of getting Paul to *see me*, the difficulty of creating a balanced marriage where I wasn't overshadowed by Paul's personality and talents. I knew he respected me deeply when we married. I knew he admired my intelligence and strength and endurance. But I didn't realize how much he didn't understand about me, my needs and desires. I think he would agree, even today, that I understand him better than he does me. In part this is because by nature he's more of an extrovert and I'm more of an introvert: he needs to talk things through aloud to know what he feels and knows, while I need time alone to contemplate my internal feelings and ideas. Paul was very gregarious when we first married, I was more private. Over the years, he's become more reclusive because of the rejection he has suffered, whereas I have become more public, though I still need lots of private time. And in part, Paul's inability to see me relates to the fact that it was difficult for him to comprehend how different my point of view was from his. How could we be so far apart in our approaches when we agreed on all the basics? I had to learn to assert myself out loud so that he could understand my objections; he had to admit he couldn't understand them without moving into another way of thinking. In Paul's own words, it took him years "to see with both eyes," to understand that my experiences as a woman gave me a different perspective from his because I had a different relationship to power structures. Caring about me caused him to put himself in my shoes. While I seemed more equipped for this kind of empathy, it was important for me not to assume the moral high ground. From Paul I learned the virtue of confrontation.

Our marriage started out on a somewhat traditional note. I got pregnant quickly (which was a surprise since I didn't have children with Guy, even though we didn't use birth control and he fathered children in other relationships). Paul and I had our four daughters in five years before we, or rather he, decided our family was large enough. From a large family myself, I felt that I should want a lot of children too. I'm glad Paul asserted his will in this regard—otherwise I couldn't have pursued my academic career. It was hard enough with four children, and I couldn't have done it at all without his support. I was already teaching classics at BYU when Paul and I got married, but I hadn't finished my master's thesis yet, in large part because I lacked confidence in my writing and ideas. Paul was just starting his law practice. I quit teaching when I first got pregnant and stayed home with the children. I cooked from scratch, canned our home-grown fruit and vegetables, and even sewed some of the girls' clothes. I liked it, though I missed the intellectual engagement of teaching.

It was Paul who insisted that I finish my master's thesis on Homer's *Odyssey*. He said it would be a shame after all the work I'd done not to finish my degree. Every night after dinner, he watched the babies while I headed to BYU's library, which stayed open until 11 P.M. It took me two years, but I completed the thesis and was proud of it. A personal breakthrough, it ended my long-standing writer's block and my sense that I wasn't good enough. It also made me eligible and sought after to teach at BYU again. So, when my third daughter was just a week old, I started teaching part-time. I continued teaching part-time until I got a full-time position at the University of Utah when my youngest was twelve.

I started my PhD when my youngest was just four. I knew by then that for the sake of my career and sense of self, I needed a doctorate, an outward sign of the caliber of my academic work that would enable me to move up in the academic system. Again, without Paul's help, I never could have finished. I needed his support in every way: financially, emotionally, and in order to care for our children. When my children were small, it would have been more economically advantageous had I not taught or worked on graduate degrees: tuition, books, and babysitters are expensive. But my job at the university is now an enormous economic advantage for us, providing security, good health care, and retirement benefits, which Paul, who is self-employed, lacks. The Mormon model of the ideal family doesn't take such complexities into consideration—despite the interest in Utah in entrepreneurialism, in starting a business and being one's own boss, and also despite the emphasis on self-reliance. It's hard to responsibly raise a large family if you can't afford health care for your children when they're ill, or if you ever become too ill to work yourself and have no backup plan.

Sometimes when I think about all that Paul has sacrificed for me to have a career and be a feminist activist, I can feel guilty, especially because I enjoy my job more than he does his. I can almost convince myself that he has given more than I have to the marriage and family, which is absolutely not true. It's true that he has always earned more money than I have, the money that made our family trips and helping our daughters possible. But I always did more childcare than he did, more housework, and all the shopping and planning for our daughters' needs and for family holidays. And I've often taken care of things at home so he can write. Men are not expected to sacrifice for women in any way but through their labor, so if they do, women are expected to feel grateful, if not outright guilty. But women are expected to sacrifice for men, so that men in general don't see the sacrifice as sacrifice. It's just the way things are. That, after all, is pretty much the definition of entitlement. Even when Paul hasn't exhibited that sort of entitlement, the dominant culture still taught me how I should view what each of us sacrifices for the other and the success of our marriage and family.

There has been so much give and take on both sides for Paul and me that in the end I think we've created a type of equality, or maybe it's more of a mutuality—mutual support and respect, which isn't to say that we don't still have our conflicts, even very big conflicts. In addition to the things all couples fight over, such as children, jobs, sex, and money, Paul and I have always had a difficult time balancing personal identity with couple cohesion. The fact that we are both public figures who speak and write about Mormon topics has brought us closer together and kept us united in important ways. But it has also been a source of competition and resentment. Our interests and ideas overlap so much that sometimes it's hard to say what belongs to which of us. Sometimes it doesn't matter, but at other times it can hurt if one of us is given more credit than the other.

I was attracted to Paul for his strong, charismatic personality, but sometimes I've felt overpowered by his presence and rhetoric. Over the years, Paul has become more aware of his tendency to overwhelm others, so at times he has tried to make himself smaller, sometimes so much that he begins to feel invisible, a feeling that was more common for me at the beginning of our marriage. I've learned how to hold my own place, to make myself larger and keep my own sense of self, but it has been a long struggle. My teaching and academic career, which are separate from anything Paul does, have been crucial in this process. The fact that our personalities and styles are so different helps too. Even when we basically agree on a principle, our approaches can make us disagree strongly. We become the battling and vociferous Toscanos, which can be frightening to outsiders, but is a source of amusement and fun to us.

Paul and I certainly didn't start out as the typical BYU couple. Though we have a photo with us standing outside the Salt Lake temple on our wedding day, we aren't gazing into each other's eyes or kissing—we aren't even touching or holding hands. We were still in the process of moving from friends to lovers, which was a little awkward at first. We have more affection now than we did then. Another change is that at the beginning, we both held on to some ideas about male priesthood leadership, though I had begun to claim feminism by then and was already developing my theology about women's right to priesthood, a theology that would intensify the more I learned, taught, and wrote. Being a successful teacher and writer gave me confidence about my own abilities and worth. And mothering daughters gave me the desire to create a better world for them, a place where it would be natural for them to see themselves as equally capable as men. Paul didn't have the option to be a Mormon patriarch if he wanted to stay married to me. And by the time his fourth daughter arrived, his view of women and girls had changed completely. He wanted to train our girls to stand up for themselves and to have their own voices. And he succeeded.

There's a certain irony that Paul and I, two well-known apostates, have created such a long-lasting marriage partnership and supportive relationship for each other and our children. It's also ironic that our success may be due in large part to our defiance of Mormon cultural norms. At the same time, I must admit that there are many positive views about marriage and family that we imbibed from our Mormon experience: the belief in sacrificing for the good of the family group, and the notion that marriage is a sacrament for eternal progress.

My marriage with Paul has also changed my views about marriage. On one level, I am much less romantic. I don't believe anymore in a *one and only* eternal love. But I do believe in eternal love—at least, I hope I have an eternity to explore my love relationship with Paul. I don't want to lose him; he is infinitely interesting and dear. But I also hope, if we live eternally, that maybe there are also parallel lives, or some kind of simultaneity that allows us to have other partnerships of equal depth and importance. On this level, I am eternally romantic, and maybe quintessentially Mormon. I believe in eternal lives and marriages (when I am in a believing mood and a cosmic consciousness). While I no longer accept Mormonism as the one true religion, in my new liberated state I can even go back to that troubling Mormon scripture, Doctrine and Covenants 132, and see in it mystical possibilities that go beyond its surface of despicable and patriarchal polygyny. I can see in it possibilities that could validate homosexual relationships and other eternal connections, but that's a discussion for another essay and another time frame. I'm very thankful for the marriage I have in the here and now. The struggle to remain faithful to and alive in a monogamous marriage is sacramental because it transforms the self and breaks open the ego from a narrow passageway to an infinite unfolding of self in relationship to other.

The Architecture of Marriage

Observations of a Bastard

GINA COLVIN

My mother, Marie, was unmarried for the first nine years of my life. When I became assistant stake historian, I was given the digitized photographs of about sixty years of the LDS church in Christchurch, New Zealand. I looked through each photograph carefully and came upon a grainy black and white picture of what looked like Mum, but I couldn't be sure—and I couldn't ask her, since she'd died a few years earlier. So when I hosted a Relief Society event, I asked some of the older women if this pretty young thing with a peroxide blonde beehive was my mother. They peered closely at the computer image.

"Yes, that's Marie," Sister Roper said firmly. "And she was pregnant with you at the time, if I recall."

Mum had been baptized while I was in utero, her sexual misdeeds happily expunged. When she gave birth to me five days after her nineteenth birthday, I was informally adopted by my church mothers, who spared no effort to make me feel at home. My early life was filled with love and kindness as a beloved member of a close Mormon congregation. I was very happy. But as I grew older, I realized that my mother was not.

My mother's loneliness cast the only shadows in my early years. She desperately wanted to marry. The church was clear about the superiority of marriage; she craved the paradise advertised so tantalizingly in church publications. But she was a single mother in an area of the church short on marriageable men. For a time she thought her prayers had been answered in the form of Jim, whose photo she carried. In stolen moments during his mission in Christchurch, he had promised to send for Mum and me after he returned to Utah. He must have been very convincing because I lived with the expectation that we would go to a magical Mormon land to be sealed in the temple to a handsome missionary, whom I hazily remembered lifting me up to a smile full of white teeth. But one postmission letter was the last Mum heard from him.

My mother's hoped-for marriage didn't weigh heavily on me, raised as I was in the homes of grandparents, couples in the church, aunts and uncles, and caregivers who looked after me while Mum worked. "Wouldn't you love to have a father?" she would ask. She had apprised me of the facts of life from an early age so I was aware that I had a living, breathing masculine parent who had happily contributed his genetic material to my conception. "Yes," I would answer, but only because her longings left little room for disagreement. What I really wanted, however, wasn't just any father; I wanted *my* father, who, having ensconced himself with another partner and being a generally disagreeable sort of chap, had to be forced to pay a monthly sum for my "maintenance." Aside from a few chance encounters, he was a name without a presence—which, above anything, confused me. I was used to being wanted; his abandonment of me was baffling.

Thus, as a young Mormon woman, Mum was socialized to hope for, wish for, and anticipate marriage as a curative for all personal ills. This wanting-but-never-getting threw her into depression, so that when she met Mike, a Catholic, she flung herself at him with grasping abandon, unlatched herself from the behavioral constraints of the church, and wound up pregnant and forced to marry. I watched her moral and emotional decline like a train wreck in slow motion. I know she felt terrible because I saw and heard her shame. The light in her eyes went out; she spoke resentfully of marriage to a husband for whom she had little affection. "I've made my bed," she would declare. "And I've got to lay in it."

Four more children were born to this injudicious marriage as it sputtered on for ten miserable years. Mike had a fierce antipathy for the LDS church and refused to allow either my mother or me to attend. He had a voracious appetite for booze and gambling, and his solution for my burgeoning aversion to him was a hostile and violent cruelty. I was wrenched away from a community and friends I loved, thrust into a home and a life as incomprehensible as it was insecure. Yet, I didn't question the state of marriage even in this harshest of contexts. I recognized this spectacular marital failure as the fault of two very silly people who had made a very silly decision and ought to divorce without delay.

As I became more independent, I made my way back to church, where a new generation of young women was being prepared for marriage, this time with more emphasis on the importance of marrying in the faith. "Marry in the church; marry in the temple; marry a returned missionary; make marriage a priority; marry your own race; marriage is for virgins. . . ." Not surprisingly, the messages sunk in.

I was seventeen when I met Andrew, the son of a mission president who had brought his family to the antipodes from the United States. We fell quickly in love and fantasized about our eventual marriage together. Our ferocious passion and mutual attraction meant that we had to find strategies to foil the imminent premarital consummation circling like a shark around the edges of our young and reckless relationship. As our physical infatuation mounted, so did our talk of the celestial world, the infallibility of the church, the wonders of the spiritual realm, and our destiny together as an eternally sanctioned and divinely bound couple. These moments of celestial dreaming escalated with our desire, ensuring that we remained, albeit tenuously, chaste. Those days were heady as we waited for his own mission call, which would eventually take him away to the other side of the world, out of marriage's reach. As I watched him disappear toward the departure gate, heartbreak gave way to anger as I turned on the church with its inducements for young women to pursue marriage but then to parry that love with a long, lonely two-year separation. I determined that I would not be the one who stayed behind, pining and waiting—particularly for Andrew, who would not return to New Zealand but to his home in Pleasant Grove, Utah. I believed from my mother's experience that, despite their declarations of love, North Americans didn't come back—ever.

I soon met Steve, a Kiwi boy who had lately joined the church. On paper he seemed fine. He was close to finishing his law degree, he came from a respectable family, and he was enthusiastic about his new Mormon identity. As a young man of twenty-one, he was eligible to serve a mission, but wanted to marry me instead, and I wanted to be married.

Marriage was my mission. I was desperate to come of age in the church, to be the kind of Mormon woman I had heard so much about as a girl. I wanted to be someone in the church, to have standing and status. As a single woman I was assigned to the in-between; I was convinced that I had nothing to contribute to the realm of Mormon womanhood until I was wed. Now when I look back, I wish someone had been there to rescue me. My only warning came from a heartbroken Andrew, who urged me in a short, tear-stained letter, to reconsider and wait the few short months before his mission ended. But I didn't know how to stop a planned marriage from unfolding. As I lay on my bed calculating and weighing this enormous dilemma, I was incapacitated by my lack of alternative discourses, resources, and support to alter the course of events before me. Mormon women simply didn't stop marriages.

I allowed the buzz and excitement of wedding preparations to allay my fears. It wasn't to be a temple marriage. Steve needed to wait the requisite one year of membership before we could be sealed, so I walked, my heart leaden, down the aisle to a good man for whom I was entirely unsuited. I did it without any real anticipation of our life together. My joy was in the anticipation of being a wife. But when I sought the advice of matriarchs I trusted and my bishop, I was assured, "Gina, two people who love the Lord can make a fine marriage."

So God was invited into our marriage. Because we had nothing else going, the church became our meeting place, the topic of our conversations, our touchstone, our point of commonality. But we enjoyed few gentle and companionable moments. The space between us crackled and sparked with irritation. I expressed that irritation in explosive rages, while he spectacularly and sulkily retreated. I admit that I'm not always a picnic to live with, but the silences and denial that characterized his response to this impossible life were just as debilitating and toxic as my anger. No amount of prayer or church service could correct our unsuitability. It was simply and categorically a marriage that shouldn't have happened.

Not that either of us would admit that. Within a year we were sealed and within two years he was called to be bishop. He was a hardworking bishop. But we were far too young to bear the weight of such a responsibility—particularly when our marriage was so brittle. Still, I believed firmly in the adage that two people who love the Lord could make a great marriage. When, shortly after our third anniversary, he announced that he wanted a divorce, I was both devastated and relieved. In truth I didn't want to be married to him every bit as much as he didn't want to be married to me. But I clung to the idea that there had to be some divine remedy that would act as a curative for our failed love, because the alternative was unthinkable. Could it be that I had not loved God enough—or was it simply that loving God wasn't enough to make a marriage work?

Within weeks he had found another woman. Within months she was pregnant with his child. While I reveled vindictively in the spiral of misfortune that followed him, I also felt moments of intense pity as his life unwound. I had known all along that we shouldn't have married and that I could have stopped it and saved us years of grief. His adultery cost us both heavily. I became convinced that Mormon marriages inevitably carried untold complications and burdens. The church gave too many assurances, intruded too much in the structure of our lives, and demanded too much from us. I became more and more skeptical of the institution of marriage—particularly Mormon ones.

At age twenty-three, one year into our two-year statutory separation period, I experienced a revelatory moment one winter's day while warming myself before the potbelly stove. In an outpouring of spiritual feeling, I breathed the expectation of marriage away in waves of divine peace. I felt for the first time in my life that I was enough alone. In this gift I had found a contented ease with myself, a confident tranquility that with or without marriage I was enough, and I hugged the possibility of singleness and a life of solitude to me like a warm and comforting wind.

I made plans: I would finish my university degree. And then I would live in Australia. Then I would go to England, take saxophone lessons, and busk on the streets of London while I did my graduate studies. Life (sans "would be/should be" husbands and church curriculum materials promising wedded bliss) began to feel promising and good and right. In many ways divorce liberated me from absolute certainty in the dogmas and expectations I had inherited throughout my young Mormon life. I found that I no longer relied upon the church for my sense of self.

Having acquired this self-assurance, I became, briefly, a brazen coquette. I jumped enthusiastically into a few non-Mormon flings—and it was fabulous. Young and sexy, I threw myself into a pastime of casual and outrageous flirtations, without any sexual follow-through. I was a cruel and heartless tease, and immensely proud of myself.

And then, a dream came to me like a revelation, unbidden, unforced, not born of any desire for an attachment. He was a different kind of Mormon man. He wasn't in awe of me, he wasn't intimidated by me, nor was he weak. There was an honest fearlessness about him. And he loved me without reservation. The dream was so startling and clear that it left me breathless. In that moment I knew that God or the universe had a course in mind for me. But rather than feeling anxious for this plan's unveiling, I was touched by the beauty of this serendipitous intervention. I calmly went about my life, preparing for a departure I planned to be permanent, while the gentle possibility of this young man of my dreams settled at the back of my mind.

Two weeks before I was about to leave, a young man four years my junior returned from his mission. Although I had known him most of my life, I had never given him so much as a passing glance. Nathan had left as a boy but returned a young man. Fresh-faced, he was in love with the world and possessed a quirky confidence that I quietly appreciated. Potential brides had buzzed eagerly around him since his return, vying for his attention. I was among the few women who weren't interested in him romantically. Sure, he was very funny, very loving, wonderfully open, vibrant, and charismatic. But he was too young, too callow, and far too unsophisticated to turn my head. He lacked depth and complexity. I thought he was cute in the way an older sister thinks her little brother's friends are cute. I told him once, "You are like an Andy Warhol painting—deeply shallow."

"Yeah," he said, with a pleasant, agreeable smile. "I know what you mean." Of course he knew full well that I was insulting him, but he was pleased that I had invested enough time into thinking about him to come up with a metaphor for his flaws.

Then one cold July morning in 1992, about a month before my departure to Sydney, he sat behind me in Sunday school. The teacher, who had travel plans coming up, tried to line up a few replacement teachers and asked me to take over class a few weeks hence. "Sorry," I said. "I'm moving to Australia."

At that moment, Nathan heard a voice say with powerful clarity, "Stop her from leaving."

In response, he whispered to me from behind, "You can't go."

I turned, flattered by the attention, and said, eyes playfully batting, "Well, kiss me then." It was meant to be a joke, but he didn't seem amused.

When the lesson ended, he followed me to the car park and implored me to reconsider. He was going home to pray, he said, and would get back to me with an explanation. "All I know is that you can't go, and I need to stop you."

I laughed, patronizingly. "Well, there's nothing stopping us from having a fling!" But in truth I didn't want a fling with him.

The next day, my birthday, he showed up at my home with a single rose and a gift. I ushered him into the living room, where I resumed watching the Olympics, which happened to be on. The air was heavy and pregnant with the weight of his nervousness. I was mute in the face of this moment of tremendous consequence. I didn't want to hear his speech, so I ignored him. Frustrated with my feigned distraction as I stared unseeingly at the television, he stood up and turned it off, seated himself at the end of the sofa, and began.

"Today I was in the florist choosing some flowers for you when the florist started telling me about her recent break-up with her boyfriend. I told her, 'You think you have problems, the girl of my dreams is about to leave forever and I don't know what to do.' The florist said, 'Tell her, just tell her exactly how you feel.' So I'm here to do that now. I think I'm in love with you and I can't imagine the rest of my life without you."

I paused for what must have seemed like an eternity for him. I silently admired his candor. I thought him naïve but his brutal honesty made me feel secure. I knew that any man who conducted himself with such sincerity would keep my heart safe. But this was all before we had been on one single date. I'm still not proud of what I said to him: "I think you've mistaken lust for love. You'll get over it."

He took this with surprising good grace but was undeterred as he explained how sure he was that I was the "one." He wasn't embarrassed. He remained calm and self-assured, telling me with his eyes and his smile that he was both unsurprised by my reaction and confident I would eventually change my mind.

I got up quickly, bringing the moment to a close. "We can date for a couple of weeks—and we'll see what comes of it," I said, relenting, as I shoved him out the door.

And date we did. Gradually the boy from my vision began to take shape and my guarded heart began to soften. He proposed to me weeks later, on bended knee under a cloudless, star-dappled sky. Our backdrop was the New Zealand Temple. Even though I thought it was a bit of a cliché, I looked down into eyes that were unfailingly true. Without a pause, I uttered my heartfelt "Yes."

Our temple marriage was a quiet affair. I didn't want it any other way. I traded in my plane ticket to Sydney for a trip to the New Zealand Hamilton Temple. Only my mother and an elderly couple from our stake attended the ceremony. As Nathan and I kneeled across the altar from each other and clasped hands, it was as if the hosts of heaven appeared, to witness an event that we choose to believe was orchestrated at the very throne of God.

I sometimes miss my dream of solitude, particularly in the swirl of six sons who vie for our time, money, and attention. But we've been married for over twenty years now and we still get excited about seeing each other when we've been away. Occasionally I rage at the injustice of our domestic inequities. Occasionally he sulks and stews when I forget his tedious dates or appointments. But we've always been great mates. He is the first person I want to share my news with, and the last person I want anyone else to criticize. Unlike my first husband, throughout our marriage he has been unswervingly honest, unthreatened, forthright, calm, and confident against my sudden hyperbolic rages at the world and its injustices. And I have appreciated knowing that if I ask him what he's thinking, he will tell me, leaving nothing out, making no embellishments. Two decades haven't dulled his sparkly, open, and friendly personality, and age has transformed him from cute to handsome. For all his affability, however, he's still a creature of habit, not naturally inclined to dash at sweeping changes or a wholesale reconsideration of his life's purpose. So in me he gets a partner who throws herself at new ideas, embraces challenges, and gets restless when life descends into a dull and unimaginative domestic routine.

Perhaps because I had used the church unsuccessfully as the glue in my first marriage, I didn't want to give the church the power to occupy the space between Nathan and me. We have therefore crafted a marriage that has taken shape in spite of the church, not because of it. I have never taken his name. We have maintained our independent interests. I have always worked, because I enjoy what I do, I'm good at it, and I like earning a salary. We don't feel the need to vote the same way—we are happy to debate and argue politics without it causing a philosophical rift in our relationship. We don't pretend that we are happy when we aren't, or try to model ourselves around the dominant discourse of Mormon marriage. He doesn't use any term of endearment that includes a sugary ingredient. I don't interfere with his need to shout excessively during rugby matches.

I'm by no means the first woman in the world to marry a mummy's boy. Nathan's mother found it difficult at times to hold back her feeling that her son needed more pampering than his fiercely independent wife was willing to furnish him. But for one thing alone I am intimately grateful. On the eve of our wedding, she took aside her virgin offspring and told him candidly, "Now, son, on your wedding night, none of this 'wham, bam, thank you ma'am' rubbish. None of this whip it in, whip it out, and wipe it. You've got to explore Gina's erogenous zones—sex has to be enjoyable for her too!"

Having been married to and divorced from one Mormon man before marrying another, I'm absolutely convinced of a few things. A marriage needs to be formed for its own sake, not for anyone else's. Mormon marriages offer no assurance of eternal bliss. For better or for worse, Mormon marriages must endure another deep level of complexity that for some is difficult to navigate. This Mormon marriage fug is often constituted by the clutter and chaos of decades and decades of advice, directives, and instructions over the podium; the historical emphasis on marriage as the ultimate occupation for women; the complications of sometimes many hours of church service; gender roles that, despite the Proclamation on the Family, remain problematic and legitimately contested; the unresolved problem of polygamy; the conflation of motherhood with womanhood; the new wave of Mormon feminist politics that raises questions over a Mormon husband's very identity; all these have rendered the business of Mormon marriage potentially thorny. In my experience, the church can be a paramour, a cuckold, a third wheel by which the growth of a vibrant, healthy, and beautiful marriage is compromised. This is not to say that the church is always an impediment to a healthy marriage, because it's not. The church can and often does provide a sturdy framework from which couples can draw support. But while the church can supply the engineering expertise, the architecture and the interior design must belong to the couple alone.

Sometimes Mormon marriages fail horrifically and cause ripples of agony for generations to come. Sometimes, despite a lifetime of hopes and dreams, marriage simply doesn't happen. Sometimes our choice of partners is so badly flawed that no amount of prayer or supplication can alter an inherent unsuitability. Sometimes being alone can be its own kind of paradise. And sometimes, just sometimes, God intervenes spectacularly and performs wondrous, perfect, homemade miracles.

PART V

Expectations: Met, Unmet, or Exceeded

Figure 7. Brad and Kira Olson, December 2001, Seattle, Washington

Kira writes: "Emerging from the temple was every bit the fantasy I had been afraid to want. Our friends and family were waiting for us, as is tradition, and the sun was shining, miraculously for December in Seattle. I didn't anticipate how wonderful I would feel walking out in a wedding dress, arm in arm with a handsome guy in a tux. I always wondered what was really going on with those pretty brides flowing out of the temple with their smiles and perfectly coiffed hair and rows of matching effervescent bridesmaids. But this moment was all mine. I was so happy. I felt so bright and so full of hope for my future with Brad. It's an absurd notion to the world, I think, to commit your eternity to someone. That day, it felt like the most right thing I'd ever done. And despite some waverings about who I am in this role of Mormon wife, I haven't regretted it for a moment."

Saying Yes

JOANNA BROOKS

Are you kidding? Of course I fell in love with him.

It began the night I saw him across a crowded patio at a UCLA graduate student party in Venice Beach: a brown-haired, blue-eyed, freckle-faced surfer type, all goodness and frenetic energy. I wore chunky black platform heels. I may have been smoking a cigar. (That happens with Mormon girls sometimes.) It was one of those autumn nights in Southern California when the Santa Ana winds blow fire down the canyons. Makes you want to jump into the ocean.

And jump I did. On our first date, he let me drive his truck—an oversized white GMC Jimmy with giant tires and eight cylinders under the hood. On our second date, David taught me to skateboard. I'd always wanted to learn. I wobbled and tilted and fell all over the parking lot across from his apartment, while David coached and chuckled. Perfect strangers hollered, "You're in love!"

That love part—it was clinched the week we spent on the picket lines of our teaching assistant union strike. Other people, I had to beg to walk one shift. Not David. I couldn't get him off the picket lines, from sunup to sundown. When he wasn't hollering and hoisting his sign, he was driving his truck from picket site to picket site, feeding and watering the strikers.

"This," I thought, "is a man who would cross the plains." He'd pull a handcart. He'd pull other people's handcarts. All the way to Zion.

"You know," I told him, matter-of-factly, three months after we met, "we're going to get married." We were sitting outside of a friend's wedding reception on a curb on a sycamore-lined LA avenue.

He peered at me through the little round glasses that made him look like an acolyte of Leon Trotsky. "Yes," he agreed, smiling. "I know."

*   *   *

Yes, I did: I fell in love with a Bolshevik. I fell in love with a handsome, intelligent, funny, compassionate man. Who is Jewish. And then I married him.

Oh, yes, I gobbled him up.

There will be no apologies from me on this subject.

And can you believe that more than a decade into the marriage, I had to draw a breath before writing that sentence? Can you believe it's still a bit tender?

It was hard for everyone in my family, my falling in love with David. There were months and then years when my mother didn't speak to him. It was a sibling who told me, "We don't know what to make of you. You knew what was right." To my father, my falling in love with David was like the final act in a drama of separation: before his eyes, I became something of a stranger. My parents paid for the wedding. My family danced at the wedding. But it changed us.

Yet isn't this how God defined marriage for Adam and Eve: that you must "leave father and mother" (and sometimes even brother or sister) and "cleave" wholly to your beloved?

*   *   *

Don't be angry with them. I'm not. OK, I may have been, once. But even then, I understood. To my family, my choosing to marry David meant I chose not to be with them in heaven. A literal reading of Mormon doctrine holds that marriage is a rite necessary to eternal salvation, to the continuity of our family ties across eternity. In the eyes of my family and many of the people I grew up with, not marrying a faithful Mormon in the temple means cutting yourself off from your ancestors. In communities of orthodox Mormons, a child who marries outside the faith can reflect poorly on parents, evidence that they did something wrong. People speculate about what the parents' errors might have been, gossip about sins the child might have committed.

But for me, choosing David meant placing my trust in a God bigger than doctrine. It meant choosing my joy, my best friend, my chance to create a family, choosing all these as indivisible elements of my own spiritual well-being.

For years, I had believed that if I were a better Mormon, if I waited more patiently, had milder thoughts, a tamer spirit, if I were just *better*, God would reward me with a good Mormon husband.

Then one Sunday, when I was twenty-five years old, I found myself in a chapel full of unmarried Mormon women who also believed that if they were better Mormons, waited more patiently, had milder thoughts and a tamer spirit, God would reward them with good Mormon husbands too. Most of the women were nearing forty.

"We often ask God over and over again what it is we should do," my gray-haired Mormon bishop said, "but sometimes we just have to do and seek God in the process."

So I did.

I chose not to bet on waiting. I chose love. I chose to say "yes."

I know the importance of sacrifice. All the great religions teach that giving something up and saying "no" can make us more holy.

But so can saying "yes." "Yes" to love, "yes" to marriage, "yes" to babies. "Yes" to the outrageous sweetness, and "yes" even to heartbreak. "Yes," I love you, Mom and Dad. "Yes," I love you, ancestors. "Yes," I love you, baby daughters.

I love, I love—yes, yes, yes—like the glass crushing under my bridegroom's heel. I gave way and I said, Yes, God, do with me what you will.

*   *   *

Of course, David's family must have had feelings about our marriage too. Their only son marrying outside the faith, to a *Mormon* woman—a religion that strikes most people as, well, a little *odd*. And the question of children: Would I raise them Jewish? Would this new daughter-in-law weaken the bonds of identity holding the Jewish people together across millennia? That's what rabbis asked in worried tones. But if my in-laws worried, they never breathed a word of it to me.

One afternoon before the wedding, we went to the local Judaica store to pick out our *ketubah*, the beautifully calligraphied marriage contract we would hang on our bedroom wall. There came some question in our filling out the ketubah, a question that revealed my non-Jewishness and the less-than-kosher quality of our marriage. The store-owner looked down his nose at me and queried whether in fact the wedding would take place after sundown on Saturday, as Jewish law required.

That was enough for my mother-in-law. She looked the store owner in the eye and told him that people talk, especially in the Jewish community of Orange County, California, and that if one friend told another that a certain store was less than respectful to its patrons, word would get around. And that was the end of that.

Because, you see, you don't mess with the Jews. Or the people they love. Their family. *Mishpucha.* Families can choose to stick up for each other. Even when love leads them outside the rules. Families too can say yes.

*   *   *

One Sunday at church a few years ago, one of the pink-haired ladies working in the library asked me about my Jewish husband. "I see he's coming to church with you and the girls," she said, handing me the chalk I'd asked for. "Is he showing any interest? Or is he doing it for you and the girls?"

I smiled and shook my head. "No," I said, my fingers touching hers as I accepted the chalk. "I think he's doing it for me and the girls." I paused, wanting to defend him, wanting to explain. "He's a very good father," I added.

"And a good husband," the pink-haired lady said, knowingly, surprising me. "You can't say that about all LDS men, you know."

*   *   *

I love, I love, I love my Mormon people, even when they annoy or distress me. They're family: *mishpucha.*

I love, I love, I love my husband, even when he leaves a trail of disorder through the house, especially when he curses while playing golf with the second counselor in my bishopric, and most especially when he lays the quilt my Laurel class made for me before I went away to BYU out on the back lawn and teaches our daughters to play backgammon in the sun.

I love, I love, I love our gorgeous freckle-faced daughters, all goodness and frenetic energy.

It's very roomy, our handcart, the one we pull every day, across the plains of quotidian misunderstanding and uninspired sectarianism, toward a Zion with room enough for all of us and our motley crew of ancestors too. It helps, of course, that the man who's pulling the cart with me has these wonderful blue eyes, a terrific sense of humor, and a heart like an ox's.

Yes, of course, I fell in love with him.

And my family? Eventually, they fell in love with him too. In their own time and their own way. He was, after all, irresistible. There was always enough love there for all of us. It was our job to find it; it was our job to say yes.

Across Racial and Cultural Divides

JAMIE DAVIS

I was always a model Mormon girl: gold medallion around my neck, scriptures on my bedside table, prophetic quotes taped to the bathroom mirror. I had a few feminist leanings involving a desire for an education and a career in addition to motherhood, but it was nothing I wasn't willing to hide when asked to give a talk at a stake Young Women's conference. I had a reputation for perfection—a part I played well as I went to BYU and on a full-time mission to Brazil.

As every Mormon knows, any hint of romance with someone living within the geographical area of your mission is strictly forbidden. If you meet someone you're attracted to, you're expected to keep a tight lid on that attraction until you're released from service. Fortunately, Leo and I did just that. We served as fellow missionaries in neighboring areas for two transfers. The ward members and other missionaries adored Leo, and I admired and respected him. He finished his mission six months before I did, giving us the opportunity to write letters back and forth as friends . . . until it developed into a connection unlike any I'd previously known.

Though we'd done nothing wrong, I quickly learned that an interracial, intercultural attraction was wrong enough. I'm a fair-skinned, freckled redhead with roots in Northern and Western Europe. Leo's skin is the color of rich chocolate, his ancestry a mix of the many races populating Brazil's history: indigenous peoples, Portuguese colonists, African slaves. Mormons would generally categorize someone like him as a Lamanite, the descendent of an ancient people in the Book of Mormon, cursed for their wickedness with a skin of darkness, to be lightened only if they repented and returned to God. The Book of Mormon explained that the curse would make them less delightsome and enticing, thus ensuring that they remained separate and didn't "mix" with the more righteous Nephites.

But Leo's chocolate skin and deep brown eyes made him all the more attractive. He was terrifically handsome, as well as different and mysterious to me, just as I was to him. Still, there was something beyond the good looks so common among beautiful Brazilians. Leo was humble. I had never met a North American Mormon man with the humility and meekness Leo displayed. He was smart and ambitious, yet gentle. Seeing these traits, I hoped to find someone just like him in the United States after my mission. But the more I got to know Leo, the more I realized that his qualities were inextricably tied to the culture he'd been raised in. I didn't love him in spite of his being different from the Mormon men I knew; I loved him *because* of it.

After my mission, the letters Leo and I exchanged turned to phone calls and soon my parents and I were planning a trip to Brazil. As my mother stepped off the plane and hugged Leo for the first time, she knew she had met her future son-in-law. My parents were as enamored as I was during the week we spent with Leo and his family. After months of prayer and fasting, each of us had received a confirmation that it was God's plan for the two of us to be together. The day before we were to leave, Leo proposed. I cancelled my return flight and deferred my scholarship at BYU. Instead of starting a new semester, I started planning a wedding to be held in the São Paulo Temple. Leo and I, along with my parents and the Brazilians from our mission, were overjoyed.

Months earlier, a few weeks before I finished my mission, I had asked my mission president what he thought of marriage between an American and a Brazilian. He told me flatly, "The brethren don't approve of interracial or intercultural marriages." His words wounded me, but they foreshadowed other responses. At the announcement of our engagement, the members of my home stake were shocked and judgmental. The American missionaries we had labored beside spread gossip that we had misbehaved. The girls in Leo's stake in northern Brazil were furious that I was stealing him from them. Our mission president let us know that we weren't welcome to celebrate our temple wedding within the boundaries of our mission. Although we were marrying in the temple, it felt like we were about to be summoned for discipline.

LDS history is marred by racism, most commonly evidenced by the policy that black males could not hold the priesthood, a policy that changed in 1978. Before then, LDS missionaries in Brazil would ask church investigators for their family photo albums to determine if an individual would be eligible for church participation based on the absence of African ancestry. In 1975, when the first temple in South America was announced as São Paulo, LDS authorities faced the difficulty of determining which Brazilians would be restricted from the temple based on race. President Spencer W. Kimball cited his experiences with faithful Brazilians of convoluted bloodlines as an important factor in the extension of the priesthood to all worthy males, regardless of race. Growing up in the church in the 1980s, after the policy change, I was still taught that blacks were less righteous because they were "fence-sitters" in the preexistence, meaning they were unsure whether they wanted to follow Jesus or Satan.

Getting married in this tense climate was daunting. Fortunately, the doubts about our marriage only united us as a couple. Being different made us feel freer to recreate marriage in our own way. Growing up in a traditional Mormon household, I was often frustrated by narrowly defined, church-assigned gender roles and shared with Leo my desire for an egalitarian marriage. Leo's experience growing up Mormon outside of North America had protected him from the cultural expectations I felt and made this type of marriage seem natural to him. His parents were an example for us—his mother had worked full-time throughout her life, establishing a career as respected as his father's.

Leo and I took care to craft our marriage the way we wanted it, not how others expected it to look. We took turns working on our educations: I first completed a BA in education, and then he pursued a BS in engineering. When he neared graduation, I began an MA, followed by his MBA and my doctorate. Throughout our marriage, we've both worked and contributed to our financial stability and family income. When a brief stint as a stay-at-home mother led to a serious bout of depression for me, Leo championed my desire to return to work. As my career has blossomed, Leo has continued to support me while coparenting our children and never once referring to it as "babysitting." While I was in school, he even did the lion's share of cleaning, all while still traveling and thriving in his own career. Our children are a beautiful mix of all that is Brazilian and American, raised to be bilingual and blessed with the sense that they can make a home for themselves in many places around the globe. From their infancies, they have been taught to be proud of their unique heritage, even when it's not valued by others.

This doesn't mean that we're perfect. We fight. Sometimes, a lot. However, I don't believe the differences in our cultures play out any more significantly in our marriage than the differences in culture that any couple faces as they attempt to create a single family unit out of two distinct backgrounds.

After ten years of marriage, I reject wholly the idea that intercultural or interracial marriage is dangerous. On the contrary, I believe that our supposedly opposing cultural backgrounds have been crucial to the success of our marriage, as they have contributed to the egalitarian relationship we desired. They've also increased our sensitivity toward each other and the people around us. Our marriage has taught us how to navigate other cultures and people, which has directly translated into opportunities for success in our professional lives. We both work internationally, traveling the world, with the confidence of knowing how to traverse languages and cultures. Our intercultural marriage has allowed each of us the freedom to find our inner voice and explore our identities in ways that wouldn't have been possible had we each married someone who was supposedly just like us. And best of all, instead of seeking approval from others, our choice to marry across racial and cultural divides has taught us to rely directly on God for personal revelation and confirmation of choices that affect our future.

The Shared Table

REBEKAH ORTON

Jack Spratt could eat no fat,
His wife could eat no lean;
And so betwixt the both of them,
They licked the platter clean.
—Traditional nursery rhyme

Picture this: me, after my first pregnancy. I am squat like deflated bread dough—
not only my stomach, but my entire body. My maternity clothes strain against
my girth; my cheeks are still pouchy. Beside my round corpulence, proudly
holding our small baby, is my husband, Chris, all angles and planes, wearing
clothes so loose he looks like a fifteen-year-old borrowing his father's best suit.

We hadn't started out so far apart in appearance, but a surprise pregnancy
on top of my first year of graduate school dramatically changed my size. I ate to
keep the nausea in check; I ate to quell anxiety about teaching; I ate whatever
I could rustle up between classes and papers and readings. Meanwhile, Chris
seemed to eat what I ate, but didn't gain an ounce. As I ballooned, he skimmed
along, dangerously sharp elbows and knees. I felt he'd need to sit atop a year's
supply of whole wheat to balance the enormity of the black silk barge beside
him.

I wanted, when people looked at my little family, to have them see us as a
set of Matryoshka dolls where each one nestles compactly inside the others, a
perfectly sloped bar graph when we stood side by side; I did not want them
to see a nursery rhyme. But the reality was I outweighed Chris by nearly forty
pounds, the amount of cheese the average American eats in a year. I saw my
body as truly grotesque for the first time in my life. I hadn't struggled with body
image issues as a teenager or a young adult, but after having a baby, the moment
Mormon doctrine tells me is the pinnacle of my creation, I felt betrayed by this
larger, unfamiliar body.

I assume that most women have some level of discomfort with their bodies: we're certainly trained to. But it's one thing to compare your thighs to an
airbrushed supermodel's, and another altogether to compare your hips to the

ones beside you in bed. In the interim between maternity pants and being back in my old jeans, I wanted to be able to slip on a pair of his pants and cinch them with a belt, or at least button them without sucking in.

I could have understood it if I married a ninety-eight-pound weakling, but Chris is broad-shouldered and coordinated, affectionately called "Stretch" for his ability to catch any throw when the guys play football. His arms are wiry and defined; his back tapers into a swimmer's V; I adore the curve of his backside into his athletic thighs. He is long and reedy, lean. And while I might not have been those things before my pregnancy, at least I hadn't been rotund, voluminous, or mushy. If I'm honest, in our engagement photos there were seeds of the Sprats: a tall, lanky guy and a plumper, moon-faced woman. I hadn't been happy with that, per se, but then I had weighed less than he did so I could convince myself that women were more curvy.

My weight loss would be more interesting had I used more exotic ways to achieve it: the human growth hormone, or liposuction, or cases of frozen meals delivered to the back door. But Chris was a BYU student, I was trying to finish graduate school with a baby, and there wasn't time or money for anything more unusual than joining WeightWatchers (paid for as a Christmas gift by my mother), along with a combination of hunger, willpower, and enough carrots to make it look like I'd hit the tanning bed once too often. One day, I stepped on the scale and weighed, with a sense of relief, the same as Chris.

Had I been married to anyone else, I might have looked at that number, familiar because I weighed it for most of high school, safely within a healthy weight range for my height, fitting me comfortably into size six jeans, and I might have stopped there. But I looked at myself, and I looked at my husband, and I still heard nursery rhyme couplets.

Because he is eight inches taller than I, a weight-to-height ratio called body mass index is the only useful way to talk about the relationship between Chris's size and my own. At the same weight, his body mass index was a feathery 18.3; mine was 23.4. All things considered, this was better than the days after I delivered my daughter, when my body mass measured 31.3: obese. Chris would have needed to gain almost a hundred pounds to match that number. Achieving an 18.3 like Chris's would take me down to a weight I couldn't remember seeing on a scale.

In the beginning, there was something in trying to match Chris's body mass index that proved to me I belonged in this marriage. I'd married young and experienced a lot of life changes very quickly that made me question my sense of self. Getting married had necessitated that I sublimate plans to go to law school by going to graduate school instead, and then having a baby so quickly shifted me from writing my thesis in the carrels to scribbling away on our kitchen table. It was hard, at times, not to resent how the changes snowballed on top of me, but not Chris. Even our roles felt unbalanced: he loped off to school with only a backpack and the unseen weight of providing for a family someday. When I met with my advisors, I carried a backpack and a diaper bag and a baby in a fifty-pound stroller along with my shrinking ambitions. Chris and I had prayed to confirm our decision to marry, and we were married in the temple, but the heady romance of getting married required a different attention than the steady compromises and persistence necessary in being married. I naively hadn't expected marriage and its attendant motherhood to bring such fundamental transformations.

Additionally, certain physiological differences between male and female bodies are reinforced by typical Mormon gender roles; in some ways, we're set up to look like the Sprats. Men's bodies are usually used to provide, and women's primarily to create and care for children. On average, women retain three pounds per pregnancy, among other changes to their bodies from bearing children. And since we're already home, it's often easier, as women, to take over operations in the kitchen, which offers an array of opportunities to eat or not eat, and those choices affect body weight as well. I remember being overwhelmed by having access to food all the time, having to regulate myself around a full pantry. It was another reason to envy Chris's role: he could eat only what he carried with him, while I had to master the difference between hormones and hunger and hankering.

It didn't help that Chris seemed to do all the weight loss and maintenance tricks naturally while I felt like I was dancing a minuet in combat boots. I envied Chris's metabolism, but more than that I envied his attitude toward food. Even though we'd both been raised in large Mormon families by convert mothers and pioneer stock fathers, Chris had no trace of my large family mentality to eat as much as you could before someone else finished it off. He would eat cookies and soda and fries if they were around, but he didn't crave them. He must never have encountered the mantra to use it up and make it do, because he felt no obligation to the stale birthday cake, and he didn't think twice about throwing away the last handfuls of chips that had lost their crunch. And he didn't share my belief that wasting groceries was a transgression. Instead, he had a tendency to let food languish in the refrigerator, forgetting about it completely, even if it was something he loved, and he never choked down leftovers that didn't interest him.

Chris likes to eat, but it has never consumed him the way that it does me. I watched him eat with equal aplomb a seared steak in a blueberry reduction and ham with funeral potatoes, both only to the point of satiety. I couldn't fathom his ability to refuse cookies at a fireside, or his capacity to turn down a dish that looked delicious but didn't interest him at that moment. Unlike him, my work never enthralled me so completely that I forgot to eat. It hurt my feelings when he didn't eat much of a dinner I'd prepared because he'd had a late lunch meeting, or when he had only a few bites of my elaborate cheesecake because it was too rich, or when he ignored the carefully portioned leftovers I frugally packed for his lunch. Most of all, I detested the nights when I sat down to dinner, famished from the mental and physical exhaustion of taking care of our kids, and reached for seconds when he hadn't finished his firsts.

After all my efforts and self-denial and vegetables, eventually I got down to within a body mass index point of Chris's weight. But then I stalled. I couldn't maintain the dieting mentality long enough to drop below a body mass index of 19. Sure, I had lost an Irish setter's worth compared to where I'd been in the days after delivery, but I still wondered what it would be like be really, actually skinny—like Chris. But I compromised: there was no reason to lose so much weight when there were more children to be born. I'd only had one baby, and the plan was to have one every other year until there were four, if not five, children in our brood.

For the next few years, I shelved my ambition to match Chris physically, but tracked my eating and exercised through pregnancies and postpartum to stay as close as possible to his body mass index number. Still, it felt like I was always two cookies away from weighing more than him. When I was diagnosed with a prolapsed uterus and prescribed a hysterectomy, I abandoned the effort of weight maintenance for Oreos and Netflix. In the months before and after my hysterectomy, food was the simplest way to soothe the blend of pain, failure, and relief I felt. My eating weighed me down literally and figuratively: I ate expansively, and I felt an immense, permanent bloat. I knew there would be no more keep-nausea-at-bay eating, there would be no more eating for two, and no more eight pounds of baby-weight losses. After six months, I'd packed on a quarter of my body weight: enough to counterbalance my husband once again.

Reaching Christopher's weight on the way up or down the scale is always a Come-to-Jesus moment for me. He steps on the scale with a sense of curiosity, but I step on with a sense of expectation that I imagine will feel familiar on Judgment Day. Through all my ups and downs, I'd already gained and lost 150 pounds, the measure of the complete *Oxford English Dictionary*, an entire average American woman. I had to lose weight one last time. But this time I was playing for keeps: no more pregnancy interruptions. I enacted every healthy living habit I could and exercised with fervor. Eventually, there was a period when I skirted the same body mass index as Chris.

But other than me, no one cared. Chris managed to compliment my slimming frame while never badmouthing my former weights. He's good at that. When I said marriage vows where I gave myself to my husband, in the back of my mind I expected him to exert some opinions on the upkeep of his property, but he seems to love every incarnation of my body, no questions asked. Like always, he kept his live-and-let-live attitude and forgot to eat the last slice of banana bread, the final scoop of ice cream. I was the one who went vegan and pushed myself until a running injury sidelined me for six long months. I watched joggers enviously while I slipped away from my lowest married weight back to a comfortable set point around a body mass index of 20.

I've stayed there for the past year, but it takes vigilance. I still keep track, loosely, of what I eat and when. I ask myself how hungry I am before I eat, or if maybe I'm just thirsty. I fill at least half my plate with vegetables. I juggle around numbers like the seasoned dieter I've become, shadows of my fat fingers hovering around my hands as I look up the calories in a Chick-fil-A sandwich and how much fiber is in an orange. I talk myself out of finishing food on my kids' plates; I scale every recipe to feed our family exactly to avoid leftovers; I go into another room to ignore the siren songs coming out of my kitchen. Meanwhile, Chris helps himself to a second cinnamon roll and tosses out cold French fries.

Growing up, I never expected to be thin after having children, and definitely not twenty pounds lighter than I was in high school. But from where I sit now, I wonder if there is really anything wrong with being Jack and Mrs. Sprat. They split what is before them in a way that leaves no waste. In comparison to other nursery rhyme relationships, they seem to have a pretty healthy relationship: No one is stuck in a pumpkin shell. No one feels the need to tumble after. There's a part of me who would have been content not trying to be so skinny. There are moments when I'd like to eat with abandon, when I want to comfort myself with food, when I get tired of chopping all those vegetables. I'd like to feel less annoyed with the constant Mormon exchange of desserts at potlucks and Relief Society meetings, of our recipes with cream of something soups and sour cream and potato chip topping.

On the other hand, because I married Chris and because I've expended so much effort over the years, overall, I genuinely like my body—and I realize plenty of women can't say that. It's nice to catch a glimpse of myself in glass doors or windows and double-take in pleasant surprise. Sure, on the morning of the resurrection, I wouldn't mind waking up tall enough to reach the top shelf in my heavenly library, but I'd be happy to come back to this size and shape, in this version of the prime of my life.

I ran twelve miles this morning as part of a routine training run, something I never thought I'd say. Chris, a high school varsity cross-country runner, was no longer interested in running himself, but when I wanted to learn, he helped me along by convincing me that I really did need to invest in good shoes, and by watching the kids when he could and then finding room in our student budget for a jogging stroller, then a double jogger, and finally a treadmill to support my habit. He pushed our two oldest in the double jogger to help me train for my first race and jogged five miles by my side with a race bib to get me to the finish line. If I hadn't married Chris, I don't imagine that I would have been running so far this morning, the errant snowflake falling and an audio book easing me along. I want to sprint up every hill and race my pace from last weekend's run, but there is the old injury to baby and no need to rush home. Chris respects this time, rearranges his Saturdays to give me the mornings to run long. I let myself relax into the pace. I love this quiet dawn, when I fall into the rhythm of my feet and my lungs, a moving cocoon, air stinging my eyes, and the whole world fading from black to blue with a yellow tint like whipped eggs. If I hadn't married my slim husband, and learned and fought to look like him, I'd miss this space, this lightness, the patter as my body is used like it won't be for the rest of the day of lifting and laundry and lunches. I know, as a Mormon woman, that I was supposed to feel the most powerful and divine when I was creating children, but instead I felt ungrateful and graceless and mostly nauseous. Here on the trail, I am thankful to have received a body, at once more and less of myself, lithe and free.

The Marriage Pact

ALISA CURTIS BOLANDER

When I was young, my family's cultural identity made it clear that being intelligent and educated was important, and although I was a good student, I thought I would need to marry someone even smarter and more accomplished than I intended to be. I think this came from having two intelligent parents who practiced traditional gender roles—my father an electrical engineer and manager, my mother a homemaker who had earned a 4.0 GPA in college. It never occurred to me to do anything but plan on having the same traditional gender dynamics in my future family, and I figured that to achieve them, I would need to marry a very accomplished and intelligent man.

Without quite being aware of it, I planned my romantic crushes accordingly. I would find the smartest boy worthy of my admiration, and then seek his attention and approval by competing with him directly in academics. This gave me someone to admire, someone to help me push myself, and it often enough led to strong friendships with these boys, as teachers paired us together in teams or competitive projects. I grew up confident and secure in my identity as a hard-working smart girl, knowing that finding a brilliant, ambitious, successful husband would justify my personal ambition.

My husband, Kevin, and I met as juniors in high school, when we had multiple classes together. I admired him from the start, and we became part of the same group of friends. I remember one dance where Kevin took a classmate of ours, a pretty, smart, popular girl. They were having a great time together, and I was curious as to what she found so fun about him. From then on I thought of him as a potential romantic partner. To my chagrin, Kevin developed affections for a girl at a neighboring school. In our senior prom dance picture, Kevin and I appear next to each other, him with this girlfriend, and me with one of his friends.

After high school, I wrote to Kevin and four of his friends on their missions while I rapidly completed my bachelor's degree at BYU. Despite having the grades and aptitude for medicine, I decided that a medical career would be at odds with the traditional gender dynamics prized by the church and Utah culture I was raised in, so I majored in English while working as a teaching assistant for the physics department. My father, urging me not to completely surrender my technical aptitude, convinced me to build a technical writing portfolio as I studied the liberal arts.

During my last undergraduate semester at BYU, Kevin started his freshman year, and we spent most of our free time together. During those two years he'd been away, he had made the wise decision of sending me photos of him standing alone on the French Riviera, his body sculpted from biking up the steep streets of seaside villages. A few days after he arrived at BYU, Kevin brought me beautiful long-stemmed roses on my birthday, which surprised me, though the surprise was by no means unwelcome. We started showing little signs of affection for each other, long hugs or holding hands, even a few sweet kisses. But I wasn't sure what I wanted to come of it. I enjoyed dating different men and wasn't interested in being exclusive.

And then one Thursday night, I went out with another man, someone I'd felt a spark with and been on five or six dates with. As we chatted over ice cream at Cold Stone Creamery, I couldn't stop thinking of Kevin: how I would rather be talking to Kevin, have Kevin's arm around me, be laughing with Kevin since he and I knew so much better how to make each other laugh.

I let this realization wash over me while I tried to decide what to do about it. I looked into my date's face and tried to muster some feeling besides mild disappointment that he was himself and not Kevin. I couldn't do it. I found a polite way to end the date early, then dashed to my apartment, anxious to call Kevin.

I told Kevin that I never wanted to go on a date with anyone else again. We acknowledged that our strong friendship hung in the balance, unsure that it could survive a romantic relationship, but we felt we could no longer give attention to other dates when we thought only of each other. Fortunately, things went as we had hoped and our romance blossomed easily from our established friendship and made for an easy transition into married life.

About a week before our Christmastime wedding in 2001, Kevin and I were required to interview with our bishops and receive live-ordinance recommends for our sealing in the temple. We lived in different wards, and his BYU student-ward bishop requested that I attend Kevin's interview. Obedient as we were, we readily agreed to the double invitation. But Kevin had lived in this large student ward less than four months, and because of frequent weekend trips home and the demands of planning a wedding, he had never before met with his bishop one-on-one.

As the interview commenced, the bishop looked at both of us sternly, moving his narrow eyes from Kevin's to mine. "Have you remained unspotted?" he asked in a tone so deliberately deep, portentous, and god-like that both Kevin and I found it hard to keep a straight face. Kevin answered him truthfully, that we had done all we could and believed we had kept ourselves worthy to enter the temple according to the standards in place. I figured that was why the bishop had asked me to attend Kevin's interview: he wanted both parties there to help him uncover any transgressions that might be glossed over easily by one party but must come to light in the presence of both partners.

The bishop then leaned conspiratorially toward Kevin and lowered his voice to a quiet but ominous tone. "Now, young man," he directed, "I want you to make me a solemn promise: from the day you marry, never allow your wife to work. Not once."

Kevin and I froze, too surprised to respond. The demand startled and confused me. I was raised to have a strong work ethic and sense of financial responsibility, which was good since I had to pay my way through college with scholarships and my own earnings. Of course I planned to contribute to our income after our wedding. I looked at Kevin and found him as speechless as I was, the bishop's words pressing down on us.

That gave the bishop time and opportunity to continue. "During my marriage, I have never allowed my wife to enter into employment, with the exception of the last two years, now that our children are grown." He suddenly stopped, realizing that he knew nothing of our educational or career aspirations, and said to Kevin, "You're almost through with school, correct?"

Kevin chuckled nervously. "No," he said. "I'm just finishing my freshman year. I waited to start college until after my mission."

The bishop turned to me. "And what about you?" he asked. It was the first sentence he had directed solely to me.

Thinking I had a chance to remedy the direction of this discussion, I eagerly replied, "I'm currently in graduate school and teach composition for the English department."

Having learned all he needed to know, he turned from me, smirking in amusement, and bestowed on Kevin this directive: "Now Kevin, I need you to promise me that you will receive at least your master's, and probably your doctorate as well."

As I heard the bishop's words, I felt myself sink into the background of the room. I felt myself wrung and squeezed like a dishrag, hardly able to breathe. I barely heard Kevin saying, "Yes, I plan to," and I realized that I wasn't there to be taken seriously or answer questions for myself, but to witness a pact between two men regarding my marriage and its power structure. I had shrunk from what I had previously assumed was a valued and essential participant in the interview to a prop. I don't remember much of the interview beyond that, but

I remember the bishop's words echoing in my ears, and I'm certain he never looked at me or addressed me again.

I arrived at my apartment that night visibly shaken. My roommate—a dear friend of two years and someone I relied on for validation—was in the kitchen as I walked in, and I told her what had happened, my voice wavering, my shoulders slumped in an attempt to make myself as small as I felt.

"You know that the person who has more education in the marriage is the one who is most likely to work," she said, as if the wisdom of the bishop's directive was obvious.

"Yes," I said, feeling a little bolder with my good friend, "but I'm an English major. Kevin could be getting a degree in computer science for all the bishop knows, and easily out-earn me with my master's. I'm not even certified to teach high school."

"Even if Kevin could make more with a bachelor's degree, if you have more knowledge than he does, it's going to be harder for him to provide and preside in the home like he should," she insisted.

I shook my head, impatient with the absurdity of it all: how could anyone imagine that my education posed a serious threat to Kevin's divine position? "I think it's irresponsible of the bishop to deal out this advice without knowing our particular circumstances," I said. "He never even met either of us before tonight."

"Alisa," she sighed, "I'm not going to convince you, am I? But it *is* right that a husband have more education than his wife, or else you'll never be satisfied staying at home while he works."

And with my roommate's conclusion, I heard the rationalization I had always been taught growing up in the church. It was why I sought out the most brilliant men to date, and for the longest time thought I couldn't respect any romantic partner who couldn't outsmart me. It was why I had shunned the medical profession for myself. I had paradoxically believed that an ideal Mormon marriage was an equal partnership that could be achieved if only one partner—the wife—made herself deliberately inferior to her husband. In my own life, because I cared so much about education, I had sought to achieve this prescribed inferiority by making the issues of career and education into competitions I planned to intentionally let my future husband win. I finally resented these long-held, almost unconscious beliefs and choices, and found myself arguing for just the reverse.

The next day, Kevin and I had come to opposing interpretations of what the pact with the bishop meant. Kevin defended the bishop's advice, saying, "At first he thought that I was in a place to be providing for you, but once he realized our circumstances and that you were so far ahead of me in school, he changed his mind. He realized you would be in a position to work and provide for me as I go through graduate school, so he wanted to make sure that I got as much education as I could with you providing for both of us."

I sighed heavily and shook my head, resisting as hard as I could the impulse to turn away. "Really?" I said, my voice tinged with frustration and a vague sense of betrayal. "I don't see how you can think that. It makes no sense for this bishop, a man who didn't 'allow' his wife to work, to suddenly decide it's optimal for me to work for the next ten years putting you through all the schooling he directed you to achieve."

But neither of us could persuade the other to budge in our view of the interview. That weekend we visited Kevin's parents in Sandy, a Salt Lake City suburb, and told them about it. Kevin's father, a bishop himself and somewhat progressive, adopted Kevin's interpretation, and Kevin's feminist, professional mother took mine. It wasn't long before Kevin asked me to shelve the issue because we couldn't agree, and he failed to see why I insisted on being so hurt by the promise he had made to his bishop.

Several years into our marriage, I couldn't keep this issue on the shelf any longer. I had built a successful career as a technical writer–turned–project manager at a corporate training and consulting firm, while Kevin was about to finish law school. I was uncertain what would happen to my career when he graduated. Never one to do well with unresolved confusion and heartache, I had to figure out why Kevin had done what he did. One night, while we got ready for bed, I braced myself emotionally for any conflict and began, "Why would you make that promise to your bishop, someone we didn't even know? We can't even remember his name now. Don't you see how this hurts me, that you would promise him something that puts me down?" As I finished, my face was averted; I couldn't bear to meet him eye-to-eye, afraid that the old misunderstanding might linger between us.

Kevin dropped what he had been doing and came to stand before me, one finger gently lifting my face and eyes to his, his tender way of letting me know he wanted me to believe what he was going to say. "I was wrong with what I thought the bishop intended then," he admitted. "But I'd never experienced a church leader giving me bad advice before, so I believed that there had to be some good reason he wanted me to get as much education as I could."

"More education than I had," I reminded him.

"I didn't see it that way at the time, but yes, I see now that he was trying to make sure things would be unequal between us."

Knowing that we had arrived at a mutual understanding of that event and jointly rejected its divisive intent, I at last felt the issue was resolved, and we moved forward without arguing about it again. Eventually Kevin did hold up the education part of the pact: he earned a master of public of administration a few years after graduating with a juris doctorate, but it wasn't to outdo me: it was to help strengthen his career path as an attorney in government practice, a path he hoped would yield a schedule that would allow him to be an equal partner with me, avoiding some of the demands a traditional law firm places on its attorneys. He spent over two years as the stay-at-home parent to our son while earning that MPA, and I arranged to work from home a couple of days a week so that we could share the load at home more equally while I was the sole breadwinner.

Despite Kevin surpassing me in education, not all of the bishop's plan nor my roommate's prediction came true. The years I was able to work and climb the corporate ladder before children came gave me an edge in earnings that supersedes the salaries available to young government practice attorneys, solidifying my role as the main provider of income and benefits for most of our twelve years of marriage.

While I have made career choices that led to greater work-life balance and flexibility rather than sprinting up the corporate ladder, I never find myself wishing I had less education or less earning potential. I can't image that I ever would have found that ideal for myself. It might have made me explicitly subordinate to Kevin in precisely the way the bishop and my roommate considered necessary to the health of our marriage, but neither Kevin nor I believe it would have made our marriage any better. It certainly would have made us poorer, which would have made life much, much harder during the many years Kevin was going to school, and would have left us without health insurance, devastating us after our son was diagnosed with epilepsy and later autism, requiring costly therapies that would have otherwise bankrupted us.

I will probably spend most of my adult life providing income to my family in some way. As a result, I often wish I had chosen my education more deliberately and had pursued a profession that would not only provide for my family, but would better suit my interests and feel more purposeful.

I often fantasize of returning to school to get a PhD in literary analysis, or consider again my earlier plans of entering the medical profession. These fantasies have nothing to do with competing with Kevin; I've always been academically minded and, given how much I enjoyed school, it makes sense that I would want to go back. I also think it matters that both Kevin and I value education for its own sake. That shared appreciation for school made it easier for me to support Kevin financially and emotionally during those years he worked so hard in graduate school.

In any event, those are prospects that I don't feel the need to act on any time soon. Right now it's enough to be an equal providing and parenting partner with Kevin, both of us experiencing the pleasures and pains of our professional lives, the juggle when we have a sick child who can't go to school, the logistics of the laundry room or full kitchen sink when overtime is required. The give and take, the communication we've learned to depend on, and the working around each other's meetings and travel schedules haven't always come easily, but it all definitely beats a life where we struggle to constantly—and artificially—keep one partner in a superior position just because that's what other people expect. It also beats the competition I always imagined myself engineering and deliberately losing my entire life. I'm much happier being the best person I am able to be, and allowing my personal success to contribute to the success of our marriage.

A Breath I Held Too Long

DEJA EARLEY

I learned recently that my Mormon great-grandmother was married to a Catholic. Or maybe lapsed Catholic is more accurate. He didn't attend the Mormon church, but he didn't attend his church either. This matters to me because I'm married to a Catholic. I'm an active Mormon and always have been, while my husband—Sam—isn't, and likely never will be. In our house, his crucifixes are on display next to pictures of Mormon temples and the Sacred Grove. And though we've been married for five years and dated for two years before that, no one mentioned my great-grandparents having any connection to us until recently.

When my aunt casually mentioned my great-grandparents' differing faiths, I asked my father via email to tell me what she meant. He said we'd better talk about it on the phone, and I called that night, not sure what to expect.

He told me my great-grandmother—Lela was her name—came from one of the most prominent pioneer families in Utah. At age eighteen, she met a man named Tom, and, long story short, had a baby a few months after they married. In those days if you had to get married, you stayed married for the long haul, he said. They weren't exactly a match made in heaven, but they stayed together anyway.

I was folding clothes while we talked, matching the shoulders of my husband's T-shirts, halving tiny pairs of polka-dot pants belonging to our infant daughter. Almost weeping, I asked, "Why didn't you ever tell me?"

"Why would it matter to you?" he asked. "Their situation has nothing to do with yours, aside from the Catholic husband."

"But that's huge, that someone else in our family married a Catholic. It makes me feel less lonely in my marriage. Like I'm not the only one."

I didn't know I felt lonely in my marriage until I said that out loud. And it's not that I feel lonely in it, just lonely to have the kind of marriage I do. I know of four women who have married outside the church and kept their faith, and

I don't know any of them well. I know people who stopped participating before they married, and several whose spouses left the church after they married, but so few like me. The fact that my great-grandmother was like me, that she married a Catholic and managed to stay both faithful and married her entire life, this makes all the difference. This means it can be done. This means, somehow, it's in my bones.

That my father doesn't think there's a connection surprises me, though maybe it shouldn't. The baby conceived out of wedlock was kept quiet all his life. No one of his generation did the math. My father and two of his sisters told me about finding out when their mother was on her deathbed. She told them, and when they asked why she never mentioned it before, she said, "It didn't seem like it mattered much."

Thomas and Lela met and married in San Bernardino, where they both grew up, in 1922. She was eighteen; he was twenty-three. He was Italian, the second generation in an immigrant family. There's some word he was tomcatting around before the pregnancy, and a sense that the family in general was unhappy about the match. The couple had three children in San Bernardino, one of whom, Marie, died before she was a year old.

During the Depression, Tom came in as relief at a bakery where workers were striking in San Diego. (When I told my husband this he said, "He was a scab." The obvious word, but one my father had avoided.) They had two more children in San Diego, and he stayed on at the bakery. My father remembers Tom's forearms, massive from kneading giant vats of dough. Tom used to ride on top of the bakery truck, and he once fell off it onto his head. He survived, but lost his sense of smell, and he used to grow very hot peppers, which Lela would turn into very hot salsa he'd slather on all his food so he could taste it.

I grew up in the house Lela and Tom built in 1947, the year before my father was born. I loved that house, which had an enormous garden with all kinds of fruit trees. Lately, thinking about Lela and Tom, I've imagined them there, Tom working in the garden and coming in with tomatoes for dinner. Maybe she's in the kitchen, getting things started, sweating some onions on the stove, and he walks in and gooses her, tells her hello.

*   *   *

Sam and I met in a PhD program in southern Mississippi. He was a fiction writer, I was a poet, and we were the only people in our program who didn't think it was fun to get drunk several evenings a week. I didn't drink because I was Mormon, and he didn't because he had done so extensively for fifteen years and no longer did it at all.

We started hanging out, and almost instantly began spending all our spare (and some not-spare) time together. This was complicated because Sam had never had a relationship that didn't involve premarital sex, and I'd never had

one that did. So we dated, sort of, on and off. To avoid being alone together in
his house or mine, we ate out. We blew through a lot of student loan money
in our efforts to avoid premarital sex. Sometimes in the early mornings, when
we'd both been up writing, Sam would pick me up and we'd drive the perim-
eter of town, watching trees through the fog. Sam would drink coffee, and I'd
sip herbal tea, and we'd talk about our classes and what we were reading and
our families and what we were writing. He'd hash out plots and I'd tell him
ideas for poems, and then sometimes he'd come in for homemade granola or
buckwheat pancakes with strawberry syrup. During seasons when we were
kissing, he'd kiss me goodbye at the door, apologizing for his coffee breath,
and I would tell him it didn't bother me, and it *didn't* bother me, though I'd
wonder if it should.

The plan was always to part. I made it clear up front that I intended to marry
a Mormon, and Sam wasn't particularly interested in marrying anyway. So we
planned to just keep each other company; to just make grad school less lonely,
and then we'd say goodbye.

I grew up a lot in the two years we hung out. I confronted the big bad world
outside Mormondom: I listened to "enlightened" ideas about sex and gender in
my graduate classes; I helped my students workshop poems about all manner
of subjects disturbing to my religious sensibility. The ward in Mississippi was
small and strange, and when my experience in that ward combined with my
education, it culminated in a crisis of faith. Sam helped me manage the crisis.
Without trying to get me to leave the church, he talked me through it until I
understood what was good about my faith, and what was imperfect. He did the
same for the world at large. I wasn't sure how I would proceed into the universe
without him, after that.

Plus, I loved him. We loved each other in that can't-wait-to-tell-you-every-
thing way. He made me laugh—I mean really bend over in breathless laughter—just about every time I talked to him. Even now that's true. He is the most
interesting person I've ever met.

I tried not to love him. Everyone I knew, in one way or another, told me to
run the other way. My Institute teacher warned me not to "settle"; my bishop
told me it may be "good" to end up with Sam, but not "better," and certainly not
"best"; my Mormon roommate lectured me; my friends back home were vocal
about their worry; my parents prayed, I think, that I'd find someone else. I tried
to find someone else. I really tried. I listed myself on online Mormon dating
websites and went on painfully boring dates. I cried—from well-wishing tinged
with jealousy—when my friends married; I spent insomniac nights thinking of
them in their Mormon homes with their priesthood-holding husbands, attending the temple on Friday nights. They seemed so safe in their Mormon homes.
I felt so unsafe, unsteady. I initiated conversation after conversation with Sam,

outlining the boundaries of our relationship and trying to establish distance. I prayed, asking God if I should cut off contact entirely, and my answer was always the same: "Why would you do that? I sent Sam as a blessing to your life. Is he not a blessing?"

And somewhere in the last year of school, the idea of parting stopped making sense to either of us. My mother had a lot to do with this. I called her one Saturday, weeping, saying over and over again that I couldn't do it, that I couldn't choose, and I was vague, but I was saying I couldn't choose between staying with Sam and staying Mormon—I felt I was being torn in half. And my mother said, kindly, wisely, in the way a parent who really loves her child would, "Deja, maybe you should think about marrying him even if he doesn't join the church." It felt exactly like the top of my head split open, in the best possible way. The pressure left me.

Sam and I graduated. Our families came out to watch. I remember standing in front of the humanities building after giving a reading. We were about to drive home to kill time before the graduation ceremony, and Sam's mother said, "Sam, you should tell Deja what time you'll pick her up this evening."

"Deja," he said, "I'm going to pick you up . . . *right now*." And he did, swooping me up into a honeymoon hold, my shoes flying off, and both our families laughing. I remember the way my laugh sounded as it echoed off the university buildings.

There was a lot of complicated praying and confusion still to come, and some of my family was disappointed and sad when it happened, but that summer we married after a three-week engagement, friends from school saying I must surely be pregnant, but the fact of the matter was, I was still a virgin on my wedding night. We made it, barely.

*   *   *

I think of Lela and Tom. I wonder what their story looked like. I wonder where they met, and who introduced them. I wonder if he made her laugh, and if they went dancing. I wonder if she told anyone about him. I wonder where they made love. I wonder when she figured out she was pregnant, and how she told her parents, and what they said, and who helped her plan the wedding, and, when she stood in the chapel, if her mother cried, and whether she cried because it wasn't in the temple, or because her little girl was getting married, or both. I wonder if Lela felt her baby move as she stood there, and I wonder what she thought, looking across at Tom. Did he look like a stranger, because he wasn't like the Mormon boys she'd grown up with and imagined marrying someday? Did he smile at her, and did he mean it? I wonder if Lela was happy to be getting married, looking forward to her baby, or if she felt terrified and trapped. Or all of the above.

*   *   *

My new bishop in a ward north of Boston asked to meet with me recently. I thought it would be for a calling, but it was more of a get-acquainted meeting, since I had just moved into the ward. I was also submitting the form for the blessing of our new daughter, my father having blessed her when we visited my parents for Christmas.

"That part, where I'm supposed to check 'yes' or 'no' on being 'born in the covenant'—the answer's no, right? Since we weren't married in the temple?" It bothered me to check that "no" box. I had half-hoped the fact I hold a temple recommend would count for something. I wanted to check a box in between yes and no.

"Right, the answer is no," said my bishop cheerfully. "Here, I'll check it for you." He was sitting in his suit on the cushioned chairs next to me, one leg folded under him. It seemed a strange way for a bishop to sit.

"But you know," he continued, "it's never too late. He might still get baptized. My sister married a nonmember, and he's baptized now."

He launched into the story of his sister, and how long it all took, and the concerns of the family, and the happy ending. I'm used to this story; I hear some version of it often.

"Sure," I said. "He might get baptized someday. But I'm not holding my breath."

I meant that in the best possible way. I meant it almost literally.

One Sunday on my way home from church shortly after we married, I felt the longing for Sam's conversion leave me. Though I'd thought as much, I finally felt that it didn't matter to me whether or not he ever baptized, that I could and would be happy in my marriage regardless of whether he joined me in my faith. It felt exactly like a breath I'd held onto for too long

*   *   *

After the conversation with my father, my aunt sent me a picture of Lela and Tom. They are clearly grandparents by this point, standing in front of the house I grew up in, leaning against a planter box I used to play in, overflowing fuchsias hanging above their heads. She's wearing a housedress and has one hand on the scruff of a big black dog. They both look happy, genuinely smiling. Tom is holding what appears to be a can of Pabst Blue Ribbon beer.

My father said they had a rocky start. Lela used to drag Tom out of bars, he said. My father and his siblings remember Tom sneaking them sips of beer when their grandmother wasn't looking. It's shocking to think of my very Mormon father as a child, his lips pursed to a beer can, his eyes curious, his grandfather waiting amusedly to see what he thinks. At Christmas, Tom would bring out a big coffee can of pennies he'd saved all year, and the men in the family would play penny-ante craps. My grandmother would shoo the children away, worried, presumably, about the influence of betting.

I would give anything to know what they said when one of their kids or grandkids asked why Dad or Grandpa wasn't coming to church with them. I want to know if they prayed over meals, and if they did, if Tom crossed himself beforehand, like Sam does, saying "I'll dial," then letting me pray. I want to know if sometimes, when Lela was folding laundry in the other room, if she heard Tom swear a blue streak, and came momentarily unmoored from her life, pausing in the middle of folding his boxers, wondering how she, of Mormon pioneer stock, ended up married to a man who routinely swore a blue streak in the living room. I want to know about Marie, the baby who died, and if Lela wished she had a husband who could give her daughter a priesthood blessing, and whether she wondered if she was being punished, somehow. I want to know if she ever forgave herself for not starting her family the way the church said to, and if she did forgive herself, I want to know how.

*   *   *

This is what it's like to be a Mormon married to a Catholic.

It's good, mostly. The way all good marriages are mostly good. Sam makes me laugh, and makes our baby laugh, and some nights he makes an excellent pasta dish with peas and lots of olive oil and Parmesan and hints of lemon and rosemary. When something at church upsets me, I come home and tell him about it and he helps me think through it, the way he did when we were dating. He's not afraid of my intellect, the way some Mormon men I dated seemed to be. And when I drift away from my intellect, thinking that mopping the floors or having his dinner on the table might be more important than writing, he's disappointed; he pulls me back; he's impatient until I want to talk about books and ideas again.

He's a clever man. Much of the time when he talks, I wish I had something to write down what he's saying. Even his casual utterances seem worth recording.

There are rough patches. Lately he's taken up smoking again, a habit he'd quit by the time we started dating. I've never seen him do it, never actually seen him bring a cigarette to his lips, but he'll come in from getting firewood from our detached garage, and I'll smell it on him. The smell is as offensive as if he'd vomited on himself. And much of that is shock, this soul-rattling shock that I, the good Mormon girl, the know-it-all kid in church, am somehow married to a man who smokes. I can hardly believe it. I walk around our house, putting this here and that there, taking care of the baby, and it's like my voice is someone else's voice, my life is someone else's life, and I'm surely just filling in for the moment. Soon my Mormon husband will come home, the one who doesn't exist, the one I'm not sure I would even like very much. And we'll get dressed in our church clothes and go to the temple for our Friday night date.

One afternoon while the baby napped, we tried to sneak upstairs for some romance. As we kissed, I said, "You taste like cigarettes." I didn't know he'd been smoking. I thought I must be tasting something else, so I thought I was just making conversation. But he confessed he'd been smoking again, and suddenly I wasn't interested in romance. I was tired. He wanted to talk philosophically about taking care of his health and why it seemed hard to do, but I was so exhausted that my eyes started to close, and he left me there, asleep in the middle of our bed. Later he came in and woke me, holding the baby, who was hungry. They were both hungry.

But even as I write what's complicated, I keep thinking about a moment when Sam and I were looking to buy a house. We were walking the streets of Jamaica Plain, darting into open house events as we passed them, and I asked Sam if we could maybe pray before we went into the next one, just so we'd be directed in such a big decision. We hadn't been married all that long, and I was worried about asking, not sure what he would think of the idea.

Sam thought for a minute and then said sure, and surprised me by putting his forehead against mine, right in the middle of the quiet street. He held my head in both his hands, his fingers tangled in my curls, and said the Our Father slowly and beautifully. I could hear the birds singing as I listened to him pray, and it felt like we were a team, like the three of us (Sam, me, God) were in a sort of prayer huddle.

That moment could have happened with a Mormon husband, sure. He could have tangled his fingers in my curls and prayed, and the birds still would have been singing, and we probably would have felt like we were in a prayer huddle with God. But there was something beautiful about the way the Our Father surprised me, the way each word was so thoroughly not my own, that made our huddle seem more remarkable. Because we're of different faiths, I'm constantly aware of our individuality, our separateness, which makes the parts where we overlap all the more astonishing, all the more sweet.

The other day we tried again while the baby napped, and I tasted the cigarettes when we kissed, but this time I didn't remark on it. I pretended it didn't matter. I kept kissing my husband until it didn't matter at all.

*   *   *

My aunt says she doesn't remember ever seeing her grandparents show affection for each other. She recalls that when they took a picture at their fiftieth wedding anniversary and Tom put his arm around Lela and kissed her on the cheek, the gestures were startling. My aunt had never seen him do that before.

They had a practical marriage, and they did things for each other. Lela made Tom his dangerously hot salsa, so hot she'd warn the grandchildren against coming near while she made it. Tom made Lela quilting frames for the Relief Society, and all the surrounding Relief Societies, too. In the afternoons they'd sit on their patio to cool off, Lela drinking lemonade, Tom with a beer.

I love them for staying married, even knowing they may have felt they had no option. They raised great kids who became down-to-earth adults who were good at letting things go and assuming the best about people. In my mind I want to stack up the church activity of their posterity against the posterity of my mother's family to see if there's some empirical evidence that marrying outside the faith affects future generations in an exact and negative way. But I don't think it works like that: families aren't tallies, and the faiths of individuals are made up of countless influences, and I'm not convinced that church activity is the most significant mark of a well-lived life anyway.

In that picture, the one with the fuchsias and the can of Pabst, they look to me like people who have been through all that, who've played out their differences over millions of conversations. They look like people who've looked divorce in the face, shrugged, and made an omelet instead.

Lucky Despite Myself

RACHEL WHIPPLE

I'm a very determined person. I was a determined child and teenager, so very driven. This isn't to say that I was goal-oriented. I *hated* goals as a young woman. None of the goals required for advancement in the Young Women's program was anything that I was remotely interested in. A dutiful young woman, I set and completed goals every year as dictated, but rather than helping me appreciate goals prayerfully set and conscientiously recorded in a journal, the process seemed empty and artificial, busy work so girls could earn some pointless recognition to make up for the fact that we weren't eligible for a real award like an Eagle Scout. Seeds of rebellion had already germinated within me: I went through the motions as expected—except that I refused to record the hours I spent doing service on the principle that service should be done for its own sake (Kant would have been proud), and thus failed to earn my award.

My personal approach to growth and development was simple and naive: I would decide to do something, then do it. A decision = a change. There was no looking back, no allowance for regrets. You suck it up and take the consequences, good and bad.

So when I arrived at BYU as a bright, blonde seventeen-year-old, I didn't make a goal to be an ideal date: I just decided that I would be and acted as though I were. I smiled so much my cheeks hurt. I listened attentively to the young men who took me out. I laughed at jokes, asked questions that allowed the guy to show off, acted suitably impressed when he did, and indicated through body language how engaged I was in the conversation. It was all practice for the role of supportive helpmeet, attractive wife and mother hanging on the arm of a righteous priesthood holder. Since I was young and unformed, who's to say that role wouldn't be authentic for me? I was willing to give up aspects of my self to be what I was expected to be. I didn't consider it a sacrifice or diminishment because I hadn't yet figured out who I was.

Where did I get the idea that this was what I needed to do? It's obvious: I absorbed the indoctrination of my church and my college experience very well. Everything in the church, from talks in sacrament meeting to Relief Society lessons to the religion classes required to graduate from BYU, all stress how important it is to go to the temple; it's really the only way to be a good Mormon. The only way an eighteen- or nineteen-year-old girl could go to the temple then was to get married. And there's also the clear message that the only acceptable outlet for a healthy sex drive is marriage. I was a healthy teenager, just as I am a healthy woman now. Given that pressure, there wasn't much chance that I would grow up before I got married. I wasn't an adult entering a marriage; I was a child playing house, but playing for keeps: no crying, no take-backs.

When I met Clint, his face still red from the permanent sunburn he got on his mission in Brazil, he was talking about Zen Buddhism, the struggle for authenticity, searching for some key that would translate faith or intention into action. His was a quest to match integrity of action with integrity of purpose. I was still pushing myself to be a good Mormon girl. I thought, "I'll never date that guy; he's clearly not orthodox enough." But then I came to know him, and as I did, I grew to appreciate his perspective. We read the poetry of Allen Ginsberg and the meditations of Thomas Merton. He lent me copies of *The River Why* and *Zen and the Art of Motorcycle Maintenance*. And I discovered how much I liked that, with him, I could admit that I had always wanted to practice yoga, to know mythology as well as Joseph Campbell did, to read the Apocrypha (the Bible dictionary entry on it, which began by announcing that the word meant *secret or hidden*, tantalized me as a teenager), but I didn't know how to start, where to begin. Clint made a good teacher for me, and I made a good student for him.

That's a fair representation of how our relationship started out: student and teacher. That's one reason I consistently read the books he loved and recommended, while he has read so few of my favorites, though he's always happy to listen to me talk about why I value and admire them. Also, I'm a fast reader whereas he is slow and deliberate. And he has so little free time that reading for pleasure is a true luxury for him.

He sacrifices leisure for his career; we all sacrifice for his career, the source of our family income. We've moved across the country a few times—for his doctoral degree, his postdoc, his job. As planned, I've stayed home with kids, all my personal ambition beyond motherhood on hold for more than a decade. The arrangement succeeds in part because I have worked, deliberately and determinedly, to make myself the best possible wife for Clint. I take care of the home. I make the meals, bake bread, pack up leftovers into containers for his lunch the next day. I take care of his clothes, purchasing them, returning them if unapproved, laundering, folding, mending. I hunt for his socks all over the house, digging them out from under the couch and the bottom of the bed. I go camping and hiking. I do all the shopping and packing, the loading and unloading and putting away. I keep track of the calendar and know where to find things. I'm pretty much always up for sex, but not pushy about demanding it. This is the role of helpmeet I chose: this is the wife I thought he would like: this is what I decided to be.

I doubt my husband has any idea how much I molded myself.

And even still, I've been nagged by the worry that Clint will realize how flawed I am, that I will disappoint. That he will judge me to have wasted my time, my talents, our money, because I certainly feel that I fail myself and my own standards in a number of ways. There are also enough voices shouting, some within my own head, that I have diminished myself, sold myself short, deprived the wider world of the contributions I could have offered had I made other choices. Is being a stay-at-home mom, a housewife, the best use of my innate abilities and potential talents? Sometimes I feel I've lost my chance to be anything I'm actually interested in, that I'm condemned to be what I thought I should be when I was a good little Mormon girl.

So I ask myself, *What do I get out of this arrangement?* There are solid benefits for me: security, home, family. Time to read what I want. Financial stability without working. I take satisfaction in the fact that I am needed. I make the majority of day-to-day decisions about our household—what we eat, wear, how our home looks, how all our money is spent—so If I'm not there, keeping order, the house falls into chaos.

I'm able to do all this, and do it well, because I determined to mold myself into a person who could.

Clint's lucky that he got a wife who would mold herself. And I'm lucky that Clint is the one I married. Because I was determined to get married.

Choosing who to marry wasn't a matter of falling passionately in love or re-markable physical chemistry. I was never the type to have crushes: they struck me as pointless exercises of emotion, self-indulgent fantasies that waste time and energy. Nor was it a matter of prayer and revelation. I didn't wait for God to tell me who my husband should be: I relied on my nineteen-year-old ideas of logic and good judgment. The patriarchal blessing my grandfather gave me before he died of cancer advised me to choose carefully the man I would marry, to be sure he would treat me with the respect I deserved. Clint had become my best friend. I knew him, as well as I could, after months of talking, hiking, and watching foreign films. I liked him and wanted to know him better. I decided to be loyal to him. He was steady, and I knew that if he committed to me, that would be that. For a desperate-to-marry nineteen-year-old, that seemed relatively responsible.

I find Clint attractive because I love him, not the other way around. I feel lucky about that as well. Certainly I had my own standards for male beauty, and I chose Clint even though he didn't fit them all: among other things, I always looked for a man with graceful hands, long fingers, and well-shaped nails. Clint's hands are about the same size as mine. His palms are broader, but my fingers are slightly longer. His hands are strong rather than attractive. I've learned what he does with his hands matters more than how they look. He plays the piano so beautifully it calms my soul. He helps with dishes, turns the compost, massages my sore shoulders, and strokes my bare skin. And when we hold hands as we walk or watch a movie or sit in church we are together, united, one. I love Clint's hands.

Every once in a while, I'll catch sight of a picture of the two of us and smile. We make an attractive couple; we look good next to each other. Sex is good too. We're not perfectly matched, but we're willing to work things out, to try something new. But mostly, we just always reach for each other. So it gets better all the time.

I love to snuggle in bed, my head on his chest, his arm around me. But to sleep, I turn my back to him, curled in my own space, distinct from his. So we fall asleep, back to back, facing away from each other, just as during the day we fall to our own challenges and work. And when we wake, we're still together, still touching, warm and secure.

As a marriage-eager nineteen-year-old, I was happy in a relationship I found safe, comfortable, and steady. I'm even happier as it has continued to develop into a mutually supportive companionship, with plenty of room for us to grow as we laugh and struggle together. We share the joy and sorrow that is loving our children. We are each other's touchstones, the one we talk to at the end of each day to set it to rest. We're so much more than friends now. We are partners, companions, lovers. He is my favorite, the one I love best.

The success of my marriage has hinged more on deciding to be a good spouse than deciding to be a good Mormon. Admittedly, there's some overlap—but far less than you might think. It's not a matter of praying, attending church, or paying tithing, though we do all that. It's a matter of communicating, attending to our marriage, and paying attention.

Clint and I have grown up together—we had to, because we certainly weren't fully grown when we married. But we didn't have to grow closer together—we could have grown apart, as many couples do. It's an old story: one spouse's growth threatens a marriage. We've survived that. I'm more confident, relaxed, independent, and assertive as a wife than I was as a single person, both because I'm an adult now and because I'm Clint's wife. I dare to voice my opinion, whereas before I was too hesitant to commit to one. The love and support of my husband, the appreciative acceptance that he has always given me, has allowed me to be confident in who I am. I no longer feel I must work to shape myself around him. I know now that he loves me, not the role I play. He would have loved me even had I not contorted myself into what I thought was the ideal mold because he loves *me*.

My determination to marry propelled me through that leap of faith required to enter marriage and learn to trust and rely on another person. And when I hit my own crisis of faith, the man I once deemed too unorthodox was supportive. In my slow-grown confidence, I've learned that I can be critical of the church and still love it.

Despite and because of all that, we're so comfortable together. We watch shows just to share the experience. We talk about news, religion, politics, philosophy, literature, music, work, school, kids. We go on dates to lectures and movies and take bright sunny hikes on borrowed snowshoes.

Sometimes we have friends over just to have a new conversation. And I love that, hearing him say something unexpected, a new response because a new person was able to frame the conversation differently. I also love helping him, filling in words, anecdotes, names that escape him. I am valuable to him. I thrum with affection and fondness when I see his face flush as he talks. His face always reddens when he's concentrating on an argument or speaking in front of others. He looks vulnerable to me then, and it makes me feel protective and proud. He's mine.

Back to back or hand in hand, with our own work, our own interests, which often complement each other's, but don't have to. We both feel undeservedly fortunate to have each other, to love each other, to be strong together.

Thirty-Three Reasons Why: A Partial List

DAYNA PATTERSON

Because the glazed strawberries at the restaurant are red hearts, waiting.

Because an hour later, beneath a brazen angel's gaze, we immortals sit on temple hill to survey a valley of promise.

Because on the sticky vinyl of the backseat, your electric little finger skims mine.

Tongues, you teach me, are soft and warm, nights dizzy with stars.

When I serve you an accidental hairball on your spaghetti, you don't run for the door.

When I serve you a volleyball, you know how to pepper— bump, set, hit.

And when we kneel at the altar, you play an allegro beat on the drum of my heart.

Because our first night together, two icebergs learn to melt.

And when we move far from the warmth of family, you are a furnace against loneliness.

Because your legs look chiseled in slick blue running shorts, Michelangelo out for a jog.

Possibly, it's the pout of your face when you read, the pucker of your brows when I spend too much, the slack of your jaw when I show you the little white stick, the parallel pink lines.

Because you pull over and don't look away when my stomach rebels. By the gas station. By the river. In the tall grass near the church parking lot.

It's our daughters' chins.

And your dark brown turning to cinnamon in their eyes.

It's Sunday afternoon when you, the new Piper of Hamlin, sway them with your music.

It has something to do with the way your resting hand makes a T in sign language.

It has everything to do with your whispered *mi amor* and my answer, *mon amour*.

Because the lure of the universe pulls you out on a cool night in March to
  witness the geometry of the moon holding hands with two planets and
  quietly singing.

Because you are a mountain boy with rivers in your veins.

And you turn over river rocks to show our girls the mayflies.

And press their eyes to binoculars to see a glacier's blue ice.

Because you revive fish after the catch, deliver them to the wet grace of second
  life.

Sometimes you come home early smelling like Old Spice and massage the place
  where wings grow.

It has a little to do with the sounds you make when you sleep and the way your
  knees make a tent of our sheets, as familiar now as a ticking clock, as the
  taste of salt.

It has a little to do with the oxytocin your sleeping form settles on me like a
  humidifier's mist.

And when the cat of my sadness leaps onto your lap casually during dinner, you
  let it sit there, feeling the bones of its shoulder blades with your thumbs.

And on Sunday nights our scriptures are heavy tomes of Shakespeare pillowed
  by our thighs, our open palms.

It's the brown and red and silver in your beard.

It's the cello of your voice, the vibration of your chest against the audience of
  my ear.

It's slow sex at midnight in soft, half-asleep dreaminess.

Because I hate to share and you don't believe in polygamy.

Because both of us are part rose, part thorn.

And because chocolate tastes better from your mouth, still warm.

Glossary

Aaronic priesthood: the lesser branch of the LDS priesthood. It includes the offices of
deacon, to which young men are ordained at age twelve; teacher, which young men
may attain at age fourteen; and priest, which they may attain at age sixteen. (Women
are currently denied the priesthood.)

Beehive: a division within the Young Women's program; girls aged twelve and thirteen.

bishop: the lay leader of a local congregation known as a ward.

branch: very small congregation; its leader is called a branch president.

celestial kingdom: the highest level of heaven in Mormon theology. People judged worthy of its glory will be permitted to be married for all eternity and to become gods.

Doctrine and Covenants: collection of writings that are purportedly revelations given,
mainly to Joseph Smith but occasionally to others, by God and Jesus Christ.

elder: the first office in the Melchizedek priesthood. Men are traditionally ordained
to the office of elder at age eighteen, and it is the title for male missionaries, who
are typically in their late teens or early twenties. Thus, in Mormonism, despite its
conventional meaning, the term often connotes youth and immaturity rather than
age and wisdom, even though it is also the title used for the highest ranking senior
members of the church's gerontocracy.

endowment: see temple endowment.

family home evening: an evening, frequently Monday, during which a family plays games,
hears a church lesson, sings church songs, and eats treats. Often abbreviated FHE.

general authority: a high-ranking leader in the LDS church; one of the few paid leadership positions in the church.

general conference: a semiannual church-wide meeting held in Salt Lake City and broadcast to congregations throughout the world. It includes six two-hour sessions, the
first of which is a women's meeting the last weekend in March and the last weekend
in September; the remaining five sessions are held the first weekend of every April
and the first weekend of every October.

God the Mother: female counterpart (and wife) to God the Father. Also known as Heavenly Mother and Mother in Heaven.

home teaching: monthly visits conducted by men to families in their homes.

inactive: used as both a noun and an adjective. Refers to a person who is still a member of record in the LDS church but does not attend meetings.

Institute of Religion, aka Institute: a building on college and university campuses offering LDS students religious instruction and social opportunities.

Laurel: a division within the Young Women's program; girls aged sixteen and seventeen.

Melchizedek priesthood: the more advanced branch of the priesthood. Its offices include elder, which men may be ordained to at age eighteen, as well as seventy, and high priest.

Mia Maid: a division within the Young Women's program; girls aged fourteen and fifteen.

mission: for men, a two-year period of service that may begin when they reach age eighteen (until 2012, the age requirement for men was usually nineteen); for women, an eighteen-month period of service that may begin when they reach age nineteen (until 2012, the age requirement for women was twenty-one).

Mormon Corridor: mainly Idaho, Utah, and Arizona, with bits of neighboring states thrown in for good measure.

priesthood meeting: a Sunday meeting for men, held at the same time that women attend Relief Society.

Primary: the LDS church's organization for children. Children enter it when they turn three and graduate from it when they turn twelve.

Relief Society: women's auxiliary organization, founded in 1842. Originally a self-governing organization within the church, it was subsumed during a mid- to late-twentieth-century program known as Correlation and is now overseen by the church's male hierarchy.

Sacred Grove: a forested area in western New York state near Manchester and Palmyra, where, in 1820, Joseph Smith went to pray about which church he should join. According to LDS belief, God and Jesus Christ appear to Smith in response to his prayers; this event is called the First Vision.

sealing: a sacred ordinance performed in the temple in which a couple or family is sealed together as a unit for all eternity.

sealing cancellation: the rendering of a sealing null and void so that a woman may be sealed to a new husband after a divorce.

sealing clearance: permission given to men to receive a subsequent sealing that leaves any previous sealing(s) intact.

seminary: daily religious instruction, often scheduled before the regular school day, for LDS high school students.

stake: a geographical collection of wards or congregations, roughly equivalent to a diocese.

stake center: a large meetinghouse in which stake offices are located and stake meetings may be held.

stake president: the lay leader who oversees a stake.

temple: a sacred building where necessary sacred ordinances are performed for both living Latter-day Saints and the dead. It is not used for regular meetings or Sunday worship.

temple endowment: sacred ritual in which Latter-day Saints are endowed with the knowledge of specific terms, tokens, and handshakes they believe they must offer the angels guarding the Celestial Kingdom in order to enter it.

temple garment: modest underwear that Latter-day Saints begin wearing after receiving their temple endowment to remind them of the covenants they have made to God. Typically referred to simply as garments.

temple marriage: a marriage contracted "for time and all eternity" and performed only in the temple. Also known as "celestial marriage" or the "new and everlasting covenant."

temple recommend: small card about the size of a driver's license showing that its holder is worthy to enter the temple.

temple recommend interview: interview covering such areas as sexual behavior, tithe-paying, honesty in business dealings, adherence to the Word of Wisdom, belief in and fidelity to the LDS church, etc., designed to assess one's worthiness to enter the temple.

visiting teaching: monthly visits to individual women conducted by pairs of women. The person who visits you is your visiting teacher; the person you visit is your visiting teachee; the person you visit with is your visiting teaching companion or partner.

ward: a local congregation.

Figure 8. Stephanie Lauritzen, October 2013, northeast door of the Tabernacle in Salt Lake City, Utah, at an event organized by Ordain Women, a group of LDS feminists seeking equality within their church. Stephanie is pictured here asking permission to attend the Priesthood session of General Conference, which was then open only to men, regardless of whether they were members of the church. LDS women's sense of exclusion from decision making and leadership within their church has been an issue as painful and divisive as American suffragists' exclusion from the vote. Courtesy of Josh Johnsen.

Word of Wisdom: the Mormon dietary code, found in Section 89 of the Doctrine and
  Covenants. Originally intended only as advice, its recommendations included eating
  less meat. In the twentieth century, it was codified as a commandment and is interpreted as forbidding the consumption of coffee, tea, tobacco, alcohol, and illicit drugs.
Young Men: the church's organization for boys over the age of twelve. They graduate
  from it at age eighteen. Also known as the Young Men's program.
Young Women: the church's organization for girls over the age of twelve. They graduate
  from it at age eighteen. Also known as the Young Women's program.

Figure 9. Daniel and Tiffany Moss
Singer, November 1993, Manti, Utah
  Tiffany writes: "The Manti Temple,
ninety minutes south of Provo, is the
closest thing to a European aesthetic
that Utah Mormonism has to offer. I
love the beautiful pioneer hand-crafted
building in the background, obscured
by the haze of a light November
rain. The rural landscape, with sheep
grazing in the pastures surrounding
the temple, was the perfect setting for
two naively romantic and artistic kids
to start their lives together. Over two
decades later, this photo still reminds
me of all the beauty we hoped, and still
hope, to create in our lives."

Bibliography

Allred, Janice. *God the Mother and Other Theological Essays*. Salt Lake City: Signature, 1997. Print.

———. "The One Who Never Left Us." *Sunstone* 166 (2012): 62–69. Print.

Andelin, Helen. *Fascinating Womanhood*. 6th ed. New York: Bantam Dell, 2007. Print.

Barber, Phyllis. *How I Got Cultured: A Nevada Memoir*. 1992. Reno: University of Nevada Press, 1994.

———. *Raw Edges*. Reno: University of Nevada Press, 2009.

Benson, Ezra Taft. "Beware of Pride." *lds.org.general-conference*. The Church of Jesus Christ of Latter-day Saints, 1 April 1989. Web. 18 October 2015.

Cherlin, Andrew J. *The Marriage-Go-Round: The State of Marriage and the Family in America Today*. New York: Vintage House, 2009. Print.

Church Handbook of Instructions 1 Stake Presidents and Bishops. *ge.tt*. 26 October 2012. Web. 21 July 2013.

"College Students More Eager for Marriage than Their Parents." *news.byu.edu*. Brigham Young University, 28 November 2012. Web. 18 July 2013.

Coontz, Stephanie. *Marriage, a History: How Love Conquered Marriage*. 2005. New York: Penguin Books, 2006. Print.

———. *A Strange Stirring: The Feminine Mystique and American Women at the Dawn of the 1960s*. New York: Basic Books, 2011. Print.

de Beauvoir, Simone. *The Second Sex*. Trans. H. M. Parshley. New York: Knopf, 1953.

Dehlin, John. "Top 5 Myths and Truths about Why Committed Mormons Leave the Church." *mormonstories.org*. Mormon Stories Podcast, 10 February 2013. Web. 20 July 2013.

"The Family: A Proclamation to the World." *lds.org*. The Church of Jesus Christ of Latter-day Saints, 23 September 1995. Web. 15 July 2013.

Flake, Kathleen. *The Politics of American Religious Identity: The Seating of Senator Reed Smoot, Mormon Apostle*. Chapel Hill: University of North Carolina Press, 2004. Print.

Freidan, Betty. *The Feminine Mystique*. 1963. New York: Norton, 2001. Print.

Goodstein, Laurie. "Some Mormons Search the Web and Find Doubt." *nytimes.com*. *New York Times*, 20 July 2013. Web. 21 July 2013.

Gottman, John, and Nan Silver. *The Seven Principles for Making Marriage Work*. New York: Crown-Random House, 1999. Print.

Hanauer, Cathi. *The Bitch in the House*. New York: William Morrow and Company, 2002. Print.

Henderson, Peter, and Kristina Cooke. "Special Report: Mormonism Besieged by the Modern Age." *reuters.com*. Reuters, 31 January 2012. Web. 20 July 2013.

Hunter, Howard W. "Being a Righteous Husband and Father." lds.org.general-conference. The Church of Jesus Christ of Latter-day Saints, 1 October 1994. Web. 18 October 2015.

Johnson, Jeffrey Odgen. "Determining and Defining 'Wife'—The Brigham Young House-holds." *Dialogue: A Journal of Mormon Thought* 20.3 (1987): 57–70. Print.

Johnson, Sonia. *From Housewife to Heretic*. New York: Anchor Press, 1983.

Jones, Daniel. *The Bastard on the Couch*. New York: HarperCollins, 2004.

———. *Love, Illuminated: Exploring Life's Most Mystifying Subject (with the Help of 50,000 Strangers)*. New York: HarperCollins, 2014.

"Joseph Smith's Teachings about Priesthood, Temple, and Women." *lds.org/topics*. The Church of Jesus Christ of Latter-day Saints, n.d. Web. 26 October 2015.

Kimball, Spencer W. "Oneness in Marriage." *lds.org*. *Ensign*. March 1977. Web. 20 July 2013.

Laake, Deborah. *Secret Ceremonies*. 1993. New York: Dell, 1994.

"LDS Church Membership Statistics." *Fuller Consideration*. N. pag., 3 May 2015. Web. 27 October 2015.

"LDS Young Women Survey Results." *LDS Young Women Survey*, N.p., 30 June 2013. Web. 18 July 2013.

Lehrer, Evelyn L., and Carmel U. Chiswick. "Religion as a Determinant of Marital Stabil-ity." *Demography* 30.3 (1993): 385–404. Print.

McKay, David O. "Structure of the Home Threatened by Irresponsibility and Divorce." *scriptures.byu.edu*. Brigham Young University. April 1969. Web. 20 July 2013.

Miller, Claire Cain. "The Divorce Surge Is Over, but the Myth Lives On." *nytimes.com* New York Times, 2 December 2014. Web. 28 February 2015.

Monson, Thomas S. "Priesthood Power." *lds.org.general-conference*. The Church of Jesus Christ of Latter-day Saints, 2 April 2011. Web. 21 July 2013.

"Mother in Heaven." *lds.org/topics*. The Church of Jesus Christ of Latter-day Saints, n.d. Web. 26 October 2015.

Nadauld, Margaret D. "The Joy of Womanhood." *lds.org.general-conference*. The Church of Jesus Christ of Latter-day Saints, 7 October 2000. Web.

Oaks, Dallin H. "Divorce." *lds.org. ensign*. May 2007. Web. 20 July 2013.

Packer, Boyd K. "Talk to the All-Church Coordinating Council." *zionsbest.com*. Zion's Best, 18 May 1993. Web. 18 July 2013.

———. "Worldwide Leadership Training Meeting: Building Up a Righteous Posterity." *lds.org*. The Church of Jesus Christ of Latter-day Saints, 9 February 2008. Web. 20 July 2013.

Paulsen, David L., and Martin Pulido. "'A Mother There': A Survey of Historical Teach-ings about Heavenly Mother." *BYU Studies* 50.1 (2011): 71–97. Print.

Pearson, Carol Lynn. *Good-bye, I Love You*. New York: Random House, 1986. Print.

"Plural Marriage in Kirtland and Nauvoo." *lds.org*. The Church of Jesus Christ of Latter-day Saints, n.d. Web. 12 December 2014.

Proctor, Melissa. "A Source of Social Capital." *patheos.com*. Patheos Mormon Channel, 1 December 2013. Web. 15 July 2014.

Rugg, Linda. "Teaching Confessions to Saints: A Non-LDS Professor and her LDS Students." *Sunstone* 18.3 (1995): 13–17. Print.

Scott, Richard G. "The Eternal Blessings of Marriage." *lds.org.general-conference*. The Church of Jesus Christ of Latter-day Saints, 3 April 2011. Web. 19 July 2013.

Tingey, Earl C. "Three Messages to Young Adults." *lds.org*. The Church of Jesus Christ of Latter-day Saints, 2 May 2004. Web. 19 July 2013.

Toscano, Margaret: "Heavenly Motherhood: Silences, Disturbances, and Consolations," *Sunstone* 166 (2012): 70–78. Print.

———. "Is There a Place for Heavenly Mother in Mormon Theology? An Investigation in Discourses of Power." *Sunstone* 133 (2004): 14–22. Print.

Welker, Holly. "Clean-Shaven: No More Beards (Straight Women, Gay Men & Mormonism)." *Sunstone* 147 (2007): 44–50. Print.

———. "Forever Your Girl." *Bitch* 46 (2010): 26–30. Print.

———. "In Our Prayers and In Our Lives." *Sunstone* 166 (2012): 79–80. Print.

———. "The Plan of Stagnation." *Dialogue: A Journal of Mormon Thought* 43.4 (2010): 223–231. Print.

———. "A Price Far Above Rubies vs. Eight Cows: What's a Virtuous Woman Worth? A Feminist Reading of Johnny Lingo." *Dialogue: A Journal of Mormon Thought* 42.4 (2010): 37–58. Print.

"When He Stopped Believing." *lds.org. Ensign*. July 2012. Web. 20 July 2013.

Yalom, Marilyn. *A History of the Wife*. New York: HarperCollins, 2001.

Figure 10. Margaret and Paul Toscano, May 2002, Salt Lake City, Utah

Margaret writes: "Here I am with my husband, Paul, when I was awarded my PhD in comparative literature at the University of Utah. The big grin on his face indicates both his pride in my accomplishment and his relief that our long ordeal was over. In fact, I could never have finished my degree without his financial and emotional support."

Contributors

Katherine Taylor Allred is a writer, a knitter, and a motorcycle enthusiast. She lives in Salt Lake City with four children, two dogs, and one husband.

Katrina Barker Anderson is a full-time mother and a part-time photographer with a degree in broadcast journalism from Brigham Young University. She currently lives in Salt Lake City with her husband, two children, and three stepchildren. She is a passionate feminist and advocate for birth and breastfeeding rights.

At age nineteen, **Viv B.** discovered the only church that would ever speak to her soul. She almost regretted that she came along 150 years too late to show her devotion by crossing the plains with the Mormon pioneers, becoming a plural wife, or living the communitarian United Order. Instead she preached modern Mormonism to the Québécois, to eight children born in the covenant, and to various seminary students and Primary children. Her eternal marriage, contracted in the Salt Lake Temple, lasted twenty-nine years.

Heather K. Olson Beal is an associate professor of secondary education at Stephen F. Austin State University, where she teaches courses in diversity, educational foundations, classroom management, and literacy. Her scholarship examines the issues of school choice, second language education, and the educational experiences of immigrant students. Heather's three children keep her busy enough that she has little time for other things she enjoys—namely, reading, eating whole pints of ice cream by herself, jogging, and going to late-night movies with her husband.

Heidi Bernhard-Bubb has worked as a freelance reporter, journalist, and a blogger. She is currently working on an MA in creative writing at the University of Essex and lives in England with her husband and three children.

Alisa Curtis Bolander is a senior instructional designer at a Fortune 100 company. She enjoys hiking and conversing with her husband in Utah's mountains and red rock wilderness. She also advocates passionately for children with special needs.

Marie Brian, also known as the Cotton Floozy, is an alternative crafter and nap Viking. Her crafts have been featured in *Slug Magazine, Catalyst,* and the *Salt Lake Tribune*. Besides making and selling subversive embroidery, Marie has written for various literary magazines, including *Dialogue: A Journal of Mormon Thought* and *Segullah*. Her poetry is included in *Fire in the Pasture: 21st Century Mormon Poets.*

Joanna Brooks is the author of *The Book of Mormon Girl: A Memoir of an American Faith* (The Free Press/Simon & Schuster, 2012) and coeditor of *Mormon Feminism: Essential Writings* (Oxford University Press, 2015). She is the associate dean of Graduate and Research Affairs at San Diego State University.

Lynne Burnett lives in a retirement community in American Fork, Utah, even though she has no intention of retiring from her work as a registered nurse at a pediatrician's office. She and her wife, Janet, love living in the heart of Zion and giving locals an opportunity to expand their worlds. Between them they have eight children and fourteen grandchildren who love them very much.

Marilyn Bushman-Carlton's latest collection of poetry, *Her Side of It*, won the Association of Mormon Letters Award for Best Poetry Collection and was a finalist in the Jesse Bryce Niles Chapbook Competition at *Comstock Review*. She has been a Utah Arts Council artist-in-residence, UAC Grant recipient, and prize winner in the UAC Original Writing Competition. She also authored *on keeping things small* and *Cheat Grass*, winner of the Pearle M. Olson Prize. *Worthy*, her biography of a plural wife who escaped polygamy, is forthcoming.

Jari Carlton Cannon received a BA in English and political science, as well as a law degree, from the University of Utah. She has practiced public finance law in Salt Lake City and Washington, D.C. She currently works part-time as an equal employment opportunity investigator and is actively involved with her children's school and extracurricular activities. She lives in Maryland with her husband, Chris, and their four children.

Gina Colvin is a lecturer at the University of Canterbury in Christchurch, New Zealand. A lifelong member of the church, she writes about LDS cultural politics at her blog, Kiwimormon (patheos.com/blogs/kiwimormon/). She and her husband, Nathan McCluskey, are the parents of six boys.

Jamie Davis is a former teacher currently working in administration. She completed a BA and an MA in education and is passionate about multiculturalism and issues of educational equity and justice. She lives in Utah with her husband and their children.

Deja Earley has published poems, essays, and stories in journals such as *Utne Reader, Arts and Letters,* and *Diagram*, and several of her poems were included in the 2012 anthology *Fire in the Pasture: 21st Century Mormon Poets*. Her first book of poems, *To the Mormon Newlyweds Who Thought the Bellybutton Was Somehow Involved*, was published in 2015. She lives in Auburn, Alabama, and blogs at dejavuearley.blogspot.com.

Bernadette Echols is an artist and grandmother living in the Southwest.

Nancy Ellsworth has a BA in recreation management and youth leadership from BYU. She is also a licensed massage therapist and currently works as a massage therapist at a Utah resort. She enjoys being outdoors and spending time with her three children. She lives a quiet, drama-free life in Salt Lake City, Utah.

Melissa G. lives in Utah.

Brittny Goodsell is a former digital journalist and professor who works in government. She boasts a legit Dundie award, her closet is color-coded, and her three sisters ground her soul. She grew up in Utah's northern mountains and can out-bake your best pie recipe.

Lia Hadley is a writer, artist, and teacher. She and her husband live life on their own terms in the Pacific Northwest.

C. L. Hanson is the alter-ego of Carol Hamer, a software engineer who has a PhD in mathematics and writes books on Java programming. C. L. Hanson writes about Mormonism in a variety of forums. She maintains a personal blog, Letters from a Broad, at lfab-uvm.blogspot.com, and has published a novel, *ExMormon*.

Erin Hill, a college English instructor and mother of two, lives in Bryan, Texas. She grew up in St. Cloud, Minnesota, attended Ricks College, then received a BA in English and an MA in English literature and creative writing from Texas A&M University. She has taught writing and literature for seventeen years. When she grows up, she wants to be Tina Fey. Or the Dalai Lama. Or both, if possible.

Christmas Jones (not to be confused with the underrated Bond girl) is a lifelong member of the LDS church. She lives and works in Salt Lake City. She is excited that her words will be part of this anthology, and would sign her own name to this essay, but she doesn't want her parents to figure out it's about them.

Stephanie Lauritzen received a BA in history from the University of Utah and an MA in arts and teaching from Westminster College. She teaches history at a Utah high school. In 2012, she organized All Enlisted, a Mormon feminist group that organized "Wear Pants to Church Day," an event by which Mormon women could quietly announce their dissatisfaction with gender inequality in the church. In only ten days, it became an international phenomenon, with women across the globe participating in their local communities. The Smithsonian Institution asked Stephanie to donate the pants she wore to church on Sunday, December 16, 2012, as an important artifact of American life and culture. Stephanie enjoys sewing at inappropriate hours and wishes President Bartlet from *The West Wing* were real. She chronicles her ongoing faith journey at mormonchildbride.blogspot.com.

Tiffany Moss holds a BA in humanities with an English emphasis and a French minor from Brigham Young University. She loves to read, write, hike, garden, and generally be in nature.

Kira Olson has a BS in social work from Brigham Young University and has spent most of her career as an adoption social worker. She pursued graduate studies at Texas A&M–Corpus Christi in English. She enjoys rousing book club meetings and raising her four children, and dreams of living near mountains again.

Rebekah Orton grew up in Utah and earned an MA in English from Brigham Young University. She lives in northern Virginia with her husband of eleven years and their three children.

Dayna Patterson is the poetry editor for *Psaltery & Lyre*. Her chapbooks, *Loose Threads* and *Mothering*, are available from Flutter Press. Recently, her work has appeared in *North American Review, Clover*, and *Weave*. She lives with her husband and two daughters in northwest Washington.

Kate Porter lives in the Pacific Northwest.

Mary Ellen Robertson earned BAs in journalism and English from Brigham Young University and an MA in women's studies in religion from Claremont Graduate University. She has decorated Rose Parade floats, worked as a substitute teacher in East Los Angeles, and spent ten years working in aerospace/government contracting. From 2008 to 2014, she was symposium director for Sunstone Education Foundation, Inc., an independent Mormon studies organization.

Amy Sorensen teaches online journaling courses and writes the occasional book review for a local literary magazine. A former high school English teacher, she works as a librarian and is always happy to recommend a good book or two. She is an avid runner and hiker and an occasional quilter. She blogs at amysorensen.typepad.com.

Anita Tanner was raised in Wyoming and has resided in Utah, Colorado, and now in Boise, Idaho. She loves to read, write, tend her yard and garden, and take classes at Boise State University. She is the mother of six and the grandmother of seventeen.

Margaret M. Toscano is an associate professor of classics and comparative studies at the University of Utah, where she also received her PhD. With her husband, Paul Toscano, she coauthored *Strangers in Paradox: Explorations in Mormon Theology*. She is also coeditor of *Hell and Its Afterlife: Historical and Contemporary Perspectives* (Ashgate, 2010).

Naomi Watkins earned a BA in English education from Brigham Young University, an MEd in language and literacy from Arizona State University, and a PhD in teaching and learning from the University of Utah. For several years, she taught endearingly awkward middle school students about English literature before working as a university professor and educational consultant. She also cofounded Aspiring Mormon Women, a nonprofit to encourage and support LDS women's educational and professional pursuits.

Michelle Weeks has a BS from the University of Phoenix. She works at a doctor's office in Salt Lake City and is the adoptive mother of two beautiful sons, now grown. You will often find Michelle exploring Utah's beautiful landscapes.

Rachel Whipple married a returned missionary she met at BYU when she was nineteen. By luck and pluck it turned out to be the best decision she ever made. She still hasn't decided what she'd like to be when she grows up, but it's likely to involve environmental humanities. In the meantime, she has become a certified yoga instructor and enjoys untangling the threads of various textile arts, Attic Greek, and philosophical discussions.

Amy Williams was born and raised in the LDS church to fifth-generation Mormons but now considers herself agnostic. A single mom of two, she teaches online English courses for a community college and writes in her spare time.